Christian Ethics in
Secular Society

Christian Ethics in Secular Society

Philip Edgcumbe Hughes

Baker Book House
Grand Rapids, Michigan 49506

Copyright 1983 by
Baker Book House Company

ISBN: 0–8010–4267–4

Library of Congress
Catalog Card Number: 82–74065

Printed in the United States of America

Unless otherwise indicated, Scripture references are from the Revised Standard Version of the Bible,
copyright 1946, 1952, © 1971, 1973. Other versions cited are the King James Version (KJV),
the New English Bible (NEB), and the New International Version (NIV). Portions of chapter 9 are based
on *Birth Control and the Christian* (Tyndale House, 1969), by Philip E. Hughes.

For
John Hewitt Rodgers, Jr.

President and Dean
Trinity Episcopal School for Ministry
Ambridge, Pennsylvania

Contents

"Since obedience is the love of God, and to do well is the life of religion, and the end of faith is the death of sin and the life of righteousness, nothing is more necessary than that we should be rightly informed in all moral notices."

> Jeremy Taylor, *Ductor Dubitantium or the Rule of Conscience,* in *The Whole Works* (1853), vol. 3, p. 49.

1

Knowing and Doing

Christian Ethics and Secular Ethics

Ethics has to do with the way people behave. The term *ethics* is derived from a Greek word (*ethos*) meaning "custom"; its equivalent, *morals,* comes from a corresponding Latin word (*mos*) with the same meaning. The concern of ethics or morals, however, is not merely the behavior that is customary in society but rather the behavior that ought to be customary in society. Ethics is prescriptive, not simply descriptive. Its domain is that of duty and obligation, and it seeks to define the distinction between right and wrong, between justice and injustice, and between responsibility and irresponsibility. Because human conduct is all too seldom what it ought to be (as the annals of mankind amply attest), the study of ethics is a discipline of perennial importance.

In postulating a divergence between Christian ethics on the one hand and secular ethics on the other, it is not intended to deny that they have much ground in common. That ethical standards are seriously regarded by the secular authorities as well as by the Christian church is not questioned. The presence of police forces and courts of law throughout the world testifies to concern for what is socially fair and equitable. Communities in which violence and intemperance are not curbed and punished become intolerable. Even in places where the agents of justice and order betray their trust by acting corruptly, the basic purpose of their appointment remains the same: namely, to protect society from those whose conduct is lawless and irresponsible. Moreover, there is general agreement that the community of mankind is best served by public officials who are just and incorruptible and by private citizens who in their businesses and professions are honest and trustworthy, and that happy homes, considerate neighbors, and conscientious citizens are a boon to society.

It would, however, be a mistake to conclude that Christian and secular ethics must be virtually identical simply because both have a concern for decency and order and profess antipathy to injustice. Practices such as easy divorce and abortion on demand, which are incompatible with Christian standards, may be widely sanctioned in the secular world. Even the apparent similarities of emphasis, valuable though they may be for the beneficial ordering of society, share the same ground only at a superficial level. For secular ethics is man-centered, that is, this-worldly and humanistic, whereas Christian ethics is essentially theocentric: its primary concern is the will of God and the advancement of His kingdom. There are some in the church today who have persuaded themselves that because both Christians and Marxists desire and strive for the removal of inequity from human society, Christianity and Marxism should not be considered enemies but blood brothers. This may sound splendid, but the fundamental incongruity of such an alliance is evident in the fact that the atheistic ideology of Marxism demands the obliteration not only of Christianity but of all religion. It is preposterous to imagine that there can be a concordat between Christianity and this or any other form of atheistic humanism.

Unlike secular ethics the primary concern of Christian ethics is not with the organization and improvement of society, but with the relationship of man to his Creator. Love of God comes first, and then love of one's fellow man. As the summary of the divine law indicates, love of God not only precedes but also is the source of love for one's neighbor; for only when man lives in harmony with his Creator can he be truly human and live in harmony with his fellow man. There is nothing surprising, then, in the observation of Helmut Thielicke that "it always happens that Christian ethics, whenever it begins with these concepts of world betterment and virtuous ideals, promptly loses its distinctive content."[1]

The only authentic basis, as we intend to show, of all Christian ethics, and indeed of all human ethics, is man's obligation as God's creature to live his life in accordance with the will of God, to whom he is answerable for all that he does. Only in willing service and obedience to God can man realize the full potential of his humanity. Genuine freedom is to be found only in this harmony with the mind and will of his Creator, a harmony which belongs to the true nature of his constitution. That is why it must be insisted that human ethics, rightly understood, is derived from God and directed toward God, and therefore is essentially theological in character.

This means that under God there is but one structure of ethics for mankind, which Christ has summed up in the twofold command to love God with all one's being and one's neighbor as oneself. The human situation, however, has been corrupted and complicated by the fall of man into sin. Human sinfulness consists basically in man's refusal to acknowledge the sovereign authority of his Creator and in his rebellious determination to live his life in a thoroughly self-centered manner. Fallen man foolishly harbors the illusion that to be humanistic is to be genuinely human, whereas in reality this involves the negation of his true humanity,

1. Helmut Thielicke, *Theological Ethics* (1966), vol. 1, pp. 18–19.

because it requires the suppression of the truth of his creaturehood. For man to deny his creaturehood is to deny the very foundation of his humanness and to tread a road that leads to subhuman or even inhuman conduct. The tragic consequences for humanity of willful isolation from God are daily before our eyes.

Since there is so much that is evil and vicious in human society which leaves out of account its creaturely answerability to almighty God, the ethical situation is far from being simple and straightforward. The stage is thus set for the gospel, for God who created and providentially sustains the world does not abandon His creation to the forces of evil. God would not be God if what He purposes should come to nothing; it is certain that His purpose in the creation of the universe cannot and will not end in failure and frustration. God indeed has taken effective action for the restoration of mankind and the reconciliation of all things through the mediation of His Son, who by His incarnation identified Himself with our humanity that He might redeem it, and conquered evil by His life of total victory and His atoning self-offering, Man for man, the Holy One for the guilty, on the hill of Calvary. Through faith in the Redeemer and grateful acceptance of His sacrifice sinful man finds justification and the renewal of harmony with his Creator. Once justified, he enters on the life of sanctification as he gives expression to the meaning and purpose of his existence by conforming himself to God's will. In other words he now begins to practice theological ethics. Christian ethics, therefore, is indissolubly connected with the evangelical message and its power, and is properly designated *evangelical* ethics.

It is essential to stress that the gospel is a dynamic force and that its effect is radical. It does not produce a mere change of attitude or a general readjustment of moral values. The transformation it achieves is so intensive that the man in Christ is described as a new creation (II Cor. 5:17); he is reborn (John 3:3; I Peter 1:3); he is totally renewed by the creative Word of God which in the beginning gave light in place of darkness (II Cor. 4:6). Thus the emphasis of evangelical ethics is not just on what one *does,* but first of all on what one *is;* for God, to whom we owe and must answer for the totality of our lives, is concerned with our entire being, not simply with our external, humanly visible actions.

This explains the severe manner in which Jesus denounced the hypocrisy of the scribes and Pharisees, who to all appearances were thoroughly moral persons, scrupulous in their religious observance, liberal in their giving to the needy, and irreproachable in the performance of their civic obligations. But the morality of those whom Jesus censured was no more than an external display designed to be seen and applauded by men—and, one may add, to impress and be applauded by God. Their pious behavior was a façade, an exhibition not of genuine righteousness but of self-righteousness. Externally their conduct seemed worthy of commendation, but they behaved as they did precisely to receive commendation. Internally their motivation was anything but commendable, for what they did contradicted what they truly were. At heart they were concerned not with the glory of God and the needs of the destitute but only with their own importance and the impression they made on others. Precisely because theirs was an ethic of hypocrisy founded upon a falsehood at the heart of their being, Jesus warned against following their example of sanctimonious ostentation: "Beware of practicing your piety before men in order to be seen by them; for then you will have no reward from your Father who is in heaven" (Matt. 6:1). Thus the poor widow's two mites, given gratefully to God from the heart and at real cost to herself, were worthful, while the lavish hypocritical displays put on, like stage performances, by others were worthless. Hence the commendation of Jesus, who saw what was actually taking place: "Truly, I say to you, this poor widow has put in more than all those who are contributing to the treasury. For they all contributed out of their abundance; but she out of her poverty has put in everything she had, her whole living" (Mark 12:43–44).

The radical character of Christian ethics is made abundantly plain in Christ's teaching that external morality is far from being the sum total of what is required of us. It is not only what we do but what we are that matters, not only our conduct but our motivation. God makes demands upon our lives in their entirety, and those demands involve far more than conformity to the canons of social convention, good and necessary though the latter may be in themselves. That we refrain from murder and adultery is desirable as well as mandatory, but Jesus went to the root of the matter when He explained that the sixth and seventh commandments are already respectively violated when the heart harbors anger which eventually leads to murder or lustful thoughts which lead to adultery (Matt. 5:21–28). But anger and lust belong to the common experience of our fallenness. Accordingly the ethical teaching of Jesus indicates the necessity of spiritual rebirth, by which the totality of our human nature is newly created and thus radically transformed.

In St. Paul's appeal to the Christians in Rome to "present your bodies as a living sacrifice, holy and acceptable to God," the term *bodies* refers not merely to the outward aspect of their lives but to the whole of their existence, which as human existence is in the nature of the case *bodily* existence. That this is so is confirmed by the admonition which follows immediately: "Do not be conformed to this world," that is, the Roman Christians are not to accommodate themselves to the pattern of secular living, "but be transformed by the renewal of your mind, that you may prove what is the will of God, what is good and acceptable and perfect" (Rom. 12:1–2). That is to say, Christians should be radically and totally restructured, the renewal of the mind involving *ipso facto* the renewal of their motivation, so that the whole of their being may be attuned to the mind and will of God.

This passage clearly teaches that there is tension between evangelical ethics and secular values. This tension, which daily confronts the Christian believer, exists because the new man in Christ is not removed from the secular scene. It is true that he is "not *of* the world," that this secular sphere ("the world") is no longer the sphere of his true citizenship, because by God's grace he has been "transferred . . . to the kingdom of his beloved Son" (Col. 1:13). Yet he is still *"in* the world": it is on the secular stage that he has to live out his new life in Christ. Indeed it is *"into* the world" that he is sent by his Lord as the bearer of the evangelical message of reconciliation (II Cor. 5:19–20), as Christ asserted in His high-priestly prayer:

> I have manifested thy name to the men whom thou gavest me out of the world. . . .
> And now I am no more in the world, but they are in the world. . . . I do not pray that
> thou shouldst take them out of the world, but that thou shouldst keep them from the
> evil one. They are not of the world, even as I am not of the world. . . . As thou didst
> send me into the world, so have I sent them into the world (John 17:6, 11, 15, 16, 18).

Christians consequently are in an interim position. The new age of the gospel has, with the coming of Christ, penetrated the old age of the secular world; but the fullness of this new age—and accordingly the termination of the secular age—has not yet come. It awaits the return of Christ (Phil. 3:20), whose coming in glory will mark the end of all humanistic secularity. As the new era then reaches its consummation, "new heavens and a new earth in which righteousness dwells" (II Peter 3:13) will be established and creation will be brought to its ever-intended destiny in Christ; for Christ, in whom all things were created, is also the One through whom God reconciles all things to Himself (Col. 1:15–20; Eph. 1:9–10). Meanwhile Christianity exists in a secular environment. Even though the Christian no longer belongs to this fallen world, he still has to live out his earthly life in the midst of its secularity, and, as we have seen, he is under orders not to withdraw from it but boldly to challenge its structures with the radical demands of the gospel.

The Ethical Implications of Christian Theology

If, as we have argued, Christian ethics is essentially theological in nature, it is only to be expected that the converse is also true, namely, that Christian theology is essentially ethical in its application. Theology as presented in Scripture invites more than intellectual assent. Addressed to man's whole being, it involves the will just as much as the mind; indeed it may be said that theology is addressed through the mind to the will, and that from the will it finds expression in action or conduct. The end of theology is practice. Doctrine is for doing, not just for hearing and learning, and that is why in Scripture it is always presented as bearing ethical consequences. The following passages will illustrate the close kinship between Christian theology and Christian living.

> Hear, O Israel: The LORD our God is one LORD; and you shall love the LORD your
> God with all your heart, and with all your soul, and with all your might (Deut.
> 6:4).

We need not argue here the fundamental significance of the doctrine of God's unity, uniqueness, and absolute sovereignty as Lord of all. But merely to know this doctrine is not the same as to know this God who is one and supreme. It is not possible for us to view this truth in clinical isolation, for this God who is the source of our being is also the Lord of our being, and it is only in harmony with Him and His will that our being has its true meaning and purpose. This harmony with God can best be expressed by the single term *love,* and truly to love God is truly to know

God. Thus the right knowledge of the doctrine of God will inevitably lead us to love God with the whole of our being. Here we see the relationship between theology and ethics, since proper knowledge of God cannot possibly be divorced from responsive behavior.

> Against thee, thee only, have I sinned, and done that which is evil in thy sight. . . . Create in me a clean heart, O God, and put a new and right spirit within me. . . . Then will I teach transgressors thy ways, and sinners will return to thee (Ps. 51:4, 10, 13).

Although David says that he has sinned against God only, he is not implying that he has not sinned against Bathsheba in causing her to commit adultery with him, or against her husband Uriah in arranging for him to be killed in battle. Rather he is using a Hebrew form of expression to assert that his sin is ultimately against God. Any sin against one's neighbor is, when seen in proper perspective, a sin against God, for, as the summary of the law indicates, love of one's neighbor follows and flows from love of God. Thus it is plain that neither ethical nor unethical behavior can be severed from theological responsibility. David's request of God to create a clean heart within him and to give him a new and right spirit shows that he has a true understanding of the radical nature of genuine ethical renewal as the dynamic work of God, which is at the same time the prerequisite for living a life that is pleasing to God and brings blessing to others: "Then will I teach transgressors thy ways, and sinners will return to thee." Good theology is the right way to good ethics. Unethical conduct points to an incorrect doctrine of God.

> O the depth of the riches and wisdom and knowledge of God! How unsearchable are his judgments and how inscrutable his ways! . . . For from him and through him and to him are all things. To him be glory for ever. Amen. I appeal to you therefore, brethren, by the mercies of God, to present your bodies as a living sacrifice, holy and acceptable to God, which is your spiritual worship [reasonable service, KJV] (Rom. 11:33, 36; 12:1).

If any passage in Scripture makes plain the indissoluble connection between Christian theology and Christian ethics, it is this one. In Romans 9–11 St. Paul has been writing about the deep mystery of God's electing grace. This doctrine is too profound for our finite minds to fathom. But this does not mean that it is an abstract truth remote from the practical realities of everyday life. On the contrary, all Christian truth, however mysterious and beyond our human understanding it may be, is truth for us to experience and, by that experience, to recognize as truth. So also with the inscrutable doctrine of God's electing grace: everyone who is brought to faith in Christ is a recipient of God's electing grace and accordingly enters into the experience and the knowledge of the truth of this doctrine. Far from being a mere philosophical formulation or intellectual construction, it is addressed to and dynamically affects the believer's whole being. Like all Christian doctrine, it conveys ethical implications and consequences. It leads logically to behavior that is distinctively Christian and glorifying to God; hence the "therefore" of Romans 12:1. The wonder and wisdom of God's "unsearchable judgments" (Rom. 11:33) cannot be a mere cerebral concept but must influence the manner of our daily living. The apostle's appeal, then, is made on the basis of the logic that connects theology with morality: *"Therefore* present your bodies[2] as a living sacrifice, holy and acceptable to God, which is your *reasonable* [logical][3] service."

> For by grace you have been saved through faith; and this is not your own doing, it is the gift of God—not because of works, lest any man should boast. For we are his workmanship, created in Christ Jesus for good works, which God prepared beforehand, that we should walk in them (Eph. 2:8–10).

In this passage St. Paul points out that our salvation is owed entirely to the grace of God and is appropriated through faith in Jesus Christ, that it is not achieved by virtue of any meritorious works that we may imagine we have performed, and that even the faith with which we believe is not of ourselves, as though it were our doing, but is itself also a gift of God's grace. In other words, all the merit of our redemption belongs to Christ alone; our justification before God depends entirely on the perfection of the Son's atoning work accomplished on the cross. As St. Paul says elsewhere with reference to the sinner's salvation: "All this is from God, who through Christ reconciled us to himself" (II Cor. 5:18). Good works, then, do not contribute to our justification before God.

But this does not mean that the doctrine of our redemption by grace alone and through faith alone is unrelated to the demands of Christian ethics. To deny justification by good works is not to deny the importance of good works for Christian living. Indeed the justification of the sinner, who merits nothing but divine condemnation, logically leads to his living his whole life henceforth to the glory of God, who has freely forgiven and restored him in Christ. "Created in Christ," the believer's will is now in tune with the will of his Creator. This new act of creation is "for good works, which God prepared beforehand, that we should walk in them."

Thus in Christ we recover the meaning and purpose of our creation. Then, and only then, are we enabled to show our gratitude to our gracious God by performing those works which are pleasing to Him—pleasing precisely because they are works He has "prepared beforehand, that we should walk in them." This shows again

---

2. For the significance of the term *bodies* see p. 14.

3. The Greek adjective here is actually *logikos,* which many contemporary scholars prefer to translate "spiritual" (so the Revised Standard Version and the New International Version). We prefer, however, to retain "reasonable" here (cf. the New English Bible and the Jerusalem Bible), which is certainly a meaning the adjective continued to keep in the first Christian centuries. The argument above, however, is not dependent on this translation, for the logical character of St. Paul's appeal is clearly shown by the conjunction "therefore" at the beginning of the sentence.

how closely theology and ethics belong together. God is at the heart not only of the Christian's theology but also of his ethics: "God is at work in you," St. Paul assures the Philippian believers, "both to will and to work for his good pleasure" (Phil. 2:13).

The relationship between knowing and doing is repeatedly stressed in the New Testament. God's Word is not merely the revelation of truth for our information; it is His command. The indicative carries with it an imperative. His Word of truth is sent forth with dynamic force which, as it redeems our whole being, cannot fail to find expression in our actions. "But be doers of the word, and not hearers only, deceiving yourselves," St. James exhorts. The person who is "no hearer that forgets but a doer that acts . . . shall be blessed in his doing" (James 1:22, 25). And this in fact echoes the teaching of Christ Himself: "Not every one who says to me, 'Lord, Lord,' shall enter the kingdom of heaven," He warned His hearers, "but he who does the will of my Father who is in heaven. . . . Every one then who hears these words of mine and does them will be like a wise man who built his house upon the rock. . . . And every one who hears these words of mine and does not do them will be like a foolish man who built his house upon the sand" (Matt. 7:21, 24, 26). In response to the information that His mother and brothers desired to see Him, He declared, "My mother and my brothers are those who hear the word of God and do it" (Luke 8:21); and to the woman who affirmed the blessedness of His mother He replied, "Blessed rather are those who hear the word of God and keep it" (Luke 11:28). The blessedness is not merely in the *knowing* but also in the *doing* of the truth. Hence the Master's admonition to His disciples: "If you know these things, blessed are you if you do them" (John 13:17).

The Human Situation

The biblical record graphically portrays not only the origin and destiny of man but also his glory and tragedy. A right appreciation of the task of Christian ethics is dependent on a right understanding of the human situation. In particular, there are four main aspects of the human situation which should be considered, namely, the creation, the fall, judgment, and redemption. These combine to give the light and shade of a total picture of man and the environment in which he functions as an ethical being. In the biblical perspective, of course, there is no room for any kind of dualism in which two equal and ultimate principles eternally and irreconcilably stand in opposition to each other, as, for example, the spirit-matter (good-evil) dualism of Pythagoreanism and some other religious-philosophical systems. There are indeed forces contrary to God and His will, but not forces equal in power and duration, since all that is opposed to and other than God belongs to the created order and is accordingly finite, temporal, and not at all independent of the divine power and purpose. For as Creator of all, God is the supreme and sovereign Lord of all "who accomplishes all things according to the counsel of his will" (Eph. 1:11). A correct view of God is a prerequisite for a correct view of man. To see man and his world in their true relationship to God is to see things in their true proportion.

The Creation

Man is a creature of God, and as such he belongs to the whole order of creation, which God pronounced "very good" (Gen. 1:31). The fact that man is a creature means that he is dependent upon God: he has no independent existence apart from God, who is the sole source of his being. Man's existence, moreover, though divinely given, is not the same as God's existence, for God is infinite and eternal, whereas man is finite and temporal. And, being dependent on God, man is necessarily subordinate to God. The true meaning of man's existence is found only in fulfilling the will of God, the key to his human freedom and self-fulfillment. Just as a machine functions in accordance with the design of its maker—an airplane to be flown, and an automobile to be driven, each in accordance with the potentialities (and limitations) of its own special construction—so man was created to live in conformity with the purpose of the Creator, to whom he owes his constitution. An airplane that rejected its pilot or a car that said, "I can drive myself," would be uncontrolled and would inevitably end up in disaster—how much more the man who refuses the guiding hand of God!

Man of course is not a mere machine. He is a *person*—precisely because he has been created in the image of God, who is Himself a *personal* being, the trinitarian being of three Persons in one God. Far from being a piece of impersonal machinery, man manifests his personhood through all the faculties of personality: he functions as a rational, moral, volitional, articulate, and responsible being. This personal distinctiveness sets him apart from and above all other orders and levels of creation; indeed, his entire life is one of interpersonal relationships. Of these the primary relationship is the person-to-Person relationship between himself and his Creator; and, second, there is the person-to-person relationship between himself and his fellow human beings. Man's personhood means that God is able to commune with him, Person to person, and to require of him that he love God with all his being and love his fellow man as himself, in that order. This is the basis and the demand of authentic human ethics, which is in the first place man's loving response to God who created him and who first loved him, and then a loving outreach to his fellows who share with him the experience of God's creating and caring love.

The uniqueness of man in the created realm derives from his creation in the image of God. Thus man enjoys a privilege and responsibility which set him apart from the rest of creation. He alone is able to know God as one person knows another, to converse with God, to love and be loved by God, to respond with conscious obedience to the command and will of God, and joyfully to live his life to the glory of God. With such rich and special endowments he is equipped to serve, in accordance with the divine will, as God's viceroy on earth, faithfully fulfilling his mandate to exercise dominion over the created order and developing its immense potentialities, always for God and under God, in furtherance of the purpose for which all, including himself, was brought into existence (Gen. 1:26–31).

As a *rational* being man is capable of receiving communication from God and understanding the design of God for the world He has created. Man has not been left in the dark to grope around tentatively for the truth about God and creation. As a *moral* being man is intended to reflect the perfection of his Maker, whose indefectible love and justice are the essence of all morality.

The divine holiness is itself the demand for the holiness of man (created as he is in the image of God), as Leviticus 19:2 shows: "You shall be holy; for I the LORD your God am holy" (see also Lev. 11:44–45). This demand is the basis of St. Peter's appeal: "As he who called you is holy, be holy yourselves in all your conduct" (I Peter 1:15). The same logic lies behind Jesus' injunctions in Matthew 5:48 ("You, therefore, must be perfect, as your heavenly Father is perfect") and in Luke 6:36 ("Be merciful, even as your Father is merciful"). Moral perfection is demanded of man because by virtue of his constitution in the image of God he is a moral creature. Morality is indispensable for the integrity of his existence as man, for the achievement of his true human identity, for the full expression of the divinely given potential of his humanness, and for the accomplishment of his mandate to have dominion over the created realm. His ethical duty is to show forth on earth the perfect goodness of the Creator. Amorality (the denial of moral obligations) and immorality (the breaking of moral standards) insult and degrade his humanity.

The Fall

The fallenness of man is the consequence of his rebellion against the authority of his Creator. There are a number of evidences that such rebellion is monstrously stupid: it disrupts the harmony of man's fellowship with God, it blights the perfection of his environment, and it destroys the dignity of his viceregal status as the crown of God's creation. The rebellion of man is suicidal because God is the sole source of man's life; it is irrational because God is the sole source of man's reason; and it is immoral because God is the sole source of man's good. Man's rebelliousness against God cuts his lifeline and inevitably precipitates him into alienation, meaninglessness, and death. Moreover, it affects not only man's relation to God but also his relationship to his fellow men and to the whole order of creation. When man separates from God, in whom his own integrity and his oneness with others consist, he is fractured within himself and estranged from others. Divorcing himself from the divine source of all love, man loses his love for others. The existence of other persons becomes a threat to his own existence and ungodly and therefore unethical emotions of suspicion, jealousy, and hatred may even drive him to commit the horrible wickedness of fratricide, so graphically illustrated by Cain's murder of his brother Abel. That alienation from God also involves alienation of mankind from one another is depicted in the accompanying diagrams. Figure 1 shows that the nucleus of our union with one another is our union in God, the Creator of all. Figure 2 shows that separation from God is at the same time separation from one another and the disruption of interpersonal relationships.

By rejecting the authority of God and His Word man denies, overtly or tacitly,

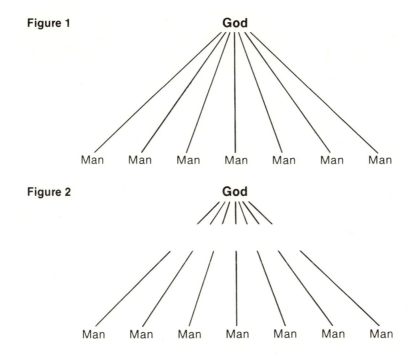

Figure 1

Figure 2

his creation in the image of God and at the same time perverts that image as he senselessly and wickedly affirms his own autonomy—in effect affirming his own deity. But despite the satanic assurance that liberation from the notion of God and His sovereignty will lead to the discovery of his own deity, what man actually discovers is his own guilt and nakedness in the presence of his holy Creator and the impossibility of hiding from Him to whom we are answerable (Gen. 3; Heb. 4:13). For man (however much he may wish it) cannot cease to be what he is by his very constitution, namely, God's creature, with the divine image stamped upon his inmost being (however much he may attempt to disavow and deface that image), finite, dependent, mortal, accountable.

Moreover, man's rebellion against the authority of God is, both in its origin and in its effects, immoral and unethical. To deny the truth and to accept in its place what one knows to be a falsehood is thoroughly immoral. Yet this is precisely what man does, for he arrogantly turns his back on what he knows to be the truth about God and with incredible stupidity welcomes instead the lie of the devil. By his arrogance man also displays incredible ingratitude, and ingratitude to Him who is our wholly beneficent Creator is thoroughly immoral. It is ironic that the satanic contradiction ("You will not die"—Gen. 3:4) of God's Word is the lie that kills! Hence Christ's denunciation of the devil as not only a liar but also a murderer from the beginning (John 8:44).

Man's declaration of autonomy and self-adequacy is his fall, not his rise. His repudiaton (futile though it may be) of the personal Creator-creature relationship, which is the source and center of man's whole being, and which alone gives meaning to his existence and fulfillment to his potential, disrupts the very heart of personhood. Man's refusal to acknowledge the sovereign rights of his Creator automatically puts him at enmity with God—and such enmity is absolutely unethical and the beginning of all else that is unethical. Enmity with God inevitably leads to enmity with his fellow man.

By definition there can be but one God. There is "room" for but one infinite being; any conception of two or more infinite beings who exist "side by side" involves a contradiction. Man in the abstract, however (even if spelled *Man* with a capital *M*), is not at all a comparable unity, for mankind is a multiplicity, composed of many individuals, mortal, vulnerable, and transient, "like the flower of the field" (Isa. 40:6–8). Therefore every would-be autonomous man is a potentially deadly rival to every other would-be autonomous man, an open contradiction of his claim to absolute self-sufficiency, and a threat to his very life. This is why enmity between man and man, ruthless rivalries, cruel injustices, and brutal fratricide are so prevalent in human society. The history of mankind, ever since Cain murdered Abel, is largely a history of manslaughter and martial conflict. But God, being one, cannot be at enmity with Himself; being immortal, He is not threatened by death; being holy and loving, He is free from all hatred and iniquity. The integrity of man is realized only in a harmonious filial relationship with the one God, his Creator; from that relationship alone follow the unity and harmony of human society, over which man was created to exercise dominion in accordance with the will and design of the Creator of all. Henry Stob has well said:

> Think of man as a completely free, autonomous personality and you isolate him and thereby destroy society. . . . There can be for him no sovereign good that engages his will, for he can recognize no law of which he is not the author. He can acknowledge no objective reality which measures and regulates his intelligence. He can only settle down in the solitude of his tiny sacred universe and resist any intervention from outside.[4]

One might say man becomes in his fallenness an existentialist, for whom the only existence that has reality and meaning is his own. His own present being alone holds significance for him: the past is past and done with, the future is unknown and unknowable. A word from the past uttered by someone other than himself cannot bind him or be determinative for him (Gen. 2:17). The only history that is of moment to him is his own. No one, not even God (if He exists), can predict what will happen in the future (Gen. 2:17 again), for the future is as yet nonexistent, subject to chance and coincidence and contingency. But this, alas, is not the heroic fulfillment but the tragic diminishment of man. He has in fact dehumanized himself by isolating himself from God and from his fellow man, since the unity of man both individually and collectively cannot be realized apart from union with

---

4. Henry Stob, *Ethical Reflections* (1978), p. 175.

God. What is more, man has "de-deified" God (insofar as he takes Him into account at all) by reducing Him to merely human proportions: he insists that what man cannot see—the future—God cannot see, and that what man cannot do—foretell and control the future—God cannot do! Self-isolation, however, can never protect or insulate man from his own finitude and mortality, nor can it in any sense nullify the reality of the supreme existence and sovereignty of God or of man's answerability to his Creator.

But there is yet another complication to the human predicament, for the rebelliousness of man affects not only his relationship to God and to his fellow men but also his relationship to his environment. Placed at the head of the created order to have dominion over it and harness its forces for the glory of God and the benefit of mankind, man dragged down his world with him when he fell away from God into sin (Gen. 1:28–31; 3:17–19). The disorder of man is inescapably communicated to the realm of nature as he pervertedly distorts his mandate by immorally and irresponsibly exploiting the lower creation for his own selfish ends. It is not surprising that man is threatened by the environment, originally so congenial to his existence, as a result of the colossal abuse to which he has subjected it. St. Paul graphically speaks of the created order as being "subjected to futility" through human folly and wickedness and as waiting "with eager longing for the revealing of the sons of God," because "the creation itself will be set free from its bondage to decay and obtain the glorious liberty of the children of God" (Rom. 8:19–22). Just as the selfishness of fallen man disturbs the course of nature, so the consummation of man's redemption, described here as "the glorious liberty of the children of God," which is fulfilled in Christ, will restore nature and the environment to their pristine harmony and accomplish their predestined glory.

Judgment

God's Word, of course, precisely because it is *God's* Word, cannot fail. Despite the devil's contradiction, the original warning of judgment has proved to be a word of truth. The problems of human society throughout history manifest that judgment which man by his rebellious ingratitude has brought on himself. Though final judgment is a terrible and ultimate reality, divine judgment is not merely future and eschatological: the disobedience of man has ineluctably woven it into the very fabric of everyday existence. This was clearly perceived by the prophets of old. Jeremiah, for example, admonished the people of his day in the following terms:

> Have you not brought this upon yourself by forsaking the LORD your God, when he led you in the way? . . . Know and see that it is evil and bitter for you to forsake the LORD your God. . . . Your ways and your doings have brought this upon you. This is your doom, and it is bitter; it has reached your very heart. . . . Hear, O earth; behold, I am bringing evil upon this people, the fruit of their devices, because they have not given heed to my words; and as for my law, they have rejected it (Jer. 2:17, 19; 4:18; 6:19).

In an important passage in the New Testament (Rom. 1:18–32) St. Paul describes how man plunges himself into the grossest stupidity by his suppression of the truth about God, truth which is fundamental not only to all existence, his own included, but also to the comprehension of the meaning of the universe, of which he is a part. By withholding the love and honor due his Creator, whom he should reverence and adore and to whom he owes his being and everything that is good, he is guilty of appalling ingratitude; despite his proud pretensions to wisdom, he makes it plain that he has taken leave of his senses. Religious by constitution (for, despite fierce denials, he is stamped with the divine image), man idolatrously worships the creature instead of the Creator, perverting not merely pure religion but also his own nature as he indulges in the unnatural lusts and passions of his fallenness. Three times St. Paul says of the ungodly that "God gave them up" to their vile and improper practices (vv. 24, 26, 28). Sinful man needs no assistance in working out his own perdition. Ungodliness unaided brings its own judgment on man and society here and now, in addition to final judgment hereafter. To be given up by God to wallow in the filth of one's own making is itself self-manufactured judgment.

But the unpleasant consequences of individual and corporate ungodliness that overtake us in this life, including such calamitous developments as the Babylonian captivity of the Jewish people, and even physical death, are interim judgments. They are but preludes to final judgment. The unease and disharmony deep within every ungodly person are symptoms of a bad conscience; for every human being, made in the image of God, knows that an account has to be rendered to Him who is the just and holy Creator of all and from whom no creature is hidden (Heb. 4:12–13). "For his eyes are upon the ways of a man, and he sees all his steps," we read in Job 34:21. "There is no gloom or deep darkness where evildoers may hide themselves" (Job 34:22). Physical death is not the end of things: it is followed by judgment (Heb. 9:27). "It is a fearful thing to fall into the hands of the living God" (Heb. 10:31). The fearfulness of final judgment is dramatically portrayed in the vision seen by St. John:

> Then the kings of the earth and the great men and the generals and the rich and the strong, and every one, slave and free, hid in the caves and among the rocks of the mountains, calling to the mountains and rocks, "Fall on us and hide us from the face of him who is seated on the throne, and from the wrath of the Lamb; for the great day of their wrath has come, and who can stand before it?" (Rev. 6:15–17).

The impenitent sinner does not fear physical death as much as he fears the day of judgment and what is called "the second death," the lot of those whose names are not found written in the Book of Life (Rev. 20:6, 14, 15). That is why St. Paul asserts that "the sting of death is sin," sin unrepented of and unpardoned, and that "the power of sin is the law" (I Cor. 15:56); for the lawbreaker knows that he must stand condemned before the judgment throne of the Lawgiver. This solemn reality explains why the ungodly man desperately attempts to persuade himself that physical death is the absolute end of his existence, that there is no judgment awaiting him beyond the grave, and above all that the God whom he has ignored or denied does not exist.

Redemption

The power and authority of God are certainly displayed in judgment, but judgment is only the obverse side of the coin. The primary purpose of creation is not that all should end in judgment and destruction, which would be indicative of failure rather than fulfillment, but that the world should be a mirror which faithfully reflects the glory and the goodness of its Creator. The function of judgment, then, is to purge creation of all that is contrary to that purpose. Being of a secondary or negative character, the function of judgment is subsidiary to the achievement of the primary and positive intention of God's work of creation which is brought about not by judgment but by redemption. Man was certainly not created in the image of God to become a slave of passion and violence, nor was the world created to degenerate into a snakepit of hatred and misery. The deadly force of evil is nullified not merely by judgment which destroys but in a vital manner by redemption in Christ which restores and regenerates. The disintegration caused by sin is counter-acted by the reintegration achieved by redemption. This reintegration involves the renovation within man of the image of God in which he was originally created, so that in the renewed creation man will finally and forever function in perfect harmony with the Creator and His sovereign will, with the rest of the created order, including his fellow men, and with himself. The restoration of man, the leader within the cosmos, brings about the restoration of the whole and the establishment of a society that is fully "ethical," or as St. Peter puts it, "new heavens and a new earth in which righteousness dwells" (II Peter 3:13).

But Christ's followers do not wait for the dawn of the new age before they start to practice Christian ethics. Here and now, as Jesus taught, Christian believers are the salt of the earth (not of course in any sense of personal superiority), whose presence in this fallen world God uses to preserve society from irreversible deterio-ration. They are also the light of the world, reflecting the pure glory of Him who in an absolute sense is the Light of the world (John 8:12), and who has commanded them to let their light shine so that others may see their good works (Christian ethics!) and give glory to our heavenly Father (Matt. 5:13–16). Secular programs for social improvement are not without importance, but radical change is effected only in the transformed lives of those who are renewed in Christ. Once reborn, Christians are destined to be conformed to the perfection of Christ; but this glorious destiny, though it will be realized only hereafter, demands ethical serious-ness during this present life. "We know," St. John writes, "that when he appears *we shall be like him,* for we shall see him as he is. And every one who thus hopes in him *purifies himself as he is pure"* (I John 3:2).

Whatever else it may be, the road the Christian is called to walk is certainly an ethical road. It is his great privilege, as a former rebel now re-created in Christ, to cooperate actively through God's grace in the fulfillment of the purpose of creation. "We are his workmanship," St. Paul explains, *"created in Christ Jesus for good works,* which God prepared beforehand, that we should walk in them" (Eph. 2:10). "Once you were darkness," he reminds the Ephesians, "but now you are light in the Lord"—such a radical contrast cannot be missed, though it may be mocked, by the world; on this basis Paul enjoins his readers to "walk as children of light," adding that "the fruit of light is found in all that is good and right and true" (Eph. 5:8–9).

Christ is the Christian's ethical goal and model. "Have this mind among yourselves, which you have in Christ Jesus," Paul admonishes the members of the Philippian church, among whom there have been disharmony and contention (Phil. 2:1–5). Christians who are in the midst of suffering are encouraged with these words: "Christ also suffered for you, leaving you an example, that you should follow in his steps" (I Peter 2:21). Christ the incarnate Son indeed displays humanity as God intended it to be: perfectly integrated, joyfully and harmoniously at one with the Father and His will, controlling the forces of the universe as He commands the obedience of both spirits and the elements, and radiating healing and blessing wherever He goes. The closer we draw to His likeness the nearer we come to the fulfillment of the immense potential of our humanity on which the image of God has been imprinted.

2

Conscience

Conscience is an inner self-knowledge which is moral in character.[1] By it man knows instinctively and constitutionally that there are at the same time a distinction between right and wrong and an obligation to choose what is right and to refuse what is wrong. That is why a person who conducts his life in accordance with what he knows to be just and honorable is called conscientious. The conscience is a line connecting man to his Creator: it is one aspect of the image of God in which man was created. It demarcates man from the rest of the animal creation as essentially a moral being who is answerable for his actions—answerable primarily and ultimately to God—and whose behavior should reflect the holiness and lovingkindness of his Creator. The fundamental nature of this relationship between God the Creator and His morally constituted creature man means that conscience, since it displays the imprint of the divine image, does not operate in a vacuum: the power of its compulsion is the innate knowledge of the perfection of the Creator and the goodness of His will.[2]

Being constitutional to man, conscience is a universal phenomenon. Both anthropology and the history of literature bear witness to this fact. The implications of the concept of conscience provide, for example, the pervasive substance or substructure of Greek tragedy, the deep concern of which is the just balance of all elements, personal and impersonal, in our world. Insolence (*hybris*), that is, disregard of the allotted order of things, inevitably is followed by retributive justice (*dikē*), because the law (*themis*) of accepted conduct has been broken. Breaking this law violates one's own fate (*moira*) or, more accurately, assigned "portion," and also that of the offended party or victim, arousing the avenging Furies (*Erinyes*) to pursue the offender with the wrath of retribution until the due penalty has been paid for his evil deed. Even Mother Earth is outraged by such crimes as inordinate passion and bloodshed, and the pollution she has suffered from them is punished by blight and plague and dearth—a notion betraying an awareness that the disorder

---

1. The Latin *conscientia* (*con* + *scientia,* knowledge) corresponds exactly to the Greek *syneidesis.*

2. Christian Maurer rightly observes that *syneidesis* "is not to be defined as a power of religious and moral evaluation or the like which can be detached from man. It is man himself aware of himself in perception and acknowledgment, in willing and acting" (*"syneidesis,"* in *Theological Dictionary of the New Testament,* ed. Gerhard Kittel and Gerhard Friedrich [1971], vol. 7, p. 914).

of human society adversely affects the order of the world man inhabits. This complex of ideas is summed up in the concept of *nemesis,* a Greek term meaning the distribution of what is due, the retribution of injustice with condign punishment—effected not so much by the human administration of justice as by the force of universal order. The sense of the reality of nemesis is heightened in Greek mythology by the personification of the concept as Nemesis, the goddess of due proportion. Nemesis represents the avenging power of deity, hating every transgression of the bounds of moderation, inevitably punishing boastful arrogance and injustice, and restoring the proper equilibrium of what has been deranged by human wickedness.

Tertullian (writing about A.D. 200) regarded the universal phenomenon of conscience, which he called the witness of the soul, as a clear proof of the existence of God inescapably present in man.[3] This evidence, he insisted, is present in all men, the humble and untaught as well as the learned and cultured, so that there is no need to turn to libraries and schools of philosophy for its verification. Whence, he asks, does the apprehension of divine judgment arise if there is no God to judge? Whence comes the soul's natural fear of God if God cannot be angry? How is there any dread of Him if nothing offends Him? What leads to watchful carefulness but the prospect of judgment? From what does judgment come but from power? And to whom does supreme power belong but to God alone? Tertullian describes nature as the mistress and the soul as her disciple: "But everything the one has taught and the other learned," he adds, "has come from God," who is "the Teacher of the teacher."

> God is everywhere, and the goodness of God is everywhere; demons are everywhere, and the cursing of them is everywhere; the invocation of divine judgment is everywhere, death is everywhere, and the sense of death is everywhere, and all the world over is the witness of the soul. There is not a soul of man that does not, from the light that is in itself, proclaim the very things we Christians are not permitted to speak above our breath. Most justly, then, every soul is a culprit as well as a witness: in the measure that it testifies for truth, the guilt of error lies on it; and on the day of judgment it will stand before the courts of God, without a word to say. Though you did not seek to know him, yet you, O soul, proclaimed God![4]

If, as we have affirmed and as Scripture confirms, conscience is universal because it belongs to the very constitution of man (to use a more technical term, it is ontological), it cannot be dismissed as something incidental or accidental in the experience of mankind. It is not the consequence of long-established custom or convention—though custom and convention may be regulated by conscience, and conscience may be influenced, perhaps wrongly, by custom. It is not an improved social sensitivity painfully developed over centuries of evolutionary advancement—

---

3. This is really a form of what is known as the argument based on the *consensus gentium,* the common consent of all nations.

4. Tertullian, *De Testimonio Animae.*

and in any case there is ample evidence to show that man is morally and socially no better today than he was two thousand years ago. And it is not an element in the hidden reservoir of the "collective unconscious" which man accumulates and draws from in the course of history. Many devices have been and continue to be invented in the endless endeavor to deny the radical nature of the conscience, but they are all futile because, conscience belonging constitutionally (ontologically) to his creaturely nature, man cannot cease to be what he is (except by altogether ceasing to be). Yet though he cannot destroy the image of God in which he is made, man in his fallenness continually perverts it and denies it, contributing all the more to his *bad* conscience, so that there is nothing he would like to be rid of more than his conscience and the unrest it causes at the center of his being.

External laws, such as the Ten Commandments or its summary enjoining total love of God and neighbor, serve to throw into relief man's guilt as a lawbreaker, but they are not essential to the formation and functioning of conscience because, as we have said, the absolute standard of God's goodness was indelibly stamped upon the heart of man at his creation. This principle of human conscience is clearly described by St. Paul in Romans 2:14–16, where he explains that the Gentiles who, unlike the Jews, do not have the law given through Moses yet "do by nature what the law requires. . . . They show that what the law requires is written on their hearts, while their conscience also bears witness and their conflicting thoughts accuse or perhaps excuse them." And, further, the apostle makes it plain in this passage that the operation of the conscience relates not only back to creation ("written on their hearts") but also forward to final judgment ("on that day when . . . God judges the secrets of men by Christ Jesus").

As has already been remarked, the conscience in essence witnesses to the status of man's relationship with his Maker. This is well illustrated in the history of our first parents: the good conscience that belongs to a state of innocence is blessed by unclouded fellowship between the Lord God and His human creatures; but the bad conscience caused by disobedience to the divine will destroys that harmonious relationship, and man in his guilt seeks to hide himself from the presence of God. Of course one may also be said to have a good or a bad conscience in relation to one's fellow man; but the interpersonal relationship between man and man (horizontal) cannot be isolated from the interpersonal relationship between man and God (vertical), for a good conscience toward God cannot coexist with a bad conscience toward man.

Thus St. Paul expressed his concern to have a conscience free from offense toward both God and man (Acts 24:16). As he himself had a clear conscience before God with regard to his dealings with the members of the Corinthian church, who knew him so well, Paul was able to commend himself "to every man's conscience in the sight of God" (II Cor. 4:2), confident that an examination of their own consciences before God would confirm the verdict of his own conscience. "What we are is known to God," he says, "and I hope it is known also to your conscience" (II Cor. 5:11). St. Peter's admonition to Christians facing persecution to maintain a good conscience (I Peter 3:16) certainly refers to their duty to live as good citizens who are careful not to give offense by lawless and irresponsible behavior. But again, the force of the conscience derives from man's answerability before God, and a good conscience in the presence of men is no more than an extension and an expression of a good conscience in the presence of God. To separate the former from the latter is to reduce reality to merely human proportions, and that is in effect to deny the Creator.

God's Vicar

The primacy of this Godward relationship is evident from the fact that an appeal to the conscience is essentially an appeal to God Himself. What could be plainer than St. Paul's protestation in Romans 9:1: "I am speaking the truth in Christ, I am not lying; my conscience bears me witness in the Holy Spirit"? Therefore Jeremy Taylor, writing in 1659, is not unreasonable when he boldly speaks of the conscience as God's vicar or substitute within us: "God is in our hearts by his laws," he writes; "he rules in us by his substitute, our conscience. . . . He hath given us conscience to be in God's stead to us . . . ; and when we call God to witness we only mean that our conscience is right, and that God and God's vicar, our conscience, know it." Like Tertullian, Taylor asserts that the possession of conscience makes atheism impossible.[5]

The commission of sin against God or of crime against man involves culpable disregard of the dictates of conscience, with the result that the conscience becomes defiled and corrupted. "To the corrupt and unbelieving nothing is pure," St. Paul advises Titus; "their very minds and consciences are corrupted." Even though "they profess to know God," by acting against their consciences "they deny him by their deeds" and thus show themselves to be "detestable, disobedient, unfit for any good deed" (Titus 1:15–16). Through addiction to lying and hatred of the truth a person's conscience may become "seared" (I Tim. 4:2): either he has become so incorrigibly rebellious that his conscience is in effect branded with the mark of Satan, or his conscience is cauterized—that is, by habitual wickedness he has rendered himself insensitive to the promptings of conscience. In the same way St. Paul speaks elsewhere of pagans who, "alienated from the life of God because of the ignorance that is in them, due to their hardness of heart," have become "callous" or insensitive (Eph. 4:18–19).

A guilty conscience is a polluted conscience, and its first need is to be cleansed of its pollution and guilt. This purgation is effected by "the blood of Christ who through the eternal Spirit offered himself without blemish to God"—that is to say, by the atoning death of Christ, the only One with a pure and guiltless conscience ("without blemish"), who at Calvary took the guilt of mankind's bad conscience upon Himself and paid its penalty. It is His blood alone which has the power to

5. Jeremy Taylor, *Ductor Dubitantium,* I,i, rule I,2,4.

"purify our conscience from dead works to serve the living God" (Heb. 9:14) and which enables us to draw near to God's throne of grace "with a true heart in full assurance of faith, with our hearts sprinkled clean from an evil conscience" (Heb. 10:22). His conscience purged and revived, the Christian, united by faith to Christ, is restored to that fellowship with his Creator which is so vital to the integrity of his being.

The function of conscience is not to will but (as the derivation of the term suggests) to know—in particular to know inwardly and instinctively that there is a difference between right and wrong, that what is in accordance with the will and character of God is right and what is discordant with the same is wrong, and that it is our duty, our moral obligation to God and also to our fellow men, to do what is right and to reject what is wrong. First of all comes understanding of the basic distinction of right and wrong, and then comes willing. Knowing that a particular decision is right and another wrong, a person may by the exercise of the will choose the former and maintain a good conscience, or he may choose the latter and engender a bad conscience. It is not the conscience but the will that chooses. Once the choice has been made and action has been taken, the conscience remains at the heart of man's being, not only witnessing for what is right and against what is wrong but also witnessing to the rightness or wrongness of the specific choice made by the will.

Thus conscience sheds the light of knowledge and instruction on the path that should be pursued; it also, once decision has been translated into action, passes judgment of either approval or disapproval on the course that has been chosen. Not that the conscience is an entity in itself—rather, and more accurately, through it the verdict of God Himself is silently and inwardly pronounced. Moreover, the expression "a guilty conscience" (and others comparably formed) does not mean that some unseen part of a person is guilty, but that the person in his entirety is guilty in the light of the witness of conscience: at the heart of his being he knows that he as a moral, responsible person is guilty before God. Within himself and inseparable from the totality of his self is this divine moral imperative whose authority is absolute and unqualified.

In no sense, then, can the conscience be treated as neutral or as subject to the accidents and contingencies of mortal existence. There are no situations in which a person is not required to love God and his neighbor. Furthermore, interpersonal communion presupposes interpersonal communication; this applies to the person-to-Person relation between man and God as well as to the person-to-person relation between man and man. The parties must be on speaking terms to experience communion. Even apart from specific commands and prohibitions, the conscience is the voice of God telling man that certain things are wrong: hatred, for instance, because it is contrary to the character of God who is love, and murder, because it cruelly deprives a fellow human being of his God-given life and therefore is contrary to the character of God who is life. And what is contrary to the character of God is *ipso facto* contrary to the will of God.

The range of the conscience may be increased and fortified by specific utterances of God. Cain's murder of Abel was monstrously wicked, even though no word had been spoken by God prohibiting fratricide, because it was an unnatural and ungodly deed and therefore a violation of conscience and a rebellion against the will of his Creator. On the other hand, God had given a specific word to Cain's parents ordering them not to eat the fruit of a particular tree, whereas apart from that command the eating of that fruit would have been inoffensive. Once that word had been uttered, however, their consciences told them that to eat that fruit would be wrong and a contravention of the divine will. It may well be observed that there are many actions which in general are morally indifferent, practices that are taken for granted, such as the eating of meals, the wearing of clothes, and sleeping at night. However, such practices are not really indifferent; normal and necessary activities of this kind are in themselves innocent and irreproachable because they are sanctioned by conscience. Yet, even though they are ordinarily done with a clear conscience, there is no custom, however necessary, which is not open to abuse: greedy excess turns eating into gluttony, extravagance in dressing becomes ostentation, and too much sleep is the mark of the sluggard. Such lack of moderation, being dishonoring to God, inconsiderate of others, and harmful to the self, is incompatible with the dictates of conscience. The totality of our being and doing is subject to the scrutiny of conscience.

Conscience and the Fall of Man

There are modern scholars who dissent from the doctrine of conscience that we have attempted to expound. Emil Brunner, for example, flatly denies that conscience is the "voice of God"; he defines it as "something sinister" which "attacks man like an alien, dark, hostile power" and which "primarily has nothing to do with God at all." Conscience in Brunner's view is "a sense of unrest, a signal of alarm," an awareness of the contradiction or disturbance of order at the center of man's existence. Thus Brunner equates conscience with what is generally known as a bad or guilty conscience.

It is true that when we say that a person "has to live with his conscience" we mean a guilty conscience; one's life is not disturbed by a clear conscience. But what is the significance of this phenomenon of conscience? To quote Goethe, "Why this rapture and unrest?" How can one maintain that the conscience primarily has nothing to do with God at all? Not even Brunner can consistently maintain such a position, for it is acknowledged that the disturbance at the heart of man's being is precisely the consequence of the disruption of his relationship with God, whose will he has disobeyed. This radical disharmony within man cannot be understood apart from the line that links man to his Creator and from the divine image which stamps every man as belonging to God. Brunner, even with his restricted definition of conscience, cannot avoid asserting that in conscience "it is the angry God who meets man" and that conscience is the fear of God which "drives the soul away from God" and which "yet is also the longing of the soul for God." When, moreover, he dismisses "the so-called 'good' conscience" as "a phenomenon which belongs to the surface of life and is therefore quite secondary" and as a reality solely in the sphere of civil justice which "has nothing to do with existence as a whole but only with isolated actions as such," he appears to make a superficial judgment which leaves out of account the profound effect of redemption in Christ on the conscience of the believer.[6]

In his remarkably penetrating though unfinished work on ethics Dietrich Bonhoeffer also presents the task of ethics as beginning with the fall of man, but the argument he develops is much more deeply rooted in Scripture than is Brunner's. Indeed, Bonhoeffer sees the knowledge of good and evil, which resulted from eating the fruit of the forbidden tree, not merely as the consequence but as the objective of the original disobedience and the scope of fallen man's ethical notions. This implies a fundamental separation between secular ethics and Christian ethics, since the latter does not treat the present state of things as normal and constant but goes back to the source of the very question of morality. "Christian ethics," he writes, "claims to discuss the origin of the whole problem of ethics, and thus professes to be a critique of all ethics simply as ethics." According to Christian ethics the knowledge of good and evil is made possible by "falling away from the origin." The one thing that man knows at his origin is God. His falling away from God has destroyed the unity of his knowledge of God, and thence of other persons and entities and of himself, for it is in God alone that man knows all things. "The knowledge of good and evil shows that he is no longer at one with his origin," Bonhoeffer states. With the destruction of the unity of his knowledge of God fallen man has lost the understanding of himself. He is now self-centered: his interest lies in his own possibilities of being good or evil, quite apart from God and in fact against God. "But," Bonhoeffer rightly insists, "man cannot be rid of his origin. Instead of knowing himself in the origin of God, he must now know himself as an origin." He arrogates to himself the divine dignity.

> Instead of accepting the choice and election of God, man himself desires to choose, to be the origin of the election. . . . He has become like God, but against God. Herein lies the serpent's deceit. Man knows good and evil, but because he is not the origin, because he acquires this knowledge only at the price of estrangement from the origin, the good and evil that he knows are not the good and evil of God but good and evil against God. They are good and evil of man's own choosing, in opposition to the eternal election of God. In becoming like God man has become a god against God. . . . Man's life is now disunion with God, with men, with things, and with himself.[7]

Jacques Ellul follows a similar path. Prior to the fall, he maintains, there was no moral conscience and no ethics, and Adam had no knowledge of the good: it was

---

6. Emil Brunner, *The Divine Imperative* (1947), pp. 156–158.
7. Dietrich Bonhoeffer, *Ethics,* ed. Eberhard Bethge (1964), pp. 142–144.

to get that knowledge that he ate the fruit. What Adam did have before alienation was "an existential communion with the good, which is quite another thing."[8] For estranged man morality is necessary and unavoidable as "part of the condition of the fall."

> Now endowed with the power to define good and evil, to elaborate it, to know it and to pretend to obey it, man can no longer renounce this power which he has purchased so dearly. He must exercise it. He cannot live without morality.[9]

Primal man is thus portrayed as grasping after and getting a knowledge he did not previously possess. This presupposes that primal man's was a rebellious humanistic understanding of knowledge. It is certainly right to postulate a radical distinction between the mind and attitude of man before the fall and after the fall; however, to affirm that in Eden Adam had no knowledge of the good but only an existential communion with the good is to impose an overelaborate interpretation on the simplicity of the text; for, since one knows what one experiences, existential communion could not have been enjoyed without knowledge of the good that was being experienced.

It is undeniable that for fallen mankind ethics has become a matter of crucial importance and anguished debate. But both Bonhoeffer and Ellul (not to mention Brunner) have overlooked a factor of extreme significance, namely that prior to the fall God treated man as an ethical being. He did so by giving man permission to eat fruit from all the trees of the garden, with the exception of one which was forbidden. This means that in his innocence Adam was addressed as a responsible person who, after receiving the permission and the prohibition, was placed in the garden on divine probation. And this could only be if he already, as created, had a moral conscience. In this state of unspoiled communion with his Creator Adam had experience, and therefore knowledge, only of good, and this in turn meant that his conscience was clear and at ease; he did not "have to live with his conscience," though he had to live by the word revealing God's will to him. From the very beginning, therefore, he was required to function as a morally responsible person capable of conscientious conduct.

The point of the Genesis account in this respect, then, is that as a consequence of the first sin man now has the knowledge of good *and evil:* to his previous knowledge of good the knowledge of evil is now added. Where before there was unclouded harmony with God and the created order, there is now conflict and discord. Where before all was life and light the dark disruption of death has entered in. The wage paid by sin is death (Rom. 6:23). The disastrous effect of the disobedience of Adam, the first representative man, is canceled only by the grace of God through the obedience, obedience unto death, even death on a cross, of Christ Jesus, the second representative man (Rom. 5:12–17; Phil. 2:8). "If," says

---

8. Jacques Ellul, *To Will and to Do* (1969), pp. 6, 14–15.
9. Ibid., p. 71.

St. Paul, "because of one man's trespass, death reigned through that one man, much more will those who receive the abundance of grace and the free gift of righteousness reign in life through the one man Jesus Christ" (Rom. 5:17). Apart from this divine grace there can be no resolution of the disharmony and contradiction by which man is bedeviled at the very heart of his being and no termination of the internal warfare which prevents him from doing what he would (Gal. 5:17). "I delight in the law of God, in my inmost self," St. Paul says again, "But I see in my members another law at war with the law of my mind and making me captive to the law of sin which dwells in my members" (Rom. 7:22–23). The heart of man has become an ethical battleground!

The knowledge of good and evil, then, which fallen man has is not really an extension in knowledge and an advancement in understanding; it is essentially the perversion of knowledge and the loss of understanding. Nor is it the achievement of human freedom and self-determination, but rather the end of freedom by the absurd choice of self-destruction. For sinful man in rebelliously and self-assertively cutting himself off from God cuts himself off from both the source and the meaning of his existence; at the same time, by taking things into his own hands and ceasing to function in accordance with the design of his Creator, he forfeits his true freedom and sinks into the bondage of his own brokenness. Hence the apostle's candid exclamation: "I do not understand my own actions. For I do not do what I want, but I do the very thing I hate" (Rom. 7:15).

Man's basic need is to recover that which he has lost; this, as we have seen, is possible only in the redemption that God has provided in Jesus Christ. The dynamic of the gospel brings reintegration as, through the mediation of the divine-human Redeemer, the penitent sinner is reconnected with his Creator from whom alone he derives his being and the purpose of his being. Now he again enjoys peace and harmony in the depth of his personhood as he delights to hear and live obediently by the word of God. No longer does he foolishly deny the absolute authority and sovereign goodness of his Creator. His conscience purged, he learns at last what true morality is. United to Christ, the believer is again on speaking— and listening—terms with his Maker. He now knows, because he has experienced its truth, that the will of God, conveyed in the word and commandment of God, defines and is identical with man's good, and that evil is identical with all that is opposed to the divine will. He acknowledges that it is precisely the goodness of God's authoritative word that sets the agenda for genuine Christian ethics.

As man was created a moral being, so in the new heaven and the new earth he will continue to be a moral being. The paradise lost will be fully regained, and more than regained, because in eternal glory redeemed humanity will not be on probation; there will be no tree of the knowledge of good and evil, but only the tree of life unfailingly yielding its fruit. Man's state will be one of ethical perfection in the renewed creation. Sin with its evil consequences of sorrow, suffering, injustice, and death will have no place in it: "Nothing unclean shall enter it, nor any one who practices abomination or falsehood, but only those who are written in the Lamb's book of life" (Rev. 21:27). All the former things that have marred and disrupted the world will have passed away for ever (Rev. 21:3–4; 22:2–5).

The Elizabethan divine William Perkins (1558–1602) speaks of conscience as having two assistants, namely mind and memory. In this connection the mind is described as "the storehouse and keeper of all manner of rules and principles," and its duty "is to prefer and present to the conscience rules of divine law whereby it is to give judgment"; the function of the memory is to recall "the particular actions which a man hath done or not done." Conscience then passes judgment on the rightness or wrongness of the man's conduct. Perkins propounds what he calls a "practical syllogism" to illustrate the reasoning by which conscience operates. In the case of a murderer it would operate as follows:

> *Every murderer is cursed,* saith the mind:
> *Thou art a murderer,* saith conscience assisted by memory:
> Ergo, *Thou art cursed,* saith conscience, and so giveth her sentence.[10]

Though an analysis of this kind may have some value, it is dangerous because it tends to be overrational and to conceive of man, or certain parts of man, as presenting particular facts to the conscience for it to pass a verdict. Logic is undoubtedly involved, but the syllogism is solely logical and could theoretically be argued quite independently of conscience. The important thing—which Perkins would not have wished to dispute—is that man in his wholeness stands before the bar of his conscience. Reason and memory, will, intention, and action all contribute to the standing of any man, but the deep inner voice of conscience does not wait upon human logic to witness to the harmony or disharmony at the very center of man's being.

The Divine Will

In the realm of human ethics there is but one authentic criterion, namely the sovereign will of God for man and the world in which man has been assigned a position of responsibility. Man in his fallenness, however, sinfully suppresses the truth of the eternal power and godhead of the Creator, devises his own system of acceptable conduct, and lapses into every kind of immoral behavior (Rom. 1:18–32). Hence the need, as we have already seen, for *Christian* ethics, which, as the ethics of redeemed humanity, is in principle the reestablishment of the original ethical relationship between man and his Creator. The ethical norm for the Christian is the will and goodness of God, no longer the will and goodness of man. The situation has been perceptively portrayed by Bonhoeffer:

> If the ethical problem presents itself essentially in the form of inquiries about one's own being good, this means that it has already been decided that it is the self and the

10. William Perkins, *A Discourse of Conscience* (1596), chap. 2.

world which are the ultimate reality. The aim of all ethical reflection is, then, that I myself shall be good and that the world shall become good through my action. But the problem of ethics at once assumes a new aspect if it becomes apparent that these realities, myself and the world, themselves lie embedded in a quite different ultimate reality, namely, the reality of God, the Creator, Reconciler, and Redeemer. What is of ultimate importance is no longer that I should become good, or that the condition of the world should be made better by my action, but that the reality of God should show itself everywhere to be the ultimate reality.[11]

The ultimate reality of God is dynamically revealed within our fallen world by Jesus Christ, in and through whom the blessedness that was lost is restored and enhanced.

The fact that humanistic ethical conduct may in certain respects approximate and even appear to be identical with Christian ethical conduct may seem to render questionable the postulate of a fundamental distinction between Christian and secular ethics. "Noble paganism," for example, has rightly been admired because of the capacity it has shown for lofty ideals, good citizenship, and just government. There is, however, a world of difference between man-centered morality, even of the most altruistic kind, and Christ-centered morality, which focuses on the glory of God for the sake of Jesus Christ. As Ellul insists, "That which constitutes Christianity is the person of Jesus Christ."

> Everything derives from the fact that Jesus is God, that Jesus Christ is Lord and Savior. Apart from that there is only talk. . . . But then one perceives that the problem is above all a problem of truth, and that it is only in this truth, recognized and assumed, that ethics can take shape. . . . For Christian ethics is going to be the relation between the person of Jesus Christ and a person who takes him as his Savior and Lord. . . . The person who does not accept Jesus Christ can only pass judgment on the good from his own point of view. . . . To him, Christian behavior will usually seem incomprehensible, absurd, sometimes bad. It can only bear the judgment which Paul referred to as "a stumbling block to Jews and folly to Gentiles" (1 Cor. 1:23). It is always a stumbling block to the humanists, the prudent, the virtuous, and the religious. It is always a piece of stupidity to philosophers, scientists, and technicians.[12]

In vital respects Christian ethics with its other-worldly perspective should be a tacit witness against the materialistic self-centeredness that is so widely accepted as ethically commendable in the secular world; this of course cannot be expected to increase the general popularity of Christianity and its standards.

As Augustine has said, "The good man is neither uplifted with the good things of time nor broken by its ills, whereas the wicked man, because he is corrupted by this world's happiness, feels himself punished by its unhappiness." As Augustine wrote he had in mind the sack of Rome and the carnage and devastation that accompanied it, afflicting all, Christians as well as unbelievers. In the face of such savage deprivation what was the advantage of Christian morality?

11. Bonhoeffer, *Ethics,* p. 55.
12. Ellul, *To Will and to Do,* pp. 88–89.

Though good and bad men suffer alike, we must not suppose that there is no difference between the men themselves because there is no difference in what they both suffer. For even in the likeness of the sufferings there remains an unlikeness in the sufferers; and, though exposed to the same anguish, virtue and vice are not the same thing. . . . And thus it is that in the same affliction the wicked detest God and blaspheme, while the good pray and praise.[13]

But the Christians in Rome lost all that they had! No, says Augustine, they lost nothing of lasting worth. "Their faith? Their godliness? The possession of the hidden man of the heart? Did they lose these, which in the sight of God are of great price?" he asks.[14] Indeed not, and it is these things which constitute the true wealth of Christians.

Augustine, who had greatly admired Plato and been strongly influenced by his philosophy, came to appreciate the radical antithesis between paganism and Christianity. Referring to the excessive veneration in which some held Plato, he expressed the following judgment:

We for our part reckon Plato neither a god nor a demigod. We would not even compare him to any of God's holy angels, nor to any truth-speaking prophet, nor to any of the apostles or martyrs of Christ, nor indeed to any Christian man.[15]

Similarly Ellul declares:

We absolutely do not deny the grandeur and value of the Platonic ideal and of its philosophy. We say only that it is in no way Christian, and that it is in no way compatible with Christianity. All efforts at conciliation have only ended by diluting the substance of Christianity.[16]

Ellul, however, overlooks the significance of God's common or general grace, which is distinct from His special or saving grace. The fact that in the secularism of our fallen society there is still a place for standards of decency, honor, and justice, and that paganism retains a capacity for noble deeds and sentiments, testifies to us that God has not abandoned His creation but continues to govern and sustain it providentially. The continuing recognition of justice and human dignity even in the midst and in the face of so much brutality and oppression bears witness that society in its fallenness has not been totally dehumanized. The protests that indignity and injustice evoke from unbelievers as well as from Christians indicate that the voice of conscience has not been utterly silenced and obliterated.

In Christ, through whom all things were brought into being, all things hold together (Col. 1:17). By His word of power the world is borne onward in accordance

13. Augustine, *City of God* 1.8.
14. Ibid., 1.10.
15. Ibid., 2.14.
16. Ellul, *To Will and to Do*, p. 74.

with the purpose of its creation (Heb. 1:3). And the wicked as well as the righteous are sustained by divine providence. From one generation to another, as Paul and Barnabas reminded the mob at Lystra, God "allowed all the nations to walk in their own ways; yet he did not leave himself without witness, for he did good and gave you from heaven rains and fruitful seasons, satisfying your hearts with food and gladness" (Acts 14:16–17). Similarly Christ assured His hearers that the heavenly Father "makes his sun rise on the evil and on the good, and sends rain on the just and on the unjust" (Matt. 5:45). Divine providence, moreover, is not limited to the seasons of seedtime and harvest, but extends over all the affairs of human society. Man's sinfulness is always busy producing its evil consequences, but God continues in control and mercifully holds human depravity and its effects within certain limits; one evidence of this is, as we have said, the continuation of a measure of law and order throughout the world. This is what St. Paul means when he says that the governing authorities have been instituted by God for the promotion of good conduct and the punishment of wrongdoing (Rom. 13:1–7). Hence also the insistence in the Book of Daniel that "the Most High rules the kingdom of men" (Dan. 4:17, 25, 32; 5:21) and Christ's admonition to Pilate that he could wield no power over Him unless it had been given him from above (John 19:11).

The seat of this rule of God in the community of mankind is the conscience: the conscience indeed of each individual member of society who is at the same time the citizen of some realm or kingdom to whose government he is subject, but the conscience also of each government whose officers are appointed to maintain order and administer justice conscientiously. The acknowledgment of ethical norms and standards is the foundation of civilization and social coexistence; the rock on which this foundation rests is the reality of conscience, which itself is an ever-present witness to the truth that this is God's world and that man is answerable to his Creator. Conscience, as Calvin has said, is "a sense of divine judgment" and "a certain mean between God and man," that is to say, a connecting point or locus of confrontation. "This awareness which places man in the presence of God's judgment is a sort of guardian appointed to notice and spy out all man's secrets so that nothing may remain buried in darkness."[17]

The Weak and the Strong Conscience

The phenomenon of conscience, then, shows that man is by constitution a moral creature. He knows instinctively that there is a difference between right and wrong. As we have said, however, the conscience is not a thing in itself: it is rooted in man's total being. The more accurately a person knows the truth, the better equipped he is to act conscientiously and the more acutely he is self-condemned if he fails to do so. His conscience is sharpened by knowledge and blunted by ignorance.

---

17. John Calvin, *Institutes of the Christian Religion* 3.19.15.

Because of the fallenness of our humanity there is a need for our conscience to be formed. The conscience is there, implanted by God, but because man sinfully loves darkness rather than light (John 3:19) he needs to be enlightened, and his enlightenment, preeminently by the gospel, results also in the enlightenment of his conscience. St. Peter, for example, had to learn that the coming of Christ implied a new and open attitude to the Gentiles since the gospel was intended for all the peoples of the world (Acts 10). This knowledge, the grasp of this truth, formed his conscience with the result that thenceforth he was able to mingle happily with non-Jews, free from conscientious scruples and misgivings.

A problem of conscience arose in the Corinthian church concerning the eating of food that had been offered to idols (I Cor. 8). An uninstructed Christian, who previously had been accustomed to the worship of idols, holding them to be real gods, would feel his conscience offended and defiled by buying and eating food that had been offered to idols in heathen sacrifice before it was placed on the market. Such a person, St. Paul says, has a *weak* conscience; it is weak because he is ignorant of certain important truths: his conscience needs to be formed by accurate knowledge. The person who knows the truth of the situation has a *strong* conscience. He knows that an idol has no real existence and is therefore a no-god, a nonentity, which follows logically from his knowledge that there is but "one God, the Father, from whom are all things and for whom we exist, and one Lord, Jesus Christ, through whom are all things and through whom we exist." He knows, moreover, that food is indifferent in itself and "will not commend us to God," and that "we are no worse off if we do not eat, and no better off if we do." Yet this does not imply that the person with a strong conscience should dominate the person with a weak conscience. The latter is behaving conscientiously even though he is deficient in knowledge, and he is not helped if his weak conscience is wounded by a blatant display of strength on the part of someone who because of superior knowledge has no scruples about eating food that has been offered to idols.

This, however, should not be taken to mean that the weaker brother should be left with his weak and misinformed conscience. On the contrary, he too can become a strong Christian with a well-formed conscience by being instructed with the knowledge that there is but one God and that idols are nonentities. Thus the person with a weak conscience should not prevail over the person with a strong conscience, for it is inconceivable that the apostle would have sanctioned any Christian's continuing weakness through ignorance when the remedy is for him to become strong through knowledge—especially knowledge of the basic truth that there is but one God. For most people in our world today the question concerning food offered to idols is not an issue, but the principle expounded by St. Paul in this passage is of permanent importance and applicable to all kinds of situations in which the knowledgeable Christian with a strong conscience has to take into consideration (and to instruct) the ill-informed Christian with a weak conscience.

Although fallen man retains his constitutional consciousness of moral responsibility, it is obvious that his rejection of the fundamental truth of his creaturely being and his acceptance of false and perverted conceptions of knowledge must have a deleterious effect on his ability to distinguish between right and wrong. To embrace error and follow falsehood does not obliterate conscience, but it does succeed in stunting and muffling it, which is itself a symptom of the perversion of the true humanity of man, a lamentable result of his denying the law of his own being. Thus man sinfully and stupidly harms himself. The remedy for this damage is grace, the grace of the gospel, by which his relationship to God is restored; thus turned from darkness to light, man now becomes attentive to the will of his Creator. But, as we have noticed, even the regenerate person has much to learn and, in order to be liberated from the erroneous notions of his past, is in need of instruction in the revealed truth of God. The formation of conscience keeps step with the formation of one's understanding of the truth. To achieve this end it is necessary to study the Word of God in both its scriptural revelation and its personal revelation in Christ (of which Scripture is also the source), because the more that Word is known and the more our lives are governed by it, the more attuned we, and with us our consciences, become to the mind of God. "All scripture," as St. Paul says, "is inspired by God and profitable for teaching, for reproof, for correction, and for training in righteousness, that the man of God may be complete, equipped for every good work" (II Tim. 3:16–17)—that is to say, it is the knowledge imparted by Scripture which forms the regenerate person as a morally responsible and conscientious person in relation both to God and to his fellow human beings.

The Moral Argument of Immanuel Kant

Deeply conscious of man's fundamental ability to discriminate between right and wrong, Immanuel Kant (1724–1804) based his argument for the existence of God on the universal moral consciousness which is natural to mankind and which distinguishes man from the rest of the animal creation. Kant spoke of morality as "practical reason" because he believed that man's sense of justice and respect for the rights of others was controlled by the exercise of reason. Accordingly, he held that the universal law of morality was at the same time the universal law of reason. Duty, which he regarded as the guiding principle of practical reason, he defined as "the necessity of acting from respect for the law."[18] The moral worth of an action, he taught, does not derive from that action in itself or from the end to which it is directed, but from the duty which requires its performance; nor does it depend on the achievement of the action's purpose, "but merely on the principle of volition by which the action has taken place, without regard to any object of desire."[19]

Kant terms the compelling demand of duty the "categorical imperative," which he describes as "that which represents an action as necessary of itself without

18. Immanuel Kant, *Theory of Ethics* 1.2.
19. Ibid.

reference to another end, that is, as objectively necessary," or, again, as "an imperative which commands a certain conduct immediately, without having as its condition any other purpose to be attained by it."[20] For him, therefore, the categorical
imperative has the force of a universal law. Thus he rejects the practice of suicide for
the purpose of putting an end to an unsatisfactory life, both because the instinct to
improve life if used to destroy life would be self-contradictory and because suicide
"cannot possibly exist as a universal law of nature, and consequently would be
wholly inconsistent with the supreme principle of all duty." Likewise the case of
someone who, to get out of a difficult situation, borrows money with the promise
to repay it although he knows that repayment will not be possible. It is obvious that
such behavior cannot be treated as a universal law of conduct, for if it were
permissible for everyone in difficulty to promise whatever he pleased without any
intention of keeping the promise, all such transactions would be ridiculous and
contradict the very notion of promise.[21]

In estimating the moral worth of actions Kant considers it "essential that the
moral law should directly determine the will." Indeed, he sees conformity to the
categorical imperative of the moral law as constitutive of man's freedom, for this
conformity is the way that man expresses his human personality, which is "the
power that elevates man above himself" and "connects him with an order of things
that only the understanding can conceive." Kant insists, further, that the moral law
is holy, and that by virtue of his autonomy man, the rational creature, is the subject
of the moral law.[22] Consequently, the force of the categorical imperative is that "a
free will and a will subject to moral laws are one and the same."[23] This may be
summed up thus: "What [one] morally 'ought' is then what he necessarily 'would'
as a member of the world of the understanding [reason]."[24] In other words, one
freely wills to do what one rationally ought to do.

The ground is now prepared for Kant's formulation of the moral argument for
the existence of God. The holy moral law raises man's mind to a principle higher
than himself and leads him to seek "the unconditioned totality of the object (or
source) of pure practical reason," which he calls the *summum bonum*— the supreme
good.[25] He defines "the supreme condition of the *summum bonum*" as that of a will
in which there is "the *perfect accord* of the mind with the moral law."

> Now, the perfect accord of the will with the moral law is *holiness*, a perfection of
> which no rational being of the sensible world is capable at any moment of his
> existence. Since, nevertheless, it is required as practically necessary, it can only be
> found in *progress in infinitum* towards that perfect accord, and on the principles of

20. Ibid., 1.6.
21. Ibid.
22. Ibid., 1.7.
23. Ibid., 2.1.
24. Ibid., 2.3.
25. Ibid., 3.1.

pure practical reason it is necessary to assume such a practical progress as the real object of our will.[26]

Thus Kant postulates that man as a rational being makes infinite progress toward total morality, and he concludes that for this infinite progress to take place the immortality of the soul is a necessary deduction.

Now, this endless progress is possible only on the supposition of an *endless* duration of the *existence* and personality of the same rational being (which is called the immortality of the soul). The *summum bonum,* then, practically is only possible on the supposition of the immortality of the soul.[27]

Kant asserts in a somewhat contradictory sentence that "it is only in an endless progress that we can attain perfect accord with the moral law."[28] He apparently holds that the soul progresses unendingly—without, however, attaining the goal of moral perfection. This failure to achieve in an absolute sense the perfection of the supreme good is evidently attributed to the creaturely constitution of man, though man is constantly progressing toward perfection. The knowledge of the reality of this *summum bonum,* which is both the object and the source of the moral law, "must lead to the supposition of the existence of a cause adequate to this effect," and that first cause, says Kant, is God:

[Such knowledge] must postulate the *existence of God* as the necessary condition of the possibility of the *summum bonum.* . . . Therefore the *summum bonum* is possible in the world only on the supposition of a Supreme Being having a causality corresponding to moral character.[29]

This Supreme Being, recognized as the cause of nature in which intelligence and will are implanted, must Himself possess supreme intelligence and will.

It follows that the postulate of the possibility of the *highest derived good* (the best world) is likewise the postulate of the reality of the *highest original good,* that is to say, of the existence of God.[30]

Obedience to moral universal law, accordingly, is glorifying to God and conducive to man's true happiness:

For nothing glorifies God more than that which is the most estimable thing in the world, respect for his command, the observance of the holy duty that his law imposes on us, when there is added thereto his glorious plan of crowning such a beautiful order of things with corresponding happiness.[31]

26. Ibid., 3.4.
27. Ibid.
28. Ibid.
29. Ibid., 3.5.
30. Ibid.
31. Ibid.

Kant thus seems to envisage the disembodied spirit as endlessly traveling and getting ever closer to the goal of moral perfection but never arriving. His doctrine of God is akin to that of deism. His system has no place for the resurrection of the body. Man he regards as under obligation to obey the moral law which flows from God and as able to do so—imperfectly, but progressively. There is no awareness of the need for the redemptive dynamic of the Christian gospel.

In his later years Kant modified his moral argument very considerably,[32] maintaining, it seems, that practical reason points to the idea of God as the source of the moral imperative, but abandoning his earlier attempt to prove the objective existence of God by theoretical demonstration. Indeed, he appears to have formed opinions not unlike those propounded by Paul Tillich, John Robinson, and others in our day, that God is to be sought in man, in the depth of man's being or in man's ultimate concern. "I, as man, am myself this Being," he wrote; "God must be represented not as substance outside me, but as the highest moral principle in me." These notions, which have nothing in common with the biblical position, are expressed in private notes, not in documents prepared for publication.

The Moral Argument of C. S. Lewis

Interestingly enough, it is essentially the force of the moral argument (discovered, however, without the aid of Immanuel Kant) that caused C. S. Lewis to abandon atheism. What he describes as "a very big question"—"If a good God made the world why has it gone wrong?"—had been a stumbling block for him in the way of belief. "For many years," he tells us,

> I simply wouldn't listen to the Christian answers to this question, because I kept on feeling "whatever you say and however clever your arguments are, isn't it much simpler and easier to say that the world was *not* made by an intelligent power? Aren't all your arguments simply a complicated attempt to avoid the obvious?"[33]

Kant, as we have seen, linked morality with reason, and Lewis had found himself doing the same. The very presence of intelligence and rationality in the world posed a problem for the atheist which required an answer. Lewis approached the question as follows:

> Supposing there was no intelligence behind the universe, no creative mind. In that case nobody designed my brain for the purpose of thinking. It is merely that when the atoms inside my skull happen for physical and chemical reasons to arrange themselves in a certain way, this gives me, as a by-product, the sensation I call thought. But if so, how can I trust my own thinking to be true? It's like upsetting a milk-jug and hoping that the way the splash arranges itself will give you a map of London. But if I can't trust my own thinking, of course I can't trust the arguments

32. See Kant, *Opus Postumum.*
33. C. S. Lewis, *Broadcast Talks* (1942), p. 40.

leading to atheism, and therefore have no reason to be an atheist, or anything else. Unless I believe in God, I can't believe in thought: so I can never use thought to disbelieve in God.[34]

The atheistic argument that is based on ethical or moral considerations is vulnerable in much the same way. To quote Lewis again:

> My argument against God was that the universe seemed so cruel and unjust. But how had I got this idea of *just* and *unjust?* A man doesn't call a line crooked unless he has some idea of a straight line. What was I comparing the world with when I called it unjust? If the whole show was bad and senseless from A to Z, so to speak, why did I, who was supposed to be part of the show, find myself in such violent reaction against it? . . . Of course, I could have given up my idea of justice by saying it was nothing but a private idea of my own. But if I did that then my argument against God collapsed too—for the argument depended on saying that the world was really unjust, not that it just didn't happen to please my private fancies. Thus in the very act of trying to prove that God didn't exist—in other words, that the whole of reality was senseless—I found I was forced to assume that one part of reality—namely my idea of justice—was full of sense. Consequently atheism turns out to be too simple. If the whole universe has no meaning, we should never have found out that it has no meaning.[35]

Earlier in the same series of talks Lewis had drawn attention to "the most remarkable thing":

> Whenever you find a man who says he doesn't believe in a real Right and Wrong, you will find the same man going back on this a moment later. He may break his promise to you, but if you try breaking one to him he'll be complaining "It's not fair" before you can say Jack Robinson. A nation may say treaties don't matter; but then, next minute, they spoil their case by saying that the particular treaty they want to break was an unfair one. But if treaties don't matter, and if there's no such thing as Right and Wrong . . . what is the difference between a fair treaty and an unfair one? Haven't they given away the fact that, whatever they say, they really know the Law of Nature [the law or rule about right and wrong] just like anyone else?[36]

The theme is developed further by Lewis in his book *Miracles.* Lewis insists that each step in an argument depends on each preceding step. To postulate that reason depends on the irrational would undermine the credentials of thought:

> It is only when you are asked to believe in Reason coming from non-reason that you must cry Halt, for, if you don't, all thought is discredited. It is therefore obvious that sooner or later you must admit a Reason which exists absolutely on its own.[37]

34. Ibid., pp. 37–38.
35. Ibid., pp. 40–41.
36. Ibid., p. 11.
37. Lewis, *Miracles* (1947), pp. 35ff.

This leads to the next stage of the argument: no reason (or anything else) that is finite can exist on its own or independently. Lewis explains that "what exists on its own must have existed from all eternity; for if anything else could make it begin to exist then it would not exist on its own but because of something else." This reason that exists on its own, then, cannot be human reason, which is imperfect and intermittent. But human minds do not come from nowhere: "Each has its tap-root in an eternal self-existent, rational Being, whom we call God. Each is an offshoot, or spearhead, or incursion of that supernatural reality into Nature."[38]

Again, if rationality is discredited on the basis of what Lewis calls naturalism, so also is morality. The nonmoral cannot be the cause of ethical standards any more than the nonrational can be the cause of reason. The only basis of moral judgments would be personal feeling or personal preference. All morality would be relativized. There could be no absolute standards. Yet, as Lewis points out,

> When men say "I ought" they certainly think they are saying something, and something true, about the nature of a proposed action, and not merely about their own feelings. But if Naturalism is true, "I ought" is the same sort of statement as "I itch" or "I'm going to be sick." In real life when a man says "I ought" we may reply, "Yes, you're right. That *is* what you ought to do," or else, "No. I think you're mistaken." But in a world of Naturalists . . . the only sensible reply would be, "Oh, are you?"[39]

At the present time, when the time-honored moral standards of society are being disdainfully dismissed as outmoded and obscurantist, and the neutral relativism of amorality is being vigorously taught and advocated, it is not surprising that social disorder and the debasement of human behavior are increasing to an alarming degree. It would be well for atheistic naturalists, at some of whose theories we shall be looking, to heed the admonition of C. S. Lewis, who was himself formerly one of their number:

> If we are to continue to make moral judgments (and whatever we say we shall in fact continue) then we must believe that the conscience of man is not a product of Nature. It can be valid only if it is an offshoot of some absolute moral wisdom which exists absolutely "on its own" and is not a product of non-moral, non-rational Nature.[40]

38. Ibid.
39. Ibid., pp. 44–45.
40. Ibid., pp. 47–48.

3

Law and Love

Law and the Conscience

The function of law is closely interlinked with that of the conscience; for the law serves to stimulate the conscience of man, to remind him that he is a responsible being who must answer to God for what he does with the life that has been given to him. The law of God is the standard of moral perfection required of man in his personal relationships with God and with his fellow men. Dignified by his creation in the divine image, man is intended to reflect the excellence of his Creator. Precisely because it is God-given, the law with its commandments is holy, just, good, and spiritual (Rom. 7:12, 14). The glory that belongs to it is divine glory (II Cor. 3:7–9). The law as given, then, is essentially a way of life. Through Moses God instructs the people to keep His statutes and ordinances, "by doing which a man shall live" (Lev. 18:5). After the humiliation of the Babylonian captivity Ezra confesses that despite warnings the people have acted presumptuously and sinfully in disobeying God's commandments, "by the observance of which a man shall live" (Neh. 9:29). The prophet Ezekiel speaks similarly of God's statutes as prescriptions for living acceptably before God (Ezek. 20:11, 13, 21). To the inquirer who asked what he must do to inherit eternal life Jesus replied, "If you would enter life, keep the commandments" (Matt. 19:17; see also Rom. 10:5; Gal. 3:12).

Here once again we come face to face with a problem that is central to the human predicament. In the presence of the law, which marks out the way of life for man, man stands self-condemned because, instead of being a law keeper, he is a lawbreaker—and to break the law is to choose death in the place of life. That is why the verdict is given that "the soul that sins shall die" (Ezek. 18:4, 20; cf. Gen. 2:17; Rom. 6:23) and death is defined throughout Scripture as the consequence of the entry of sin (in other words, disobedience to the divine law) into the world (Rom. 5:12). This means that for sinful mankind the law is no longer the road which leads to life but a dispensation of condemnation and death—not that there is any change in or anything wrong with the law, which, as we have seen, is good and glorious. It is with us men, as breakers of God's holy law, that the wrong and the evil lie; it is not the law but ourselves that we must blame (II Cor. 3:7–9). Thus while on one hand St. Paul explains that "it is not the hearers of the law who are righteous before God, but the doers of the law who will be justified" (Rom. 2:13), there is also the tragic reality that "none is righteous, no, not one. . . . No one does good, not even one" (Rom. 3:10, 12)—in this respect "there is no distinction; since all have sinned and fall short of the glory of God" (Rom. 3:22–23). All are lawbreakers and subject to divine judgment for that reason. Since we have broken the law, some means other than the law is needed if men are to be justified and to live before God. That "new and living way" has been opened for us through the reconciling life and work of Christ (Heb. 10:19–20). It is the way of the gospel.

The essence of the law is set forth in the Decalogue (the Ten Commandments), which Moses received on Mount Sinai (Exod. 20). Of these commandments the first four, comprising the first table, concern man's duty to God; they insist on the sovereign uniqueness of God's being and majesty, the wickedness of idolatry—the worship of other gods, which are no-gods, instead of the one true God—the reverence due to God's name, and the sanctity of the Sabbath as a day of rest which God has blessed and hallowed. The last six, comprising the second table, concern man's obligations to his fellow men; they enjoin the honoring of one's parents, and forbid murder, adultery, theft, lying, and the coveting of other persons' possessions. Though brief in themselves, these commandments are comprehensive in their application. They obviously provide an admirable prescription for a peaceful and well-ordered society, but properly understood they intend something more than outward conformity to certain standards of reverence and neighborliness.

This is suggested by the words which introduce the Decalogue, for they plainly indicate that God speaks to His people not as a sternly demanding Lawgiver but as their loving Savior: "I am the Lord your God, who brought you out of the land of Egypt, out of the house of bondage" (Exod. 20:2). He is their Creator who has unfailingly manifested His love for them and who, like a father, expects their love in return. He is their Redeemer who sets them free and cares for them and whom they should delight to obey and honor. To regard the Decalogue, therefore, as an assemblage of burdensome and dictatorial prohibitions is seriously to misunderstand it (in any case, not all the commandments are negative or prohibitive in form). There is an inner motive that provides the impulse for the observance of these ordinances, and that inner motive is *love*. The acknowledged summary of the two tables of the law makes this absolutely plain. To the question, "Which is the great commandment in the law?" Jesus responds,

> You shall love the Lord your God with all your heart, and with all your soul, and with all your mind. This is the great and first commandment. And a second is like it, You shall love your neighbor as yourself. On these two commandments depend all the law and the prophets (Matt. 22:35–40).

This answer not only accords perfectly with the teaching of the Old Testament (see Deut. 6:4–5; Lev. 19:18), but also instructs us that the revelation of God's will in its entirety is subsumed under the single heading of *love*.

In similar vein St. Paul declares that the prescriptions of the second table of the law may properly be epitomized by the single word *love:*

> He who loves his neighbor has fulfilled the law. The commandments, "You shall not commit adultery, You shall not kill, You shall not steal, You shall not covet," and any other commandment, are summed up in this sentence, "You shall love your neighbor as yourself." Love does no wrong to a neighbor; therefore *love is the fulfilling of the law* (Rom. 13:8–10).

Also, Paul exhorts the Christians in Galatia to be "servants of one another through love," explaining that *"the whole law is fulfilled in one word,* 'You shall *love* your neighbor as yourself'" (Gal. 5:13–14). That "one word" St. James calls the royal law, by which our associations with other persons should be governed (James 2:8).

The dynamic principle, then, in the fulfillment of the law's demands is love. The true observance of the law engages the very heart of man's being. External conformity must spring from the innermost source of love. An ethic that is merely external is identical with hypocrisy. Obsessed with self-esteem and self-righteousness, the hypocrite covers over the truth that he has no love for others with a façade of piety and charitableness. Such persons are a walking, living lie; for them Christ, whose gaze penetrates beyond the outward appearance to the lovelessness in their hearts, reserves His sternest denunciations:

> Woe to you, scribes and Pharisees, hypocrites! for you are like whitewashed tombs, which outwardly appear beautiful, but within they are full of dead men's bones and all uncleanness. So you also outwardly appear righteous to men, but within you are full of hypocrisy and iniquity (Matt. 23:27–28).

By contrast, not only the whole teaching of Jesus but also the whole living of Jesus was genuine through and through. He Himself is uniquely and pre-eminently the manifestation, indeed the personification, of love. It was love that brought Him into our world, love that motivated Him to fulfill the Father's will perfectly, and love that took Him to death on the cross for our redemption. We see the total victory of love displayed in His life and death of total obedience.

In conformity with His own example Christ taught that the observance of the law must be inward as well as outward. The roots of murder and adultery are hatred and lust in the heart (Matt. 5:21–28). The commandments may be broken in thought and intention as well as in commission of the deed. This conception of the law is in fact built into the Decalogue itself, for the tenth commandment, which forbids the coveting of what is not ours (the prelude to acquisition by murder, theft, or dishonesty), whether it be another person's house and possessions to make them our own or his wife to commit adultery with her, condemns the inward lusting that leads to unethical actions. This is more fully expounded in Jesus' emphatic warning that "from within, out of the heart of man, come evil thoughts, fornication, theft, murder, adultery, coveting, wickedness, deceit, licentiousness, envy, slander, pride, foolishness": no matter how much they may receive outward expression, all the evil things that defile a person and destroy the harmony of human society have the heart of man as their inward source (Mark 7:21–23). Only by getting right with God (the great and first commandment) can the heart of man become right with his fellow men. "We love," St. John says, "because he first loved us" (I John 4:19); and "if God so loved us" as to send His Son to be the propitiation for our sins, "we also ought to love one another" (I John 4:11). Hence, too, the penetrating question: "If any one has the world's goods and sees his brother in need, yet closes his heart against him, how does God's love abide in him?" (I John 3:17). Christians rooted in the love of God bear the fruit of love for their fellow men.

Love Unopposed to Law

Yet despite the biblical teaching that love is the fulfillment of the law and that there is no antagonism between law and love, the notion is widespread, not least in some theological circles, that law and love are antithetical. According to this view, law is by nature unloving, rigid, harsh, and inflexible; contrariwise, love is gentle, pliable, unconstrained by rules, and indeed completely unconcerned with law. Justice is held to be incompatible with mercy, with the consequence that God has to choose between being just (law) or being merciful (love): if He chooses to be just, He must be unloving; if He chooses to be merciful, He must be unjust. For God to choose injustice for the sake of showing mercy, however, is not regarded as a failure or an inconsistency, but is praised rather as a virtue or an achievement on God's part—a triumph of love over law. Moreover, this logic is extended to the cross of Christ, which is presented as a demonstration of divine love which set aside the law and its claims, and to the Christian life, which is envisaged as a way of love, free from the tyranny of law.

Now it is true that love is the essential principle of Christian conduct, as, for example, St. Paul shows in a famous passage on love (I Cor. 13), and that the specific commandment given by Christ to His disciples was that they should love one another as He had loved them (John 13:34; 15:12). In the teaching of Christ, however, love, supreme though it is, is not something that resists being shaped by law. "Abide in my love," He exhorts His followers, but immediately adds, "If you keep my commandments, you will abide in my love" (John 15:9–10); this corresponds with the admonition, "If you love me, you will keep my commandments" (John 14:15). It is plain that to say this is not the same thing as saying, "If you keep my commandment to love, you will love" (which would be an otiose tautology), for Christ speaks of the keeping of His commandments (plural), and there are many precise ethical commandments of His recorded in the Gospels, a number of which we have already noticed. Nor is the statement "God is love" a reversible statement. Herbert Waddams has rightly reproached those who wish "to change the phrase 'God is love' into 'love is God' and to twist its meaning into a statement that human love, whatever form it may take, is as good as God, and that is all we need to consider." Waddams deplores this as "another of the many forms of idolatry which sets up in the place which God alone ought to occupy some human standard or image to replace him."[1]

It is true also that St. Paul tells Christian believers that they are "not under law but under grace" (Rom. 6:14) and that "Christ is the end of the law" (Rom. 10:4). The contexts in which these assertions occur, however, plainly show that the apostle does not mean that the law no longer has any place in the lives of those who have experienced the grace of the gospel. If that were in fact the case, a treatise on Christian ethics could be limited to a single sentence: "Be loving and do as you please!" (a sentiment lifted from Augustine to which we shall return).[2] In both of these passages St. Paul is expounding the doctrine of Christian justification. In Romans 6 he reminds his readers that their baptism signifies dying to sin and rising to newness of life through union with Christ, with the result that they are "no longer . . . enslaved to sin," as was the case when they were inveterate lawbreakers (vv. 3–6). Christian believers accordingly must consider themselves "dead to sin and alive to God in Christ Jesus," yielding their members not to sin as "instruments of wickedness," which is lawbreaking, but "to God as instruments of righteousness," which is law keeping. To be "not under law but under grace," then, does not imply that Christians are no longer bound by the obligations of the law and should regard themselves as free to ignore what the commandments prescribe. There is no possible compatibility between "continuing in sin" or lawlessness and "living to God" (vv. 11–15). St. Paul therefore gives thanks to God that the members of the church in Rome "who were once slaves to sin have become *obedient from the heart* to the standard of teaching to which [they] were committed" (v. 17).

In Romans 10 the apostle is speaking in particular of his Jewish compatriots for whose salvation he longs; he knows that, like himself prior to his conversion, their zeal for God is "not enlightened," since they are "ignorant of the righteousness that comes from God" and mistakenly seek to establish their own righteousness by observing the letter of the law (vv. 1–3). Although "Moses writes that the man who practices the righteousness which is based on the law shall live by it" (v. 5; Lev. 18:5), this is exactly where the problem lies, for, as we have seen, St. Paul has already demonstrated that there is not a single person in the whole world, whether Jew or Gentile, who is righteous before God. The holy standards of the law simply throw into relief the sinfulness of man as a guilty lawbreaker: "For no human being will be justified in his sight by works of the law since through the law comes knowledge of sin" (Rom. 3:20; cf. 5:20–21). By contrast "the righteousness of God," St. Paul explains, "has been manifested apart from law," and has been defined as "the righteousness of God through faith in Jesus Christ for all who believe" (Rom. 3:21–22). The sinner's justification before God can never be through the supposed righteousness of his own works but only through faith in Christ and

---

1. Herbert Waddams, *A New Introduction to Moral Theology* (1965), pp. 87–88.
2. See pp. 69–70.

the perfection of His finished work of redemption. This is the central truth of the gospel on which St. Paul insists in Romans 10:4, where he declares that "Christ is the end of the law, that every one who has faith may be justified." Justification through faith in Christ means, and must mean, the end of the futile search for justification by the works of the law. The apostle, then, is speaking of the end of the law as a way to life for the sinner, who by definition is a lawbreaker and therefore can never hope to be justified "under law." He is not inviting us, however, to say good-bye to the law as though it were itself ended and discarded as a thing of the past.

There are two further considerations which confirm this conclusion that the God-given law, far from being abrogated, continues in force as the divine standard of holiness and morality. Firstly, our justification before God is integrally dependent on the keeping of the law—not indeed on our part (for, as we have seen, being all lawbreakers we cannot be justified by the law), but on the part of Christ, the incarnate Son, whose perfect keeping of God's law as our fellow man was the essential preliminary to His suffering and dying on the cross in our place as the Righteous for the unrighteous (I Peter 3:18; I John 2:1–2). He Himself, the unblemished Lamb of God by whose precious blood we have been redeemed (I Peter 1:18–19; John 1:29), is our righteousness (I Cor. 1:30); our acceptance before God is in Him and not in ourselves. He who is the last Adam (I Cor. 15:45) first had to gain total victory where the first Adam had suffered defeat before He could offer Himself as an atoning sacrifice in our stead. In this way the demands of divine righteousness were met by God Himself in the person of the incarnate Son, and we see that the justifying grace of the gospel is in no way the consequence of the disregard or setting aside of the law.

Secondly, although the Christian believer is justified not by the law but by grace, the law remains the standard of the divine will in the process of sanctification—not, of course, in a condemnatory capacity, for the justified believer evermore enjoys peace with God (Rom. 5:1) and will never be separated from the love of God in Christ Jesus (Rom. 8:31–39). The change that takes place is not in the law but in the Christian and in the "location" of the law. What was previously an external ordinance standing over against the sinner and condemning him has become an internal principle, engraved as it were on the living tablets of the believing heart (II Cor. 3:3), so that in contrast to his unregenerate days he now loves the law of God and delights to fulfill its commandments. He joins with the psalmist in exclaiming, "Oh, how I love thy law!" (Ps. 119:97; cf. Ps. 19:7–11). All this is in fulfillment of God's ancient promise concerning the new covenant, that He would put His law within His people and write it on their hearts (Jer. 31:33; Ezek. 11:19; Heb. 8:10). The more the believer, through the enabling grace of the Holy Spirit, conforms to this standard of God's holiness, the closer he approaches that likeness to Christ which will be complete when he sees his Redeemer face to face (I John 3:2–3). It is then that the image of God in which man was created will be fully restored (II Cor. 3:18) and the harmony of law and love eternally established.

This face-to-face encounter will take place when Christ returns at the end of the present age. It is important to notice that this culminating event, which has been so ill served by date fixers and sensationalists, has a special significance for Christian ethics—so much so that the main emphasis in the teaching about Christ's second coming, pervading the New Testament from beginning to end, may be said to be an ethical emphasis. For example, after St. John says that "we know that when he appears we shall be like him, for we shall see him as he is," he adds, "And every one who thus hopes in him purifies himself as he is pure" (I John 3:2–3). In other words, this glorious prospect should powerfully influence our daily living here and now. The apostolic insistence on the importance of this culminating event for Christian morality is rooted in the teaching of Christ Himself, who stressed that the day of His return was known to no man. Whether the return is soon or long delayed, the point is that *it is always imminent,* and it is this perennial imminence that sounds the note of ethical urgency which powerfully persuades us to maintain constant zeal and watchfulness. "Watch therefore," Christ urged His disciples, "for you do not know on what day your Lord is coming. . . . Therefore you also must be ready; for the Son of Man is coming at an hour you do not expect" (Matt. 24:42, 44; cf. Matt. 25:13; Mark 13:33, 35–37; Luke 12:37, 40, 43; 21:34–36). Paul writes to Titus that our proper preparation as we await "our blessed hope, the appearing of the glory of our great God and Savior Jesus Christ," is for us "to renounce irreligion and worldly passions, and to live sober, upright, and godly lives in this world" (Titus 2:12–13).

If, as the generations succeed each other, the return of Christ seems to be subject to protracted delay, this must be attributed to the limitations of our human perspective. What man judges to be a long time is a brief day to God. The prolongation of the present age should be seen as the prolongation of the day of grace, thanks to the mercy and longsuffering of God. Thus we are assured that "the Lord is not slow about his promise as some count slowness, but is forbearing toward [us], not wishing that any should perish, but that all should reach repentance" (II Peter 3:9). Nevertheless, the coming of "the day of the Lord" is a certainty: its arrival, so far as we are concerned, is always at hand. And this knowledge leads to a challenge: "What sort of persons ought [we] to be in lives of holiness and godliness, waiting for and hastening the coming of the day of God!" (II Peter 3:11–12). It arouses one's determination to "be found by him without spot or blemish, and at peace" at His appearing (II Peter 3:14). This is another of the many passages which urgently propound the implications which the expectation of Christ's return has for Christian conduct. Christian living, in short, should be living in the light of His coming, and all the more so as the day of His coming is unknown to us and therefore always impending throughout the history of the church.

Merit and Reward

The question arises as to the place and the meaning of merit and reward in connection with the ethical teaching of the New Testament, which speaks of faithful service being rewarded at the return of Christ and in the future life. In the Sermon on the Mount, for instance, Jesus proclaimed the blessedness of those who suffer hatred and persecution for His sake, encouraging them with this assurance: "Rejoice and be glad, for your reward is great in heaven" (Matt. 5:12). Similarly St. Paul judged that "the sufferings of this present time are not worth comparing with the glory that is to be revealed to us" (Rom. 8:18), for he was convinced that "this slight momentary affliction is preparing for us an eternal weight of glory beyond all comparison" (II Cor. 4:17). Jesus, again, warned His hearers against "practicing their piety before men in order to be seen by them," since that would mean that they would "have no reward from their Father who is in heaven" (Matt. 6:1). Charitable benefactions and devotional exercises such as prayer and fasting should be performed not with public ostentation to win the admiration of men, but privately and in secret, for then, Jesus asserted, "your Father who sees in secret will reward you" (Matt. 6:18). To love and do good to all without discrimination, enemies as well as friends, also will not go unrewarded: "Love your enemies, and do good, and lend, expecting nothing in return; and your reward will be great, and you will be sons of the Most High; for he is kind to the ungrateful and the selfish. Be merciful even as your Father is merciful" (Luke 6:35–36). In the parable of the talents, the servant who has profitably used the money entrusted to him is commended by his master with these words: "Well done, good and faithful servant; you have been faithful over a little, I will set you over much; enter into the joy of your master" (Matt. 25:21).

In these and similar passages the concept of reward is presented by way of comparison. For the Christian, the troubles and afflictions of this present life are fleeting and insignificant in comparison with the glory of the eternal bliss that lies ahead. This means, further, that to turn away from the selfish pursuit of pleasure and power that is the mark of worldliness is to suffer no loss. In the light of eternity the blandishments of this passing world are seen in their true proportion. Thus Moses chose "rather to share ill-treatment with the people of God than to enjoy the fleeting pleasures of sin," for, we are told, "he considered abuse suffered for the Christ greater wealth than the treasures of Egypt, for he looked to the reward" (Heb. 11:25–26). It is a matter of laying up treasure in heaven instead of on earth. Inevitably, then, the Christian's perspective must be different from the worldling's; for, as Jesus said, "Where your treasure is, there will your heart be also" (Matt. 6:21).

At the same time this comparison between present hardship and future joy means that the reward which awaits the Christian is an incentive to be faithful and to persevere to the end. Like an athlete under rigorous training and discipline, he willingly endures the pain and exhaustion of the contest with his gaze fixed on the glorious goal. With St. Paul he can declare, "One thing I do, forgetting what lies behind and straining forward to what lies ahead, I press on toward the goal for the prize of the upward call of God in Christ Jesus" (Phil. 3:13–14). This is common sense, certainly not self-seeking, since all is done and endured not for the sake of self but for the sake of Him who is Himself the goal and the treasure, Jesus Christ the Redeemer and Lord. All is done and endured in response to the love and suffering that bought the believer and in gratitude to the God of his salvation. All is done and endured, moreover, with the supreme example ever before him of his Redeemer, who at untold cost to Himself has opened the way to eternal glory: "Let us run with perseverance the race that is set before us," exhorts the writer of the Epistle to the Hebrews, "looking to Jesus the pioneer and perfecter of our faith, who for the joy that was set before him endured the cross, despising the shame, and is seated at the right hand of the throne of God" (Heb. 12:1–2).

The Christian ethic is one of love and obedience to Him who first loved and obeyed for our redemption. Christ Himself is the Christian's eternal reward. And nothing could be sweeter at the end of this earthly course than to hear the Master say, "Well done, good and faithful servant!" The anticipation of this reward should spur the Christian on to persevere earnestly in daily taking up his cross and following his Master; for the believer, though his security is in Christ and not at all in himself, is answerable for the quality of his life and witness. There is the possibility of carelessness and backsliding on his part and of his being ashamed before Christ at His appearing (I John 2:28). St. Paul admonishes the members of the Corinthian church not only that there is but one foundation on which to build, namely Jesus Christ, but also that each person should take care how he builds on it, because his work will be put to the test. Using the analogy of fire, which consumes materials like wood, hay, and stubble, but not gold, silver, and precious stones, he affirms that "if the work which any man has built on the foundation survives, he will receive a reward," but warns that "if any man's work is burned up, he will suffer loss, though he himself will be saved . . ." (I Cor. 3:14–15). St. Paul here quite plainly does not propound the possibility of the loss of salvation, for the man whose work is consumed will be saved because he is on the one foundation. Precisely what is signified by *reward* and *loss* is not specified. The main point is, as the apostle says later in the same letter, that those who are building on the Rock should be "steadfast, immovable, always abounding in the work of the Lord" (I Cor. 15:58). It is a sad thing for a Christian's life to be discordant with his profession.

The concept of reward ordinarily carries with it that of merit: merit is crowned with reward. The Christian reward is indeed merited. But it is merited *for us,* not by us; the merit is Christ's, not our own. The talents the faithful servant uses have been given to him, and he is commended for his faithfulness, not for his merit. We have nothing that we have not received. "What have you that you did not receive?" St. Paul asks. "If then you received it, why do you boast as if it were not a gift?" (I Cor. 4:7). There is no place for self-approbation. The resources freely given to us demand faithful and responsible stewardship. And it is not only his talents that do not belong to the Christian man, but his very self as well, for he belongs in his entirety to God who created him and who now has graciously redeemed him. Accordingly, all the glory for everything that he is and does must be ascribed to

God alone. To quote St. Paul again: "You are not your own; you were bought with a price. So glorify God in your body" (I Cor. 6:19–20). Being ourselves utterly devoid of merit in the presence of God, we can stand before Him solely in Christ and His merit, and our boasting can be only in the Lord (I Cor. 1:26–31). Therefore, however faithful, diligent, and conscientious we may be in the discharge of our responsibilities, we owe everything to the grace of God. Thus St. Paul, despite the phenomenal intensity of his labors and sufferings in Christ's cause, disclaims any merit or worth whatsoever for himself: "By the grace of God I am what I am," he testifies, "and his grace toward me was not in vain. On the contrary, I worked harder than any of them, though it was not I, but the grace of God which is with me" (I Cor. 15:10).

Hence the Christian's reward is merited for him by Christ. The inheritance that awaits him is the inheritance of Christ, the only Son and Heir, with whom he by grace has been made one (Rom. 8:17). The joy and the glory into which he will enter belong to Christ. It is in Christ that God has "blessed us . . . with every spiritual blessing in the heavenly places" (Eph. 1:3). The good works we perform as Christians are good works in Christ, "for we are his workmanship, created in Christ Jesus for good works, which God prepared beforehand, that we should walk in them" (Eph. 2:10). It is only in Christ, who strengthens him, that the Christian can do all things (Phil. 4:13). "Works must proceed out of faith," wrote William Tyndale; "that is, I must do them for the love which I have to God for that great mercy which he hath showed me in Christ, or else I do them not in the sight of God." As for the promise of the reward, "All that I do and suffer is but the way to the reward, and not the deserving thereof."[3] To assign any degree of merit to myself is to rob Christ of what belongs entirely to Him, since He gained salvation for me when I deserved nothing but condemnation. Thus Tyndale explains further:

> Christ is Lord over all, and whatsoever any man will have of God he must have it given him freely for Christ's sake. Now to have heaven for mine own deserving is mine own praise, and not Christ's. For I cannot have it by favour and grace in Christ and by mine own merits also; for free giving and deserving cannot stand together.[4]

Unevangelical Developments

In the Middle Ages a doctrinal system of good works which merit the reward of grace was elaborated and became part of the approved teaching of Roman Catholicism. According to this system man, when he fell into sin, suffered the loss of original righteousness, which, it is held, was a gift divinely added to our human nature; this loss meant that man was left in a purely natural, quasi-neutral state, with the ability to contribute to his own justification before God. Thus the door was opened for human cooperation with divine grace, and the following beliefs

---

3. William Tyndale, *Prologue to the Book of Numbers,* in *Doctrinal Treatises* (1848), p. 434.
4. Ibid., p. 436.

were incorporated into the official teaching of the Church of Rome: (1) by freely cooperating with grace prior to justification the sinner's good works merit an increase of grace and then the grace of justification itself; (2) by good works performed after justification a person may merit for himself an increase of sancti- fying grace, the reward of eternal life—provided he is in a state of grace when he dies—and an increase of heavenly glory; (3) should a person forfeit grace through the commission of mortal sin, grace may be recovered by the merit of further good works; (4) it is possible for the justified person to merit grace for others as well as himself.

In striking contrast to the assurance of the New Testament, which presents the work of salvation from beginning to end as the work of God and therefore as incapable of frustration, this system is clouded with uncertainty; this is only to be expected when it is taught that the achievement of salvation depends to any degree on man rather than solely on God. Indeed, the Council of Trent pronounced an anathema against anyone who claimed to have absolute certainty of perseverance to the end,[5] maintaining that everyone, "when he considers his own weakness and indisposition, should be fearful and apprehensive concerning his own state of grace, since nobody knows with the certainty of faith which cannot be subject to error that he has achieved the grace of God."[6]

A further development in the medieval system of works and merit involves the concept of supererogation, which affirms the possibility of performing good works in excess of what God requires and thus of accumulating a surplus of merit. It is taught that some saints actually succeed in performing works of supererogation and that the excess grace they earn in this way is stored in a heavenly bank of merit. This surplus merit can then be made available to others whose balance sheet of merit shows a shortfall. Perhaps indulgences can be sold or masses offered for those who are said to be suffering in the flames of purgatory. Support for this teaching was sought in passages like Matthew 19:16–22, where Jesus counsels the rich young man who claimed to have kept the commandments, "If you would be perfect, go, sell what you possess and give to the poor, and *you will have treasure in heaven;* and come, follow me." Verses like this led to the view that poverty is a "counsel of perfection," a meritorious way of life beyond what has been com- manded. Another such counsel, that of virginity (or chastity), is based on passages like I Corinthians 7:25, where St. Paul says, "Now concerning the unmarried, I have no command of the Lord, but I give my opinion [or counsel] as one who by the Lord's mercy is trustworthy." The third of the counsels of perfection—or "evangelical counsels" as they were also called—is obedience, and, in particular, obedience to the new law of Christ through hearing His voice and following Him, as distinct from and in addition to the old law (John 10:27; 15:10). Thomas Aquinas, for instance, saw these three evangelical counsels as the renunciation of

---

5. Session 6, Canon 16.
6. Session 6, chap. 9.

the three worldly attractions specified in I John 2:16: "Every form of the religious life that professes the state of perfection is based on these three," he wrote, "since riches are renounced by poverty; carnal pleasures by perpetual chastity; and the pride of life by the bondage of obedience."[7]

We have already shown that in the New Testament there is no room for the notion that our good works place God under obligation to reward us with grace or are instrumental in earning our salvation. As Tyndale insisted, grace and works do not belong together in our justification before God, since grace is freely given to the undeserving, whereas to claim that our works are meritorious is to deny that we are undeserving. Moreover, the call of Jesus to follow Him and be wholly committed to Him is a call to all, not just to the exceptional few; it was all, not merely one or two, whom He counseled to lay up treasure in heaven (Matt. 6:19–21), and all are summoned to obey Him. As for St. Paul's advice against marrying, this was hardly a counsel of perfection, for he explained that it related to the stress which the Corinthian church was experiencing ("in view of the impending distress it is well for a person to remain as he is"—I Cor. 7:26), and the passage contains counsels addressed equally to the married and the unmarried. Besides, the proposed interpretation has the effect of disqualifying St. Peter and other married apostles from attaining the "perfection" of virginity; indeed, St. Paul a little further on makes it plain that this was not a counsel the apostles were expected to follow: "Do we not have the right to be accompanied by a wife, as the other apostles and the brothers of the Lord and Cephas?" he asks (I Cor. 9:5). Yet of all people the apostles would surely be the last to be exempt from any counsel of perfection! Once again, and above all, such doctrines of human merit detract from the sole sufficiency of the merit of Christ for our redemption and thus deprive us of the assurance of our eternal security in Him. As W. H. Griffith Thomas has said, "From first to last, everything connected with our thinking, speaking, and doing, we need the infinite merit of our Lord and Saviour to meet and cover our own utter demerit."[8]

Man is commanded, in both the Old and New Testaments, to love God with all his being and his neighbor as himself. To do more than this is an impossibility; furthermore, no one has succeeded in doing it—with the vital exception of the incarnate Son of God, who alone could say to the Father, "I glorified thee on earth, having accomplished the work which thou gavest me to do" (John 17:4). The fourteenth of the Thirty-Nine Articles of Religion asserts that works of supererogation, which it defines as "voluntary works besides, over, and above God's commandments, . . . cannot be taught without arrogancy and impiety," because "by them men do declare that they do not only render unto God as much as they are bound to do, but that they do more for his sake than of bounden duty is required." The article then cites what "Christ saith plainly" in Luke 17:10: "When you have done all that is commanded you, say, 'We are unworthy servants; we have only done

7. Thomas Aquinas, *Summa Theologica* 2.1, Q.108, art. 4.
8. W. H. Griffith Thomas, *The Principles of Theology* (1930), p. 219.

what was our duty.'"[9] What is commanded us is in fact perfection: "You, therefore, must be perfect, as your heavenly Father is perfect" (Matt. 5:48; cf. Lev. 19:2; I Peter 1:15). There can be no counsel higher than or in excess of that. And this standard of perfection inescapably emphasizes the depth of our own inadequacy and our need to depend totally on the grace that flows to us from Him who alone is perfect.

Uncertainty regarding perseverance and the attainment of heavenly bliss is also, of course, widespread in Protestantism, especially in those circles which, even though they may hold to the sole sufficiency of divine grace for the sinner's redemption, yet make salvation depend on the will of man rather than the will of God. According to this view man decides not only whether to accept salvation but whether he will continue in it. For a person who has chosen saving grace for himself may at any time choose to renounce it and refuse to persevere to the end. By his own decision he may pass from death to life and then back from life to death; and there is the possibility of his doing so repeatedly, so that there is no saying how he will end up. This has the strange consequence of giving the will of finite man priority over the will of almighty God in this most important area of salvation. If correct, this view renders God as uncertain as man about the outcome of things, for God cannot even be sure whether those who are now recipients of His grace will continue to be so; He cannot know who, if any at all, will decide to become or remain citizens of His eternal kingdom. In this situation the will of man takes the place of the works of man in the scheme of salvation, and the degree of uncertainty is equal. The apostolic teaching declares, however, that "God's firm foundation stands, bearing this seal: 'The Lord knows those who are his'" (II Tim. 2:19). As we have already seen, our salvation is all from God (II Cor. 5:18–19), and it is for that reason that we are assured that God "who began a good work in [us] will bring it to completion" (Phil. 1:6). In other words, the doctrine of God should always be our starting point, since it is the doctrine of God, not the doctrine of man, that is of primary importance and enables us to see man and creation in their true perspective.

It is hardly surprising that the notions of merit and supererogation engendered the conception, which was long prevalent in the church, that there are two levels of piety and saintliness; the higher level, attainable only by a few who thus establish a special claim to sainthood, and the lower level, above which the vast majority of the church's membership cannot rise. The superior level is in the main reserved for those who separate themselves from the world and its seductions either by choosing solitary existence as hermits in the desert or by segregating themselves in monastic communities under vows of poverty, chastity, and obedience. There have been remarkable persons in their number, but however good their intentions, they have not been able to isolate themselves from the temptations that rise from the depth of the being of each individual (Mark 7:14–23). As Basil the Great wrote to

9. The article omits the last clause.

Gregory of Nazianzus, "I have left my life in the city, as one sure to give rise to countless evils, but I have not yet been able to leave myself behind."[10] Even the best of these people who have withdrawn from the world tend to be impelled by the hope that their subjugation of the flesh, assisted by self-inflicted indignities, hardships, and chastisements, will render them acceptable to God. This attitude, which reflects a defective grasp of the all-sufficiency of the grace of God in Christ Jesus for our justification, exemplifies the confusion between justification and sanctification so frequently present in the history of the church.

There were other formal distinctions that through long use became entrenched in the ethical teaching of the church. One was the distinction between the "cardinal" and the "theological" virtues. The four cardinal virtues, prudence, justice, fortitude, and temperance, were regarded as naturally attainable quite apart from divine grace and therefore not limited to the community of Christians, whereas the three theological virtues, faith, hope, and love (I Cor. 13:13), were held to be supernatural and infused by the grace of God. It is true that the so-called cardinal virtues were praised by pagan philosophers of antiquity; but the distinction is misleading, for the ancient systems certainly gave love an important place in their definitions of morality, though their concepts of faith and hope, where they occurred, tended to be more nebulous.

But the distinction between cardinal and theological virtues has no basis in the biblical revelation. For the Christian, all virtues are owed to the goodness of God as Creator and Redeemer. The nine virtues which constitute the fruit of the Spirit, and which therefore are produced in the regenerate life by divine grace, include joy, peace, patience, kindness, goodness, gentleness, and temperance as well as love and faith (Gal. 5:22–23); love, at the head of this list, embraces all other virtues. Thus in the famous hymn of love in I Corinthians 13, love expresses itself in patience, kindness, faith, hope, and endurance, and in joyfulness over what is right; it is the antithesis of jealousy, boastfulness, arrogance, rudeness, self-assertiveness, irritability, and resentment. To love God with all one's being and one's fellow man as oneself embraces all the virtues and guarantees their practice. Indeed, this is the product of the grace of the new covenant which inscribes the divine law of love in the believing heart. Herbert Waddams has put it well:

> The overarching and revolutionary fact of the Christian Gospel is that Christ transforms everything by renewing living contact with God. This transformation entirely changes the emphasis on all virtues so that the cardinal virtues to a Christian are just as much supernatural as natural. Moreover for a Christian the supernatural is not the antithesis of the natural, but the bringing of the natural home to God. He therefore sees all life as coming under the command of the Spirit, and as understandable only in the light of the death and resurrection of Jesus Christ.[11]

10. Basil, Letter 2, to Gregory.
11. Waddams, *Moral Theology*, p. 124.

It became customary to set against the seven cardinal and theological virtues what are called the seven capital vices, more popularly known as the seven deadly sins: pride, avarice, lust, envy, gluttony, anger, and accidie. As the virtues were to be cultivated, so the vices were to be shunned. There is no necessity to comment on these vices here—they are adequately covered by the requirements and prohibitions of the Decalogue—except to point out that "accidie" means sloth, unconcern, supercilious boredom, the unwillingness to be involved (conveyed well by the expression "I couldn't care less"). This attitude, obviously, is very selfish and unloving and therefore very un-Christian.

Another distinction in force in the Church of Rome is that between mortal sins and venial sins. The former term is applied to grave sins which result in the loss of grace, while the latter term designates lesser sins which are readily pardoned. The classification of sins into categories is pernicious, however, since the "lesser" sins may have consequences for the individual and for society no less harmful than those brought about by the "greater" sins. Moreover, it readily suggests that certain types of sins may be committed without compunction because they are of little or no consequence. As Waddams points out, "To divide sins in this way is bound to give the impression that there are some sins which matter and some which do not." Consequently, "there can be no doubt that the general effect of this distinction is unhealthy, and that it introduces into the heart of the Christian life a legalism which can only be harmful." We concur with his judgment that "it is high time that it was altogether abolished."[12]

Casuistry

The classification of sins, moreover, is conducive to extreme forms of casuistry. Casuistry is the codification of a system of rules to fit the requirements of particular cases.[13] It is commonly acknowledged that the same action may vary in its degree of culpability because of the presence of different circumstances, different objectives, and different motivations, so that in assessing the seriousness of an offense a variety of factors has to be taken into consideration. Viewed in this light, casuistry is in itself neutral and indeed a familiar component in the formation of moral and legal judgments. In the law courts, for instance, one must take into account extenuating circumstances in which a crime was committed. All agree that there is a great difference between killing that is accidental and unintentional and killing that is brutal and premeditated. Similarly, in Scripture there is an important difference between undesigned or unwitting sinning and deliberate and rebellious sinning (cf. Lev. 4; Num. 15:22–31; Acts 3:17; I Tim. 1:13).

But the term *casuistry* now usually carries a pejorative connotation and is commonly understood to imply the manipulation of the truth or the placing of an

---

12. Ibid., p. 100.
13. Latin *casus*.

interpretation on a statement which is not in accord with its plain and intended sense. In its perverted form casuistry has a long history. Indeed, from the very beginning it has been a mark of human sinfulness to seek to exonerate oneself from misdeeds by resorting to subterfuge and attempting to shift the blame on to others; Adam did so in the garden when, in answer to God's awkward question, he said, "The woman whom thou gavest to be with me, she gave me the fruit of the tree" (Gen. 3:12), thus setting the pattern for future sophistry by devising an answer which, though formally true in itself, was actually evasive and self-serving. The intricate casuistical system that had been elaborated by the rabbinical and legal scholars of Judaism met with severe censure in the teaching of Christ. He denounced, for example, the sophistry which allowed a person to consider himself free from the fifth commandment and its implications merely by saying to his parents, "What you would have gained from me is *corban*"—that is, given to God—and thereby to divest himself of any responsibility to make provision for them. To indulge in such casuistry was, Jesus charged, to reject God's commandment and to make His Word void (Mark 7:9–13).

The summary of the second table of the Decalogue, enjoining love of one's neighbor, had also been subjected to casuistical qualifications. The concept of neighbor, which was intended in a comprehensive sense, had had restrictive interpretations imposed on it, with the result that various categories of persons had come to be regarded as rightly excluded from the status of neighbor. Rabbinical codification made it permissible, for instance, to conclude that an enemy was not a neighbor to be loved. Rationalization of this kind was assailed by Jesus as immoral and ungodly and in fact subversive to the benevolent purpose of the Creator: "You have heard that it was said, 'You shall love your neighbor and hate your enemy'"—Jesus was referring to the current casuistry—"But I say to you, Love your enemies and pray for those who persecute you, so that you may be sons of your Father who is in heaven; for he makes his sun rise on the evil and on the good, and sends rain on the just and on the unjust" (Matt. 5:43–45). If hatred of enemies governed the attitudes and actions of God, we would be in a state of utter hopelessness, without His grace and without salvation; for, as St. Paul observes, "God shows his love for us in that *while we were yet sinners* Christ died for us," and in that *"while we were enemies* we were reconciled to God by the death of his Son" (Rom. 5:8, 10). Thus to love our enemies is truly a mark of godliness.

When a lawyer who had been schooled in the refinements of this sort of casuistry asked Jesus the question, "And who is my neighbor?" it was doubtless his intention to initiate a technical discussion giving him an opportunity to display his own dialectical skill. Samaritans would certainly have been numbered among the nonneighbors, since the Jews had been taught to regard them, like the Gentiles, as outsiders (cf. John 4:9; 8:48). The parable of the good Samaritan, which was Jesus' response to the lawyer's question, shows the unacceptability of such distinctions. The priest and the Levite, who passed by on the other side instead of coming to the assistance of their fellow countryman, presumably had no difficulty in persuading themselves that the victim of the assault, though a Jew, must have been a bad man, perhaps a tax collector or an adulterer, for this misfortune to have overtaken him, and therefore that they who were good men were under no obligation to endanger themselves by treating him as a neighbor and showing loving concern for him. The Samaritan who stopped to bind up the injured man's wounds and bring him to safety would, on the basis of their casuistry, have had even more justification for passing by. But he treated this afflicted Jew as his neighbor and ministered to him in his need. By this story Jesus condemned outright all sophistical evasion of the responsibility of love. A neighbor is "one who is nigh": it is one's duty and privilege to be a neighbor, that is, to be nigh with love and care to every one in need of help (Luke 10:25–37).

Another example in the New Testament of the irrational and unethical absurdities to which casuistry is capable of descending is connected with the swearing of oaths. To swear by the temple was held to be an oath that was not binding, whereas to swear by the gold of the temple made it a binding oath. "You blind fools!" Jesus expostulated. "Which is greater, the gold or the temple that has made the gold sacred?" It was also taught that an oath sworn by the altar was not binding, but that one sworn by the gift on the altar was binding, which caused Jesus to exclaim: "You blind men! For which is greater, the gift or the altar that makes the gift sacred?" (Matt. 23:16–22). Oaths had become part of a trickster's game, and not surprisingly Jesus counseled His hearers not to swear at all but always to speak the plain truth (Matt. 5:33–37).

In more modern times casuistry has so frequently been associated with the Jesuits that the terms *jesuitry* and *casuistry* have become virtually synonymous. It is true that the Jesuits had a large share in the building up of the elaborate Catholic system of moral theology, but ecclesiastical casuistry had its beginnings before the time of Ignatius Loyola and the founding of the Society of Jesus in the sixteenth century. The establishment of the practice of auricular confession, which the Lateran Council pronounced obligatory in 1215, made casuistical instruction a necessity, for the priest in the confessional needed the guidance of prescribed rulings and evaluations to enable him to judge between the different cases to which he listened and to impose condign penances for the offenses confessed. As was to be expected, the variety of these cases was practically limitless, and led to the preparation of intricately detailed manuals for the priests to use in their capacity as confessors.

The most notable authority in the systematization of casuistical theology was Alfonso de' Liguori (1696–1787), founder of the Congregation of our Most Blessed Redeemer (the Redemptorists) and author of a large work on moral theology (*Theologia Moralis*). His earnestness and self-discipline are not in question, but the tariffs or schedules he drew up to enable priests to determine whether particular offenses should be classified as mortal or venial sins show very clearly the dangers and absurdities of a detailed casuistical system. The following table illustrates the exaggerated precisionism of the system Liguori formulated. It specifies different classes of persons and the amount of money which must be stolen from them to constitute a mortal sin. Less than that amount makes the theft no more than a venial sin.[14]

Beggar	$2.00
Laborer	$4.00
Artisan	$5.00
Moderately rich man	$7.00
Very rich man	$12.00
Very rich nobleman	$25.00
Very rich community	$40.00
King	$60.00

According to this system, then, the breaking of the eighth commandment may be either a venial or a mortal sin. It depends, first of all, on the amount stolen and, secondly, on the classification of the person who has been robbed. If, for example, the sum is $15.00 and it has been stolen from someone in the first five categories, then a mortal sin has been committed, causing the loss of grace and eternal death; but if the sum has been stolen from someone in the last three categories, then a venial sin has been committed—it need not even be confessed and does not threaten the thief's continuance in the favor of God. All this, moreover, is prescribed without regard to the fact that in either case the thief may be fully aware that he is breaking God's commandment and may deliberately intend to do so.[15]

Historically, the most devastating exposure of the mental acrobatics and verbal manipulations of jesuitical casuistry was that of the satirical *Provincial Letters* of Blaise Pascal (1623–1662). He refers, for instance, to "the most acute and ingenious of all the new methods" for the reconciliation of contradictions, namely the concept of probability: since the affirmative and the negative of most opinions have each some probability, they are both probable and consequently safe. Among the rulings cited from Jesuit authorities is one regarding the obedience owed by monks to their superiors, which asserts that "it is not disputed that a monk who has a probable opinion in his favor is not necessitated to obey his superior, though the superior may have a more probable opinion."[16] The perverted form of casuistry which Pascal is attacking evokes from him an impassioned expostulation addressed to the imaginary Jesuit priest who has been explaining the methods and arguments of his society in response to Pascal's questions:

"Oh, Father," I exclaimed, "you exhaust all patience and it is impossible to hear without horror the things I have been listening to." "It is not I who am responsible,"

14. The amounts designated are contemporary American equivalents; it is inevitable in these days of spiraling inflation that these figures are only approximate, but this does not compromise our present purpose.

15. Alfonso de' Liguori, *Theologia Moralis,* vol. 3, § 528.

16. Blaise Pascal, *Provincial Letters* 6.

he said. "I am well aware of that, my Father, but you express no disapproval of them, and far from detesting the authors of these maxims, you hold them in high esteem. Have you no fear that your concurrence renders you a partaker of their crime? Can you be ignorant that St. Paul judges worthy of death not only the authors of wickedness but also those who consent to it?"[17]

Pascal expresses his dismay that "the liberty taken in overturning the most holy rules of Christian conduct has been extended to the entire subversion of the law of God."

> The great commandment which comprises both the law and the prophets [Matt. 22:36–40] is violated; piety is stabbed to the very heart; the spirit which gives it life is taken away; to love God is said to be unnecessary to salvation; and it is even asserted that this exemption from loving God is the benefit which Jesus Christ conferred on the world. It is the height of impiety. The price of the blood of Jesus Christ is to obtain our exemption from loving him! Prior to the Incarnation one was obliged to love God; but, now that God has so loved the world that he has given his only Son [John 3:16], the world, redeemed by him, is to be discharged from loving him! Strange theology of our days! . . . In this way those who have never loved God in all their life are made worthy of enjoying God's presence in eternity![18]

The danger inherent in the codification of ethical laws to fit particular cases was identical with the danger inherent in the punctilious formalism of the scribes and Pharisees so sternly condemned by Christ. Even though well intentioned in its origins, the prescription of minutiae designed to cover the endless variations of conduct and motive in a potentially endless number of cases leads almost inevitably to barren trivialization, ingenious sophistry, and cold legalism, and thus to the defeat of what should be the true purpose of moral theology: the love of God and man. The preoccupation with the tithing of "mint and dill and cummin" becomes an end in itself and brings about the neglect of "the weightier matters of the law, justice and mercy and faith" (Matt. 23:23). This is the reversal of right judgment. The picture of the ethicist who is so busy "straining out a gnat" that he fails to notice that he is "swallowing a camel" is indeed laughable, but in a way that draws attention to a state of affairs that is in reality terribly tragic (Matt. 23:24).

17. Ibid., 10.
18. Ibid.

4

The New Morality

Anthropological Ethics

"The New Morality" is the heading of chapter 6 in John A. T. Robinson's book *Honest to God.* In the preceding chapter Robinson propounded a "non-religious" understanding of prayer as people giving themselves to people, the "unconditional love of the neighbor, of 'the nearest *Thou* to hand,'" so that the *Thou* addressed in prayer is not the transcendentally other personal being of God (who has previously been defined as the immanent ground of human personality) but the *Thou* in one's fellow man.[1] The author now is able to assert that "prayer and ethics are simply the inside and the outside of the same thing," since "assertions about God are in the last analysis assertions about Love—about the ultimate ground and meaning of personal relationships."[2] Once we have deposed God and denied Him to be a supreme Being other than ourselves, all that is left are the word *God,* used as a symbol denoting "the ultimate depth of all our being," and the admonition, borrowed from Paul Tillich, that "you must forget everything traditional that you have learned about God, perhaps even that word itself."[3] It follows from this that "theological statements are not a description of 'the highest Being' but an analysis of the depths of personal relationships." Consequently Robinson assures us that "in a real sense Feuerbach was right in wanting to translate 'theology' into 'anthropology.'"[4]

Christian "theology," then, having been purged of every supernatural element and thoroughly secularized, so that even an atheist need not feel himself to be an outsider,[5] has to all intents and purposes been made synonymous with human ethical interaction. St. Paul's "new man in Christ Jesus" is redefined as "nothing peculiarly religious," but as "the love whereby we are brought completely into one with the Ground of our being, manifesting itself in the unreconciled relationships of our existence." Here, we are told, "in however 'secular' a form, is the atonement

---

1. John A. T. Robinson, *Honest to God* (1963), pp. 99–100.
2. Ibid., p. 105.
3. Ibid., p. 47.
4. Ibid., pp. 49–50.
5. See Robinson's approving references to the atheistic thought of Julian Huxley on pp. 31–34, 37–38, and 40–41 of *Honest to God.*

and the resurrection."[6] In short, the first table of the law has been smashed as a blunder and a delusion, and its fragments have been compounded with the second table. There is no possibility of loving God as "the highest Being" distinct from ourselves because there simply is no such "highest Being," but it is possible and indeed imperative to love one's neighbor; we may, if we wish, equate loving our neighbor with loving God, "God" being understood as the ground of human existence.

It is the summary of the second table—"Thou shalt love thy neighbor as thyself"—rather than the actual commandments, that Robinson finds congenial; indeed, he warns against the danger of identifying Christianity with "the old, traditional morality," naively conceived as having been "derived 'at second hand' from God."[7] He derides, for example, the notion of "the sanctity of marriage," assuring us that "there is nothing specifically Christian about it," and dismissing it as "simply the metaphysic of a pre-scientific age" which was befogged by "this supranaturalistic ethic."[8] The "revolution in ethics," on which Robinson looks with approval and which, he maintains, is now irrevocably established, has involved the rejection of "an ethic" that "is 'heteronomous,' in the sense that it derives its norm from 'out there,'" standing for "'absolute, objective' moral values" and presenting "a dyke against the floods of relativism and subjectivism." The rejection of this ethic is regarded as a significant gain, since, "except to the man who believes in 'the God out there,' it has no compelling sanction or self-authenticating foundation." And so Robinson applauds "the revolt in the field of ethics from supranaturalism to naturalism, from heteronomy to autonomy," and welcomes various kinds of ethical relativism—utilitarianism, evolutionary naturalism, and existentialism are mentioned—because "they have taken their stand, quite correctly, against any subordination of the concrete needs of the individual situation to an alien universal norm."

Yet at the same time Robinson claims to be able to avoid the "morass of relativism and subjectivism" by postulating the objective standard of Tillich's concept of "theonomy," according to which "the transcendent is nothing external or 'out there' but is encountered in, with and under the *Thou* of all finite relationships as their ultimate depth and ground of meaning." This means for the Christian, Robinson says, "the unconditional love of Jesus Christ, 'the man for others.'" But "this utter openness in love to the 'other' for his own sake" is also and "equally the only absolute for the non-Christian." Even though the non-Christian "may not recognize Christ in the 'other,'" yet "in so far as he has responded to the claim of the unconditional in love he has responded to him—for he is the depth of love." Thus, through this "ethic of radical responsiveness, meeting every situation on its own merits, with no prescriptive laws," the distinction between Christian and non-Christian is abolished—otherwise stated, the non-Christian is perceived to be

6. Ibid., p. 82.
7. Ibid., p. 106.
8. Ibid., pp. 108–110.

a Christian after all. God and theology have been metamorphosed (or, to coin a term, anthropomorphosed) into "an ethic of the situation" limited to the merely human dimension of interpersonal relationships.[9]

Robinson borrowed his definition of "situation ethics" at least in part from Joseph Fletcher's 1959 lecture, "The New Look in Christian Ethics," which was published in the *Harvard Divinity Bulletin.* Fletcher subsequently expounded his ethical position at greater length in his book entitled *Situation Ethics: The New Morality.* Both Fletcher and Robinson flourish Augustine's well-worn saying, "Be loving and do as you please."[10] This may be said to have acquired the sanctity of a proof text in antilegalistic circles as distinguished support for the doctrine that "nothing can of itself always be labelled as 'wrong.'"[11] Both Fletcher and Robinson profess respect for "guiding rules," "cumulative experience," and "principles" of conduct, provided they are not treated as hard and fast laws. Fletcher describes his position as that of "principled relativism"; though treating "the ethical maxims of his community" as "illuminators of his problems," he is always prepared "to compromise them or set them aside *in the situation* if love seems better served by doing so."[12] Robinson, while acknowledging an appearance of paradox, asserts that "whatever the pointers of the law to the demands of love, . . . there can for the Christian be no 'packaged' moral judgments—for persons are more important even than 'standards.'"[13]

Augustine, however, was far from being a "situationist" for whom ethical rules and regulations, and in particular those prescribed in Scripture, were of secondary importance and could be set aside at any time for the sake of loving others. He rightly perceived that obedience to the commands of the law and the precepts of Christ is itself an expression of love—love shown in the first place to the Giver of the law and only then love to one's fellow men. Without love, of course, obedience is no better than external self-righteousness and pharisaic formalism. Thus, with reference to Christ's admonition to His disciples, "If you keep my commandments, you will abide in my love" (John 15:10), Augustine writes, "Let no one deceive himself by saying that he loves him, if he does not keep his commandments; for we love him only to the extent that we keep his commandments."[14] He also insists that "all God's commandments, of which 'Thou shalt not commit adultery' is one, . . . are performed aright only when we are motivated by the love of God and of our neighbor for the sake of God, both in this world and in that which is to come."[15]

9. Ibid., pp. 112–116.

10. Joseph Fletcher, "The New Look in Christian Ethics," *Harvard Divinity Bulletin,* October, 1959, p. 10; *Situation Ethics* (1966), p. 79; Robinson, *Honest to God,* p. 119. The reference in Augustine is *Tractatus in Epistolam Ioannis* 7 (J. Migne, *Patrologia Latina* 35, col. 2033): *Dilige et quod vis fac.* Fletcher explains—what surely is obvious—that Augustine means, "Love, and *then* what you will, do."

11. Robinson, *Honest to God,* p. 118.

12. Fletcher, *Situation Ethics,* pp. 26, 31.

13. Robinson, *Honest to God,* pp. 119–120.

14. Augustine, *Tractatus in Ioannis Evangelium* 82 (J. Migne, *Patrologia Latina* 35, col. 1843).

15. Augustine, *Enchiridion* 32.

Nowhere does Augustine suggest that what the law commands is no more than a pointer to the demands of love, with the consequence that it is the particular situation which determines whether the law is to be observed or disregarded.

Situation Ethics

Fletcher strenuously opposes any attempt to build an ethical system, and propounds instead "a method of 'situational' or 'contextual' decision-making"; indeed, he expresses the opinion that *"any* ethical system is unchristian or at least sub-Christian, whatever might be its claim to theological orthodoxy."[16] He defines three "alternative routes or approaches" that may be followed in making ethical decisions: (1) the legalistic, which enforces a code of laws; (2) the antinomian, which acknowledges no ethical laws or principles; and (3) the situational, which he advocates, and which, he explains, comes in between legalism with its codifications and "antinomian unprincipledness."[17]

Being "sensitive to variety and complexity," situation ethics is "antimoralistic as well as antilegalistic"; because it is thoroughly "case-focused" it may be described as "casuistry," but "in a constructive and non-pejorative sense of the word." Fletcher in fact calls it "neocasuistry," with the proviso, however, that "unlike classical casuistry, this neocasuistry repudiates any attempt to anticipate or prescribe real-life decisions in their existential particularity."[18] When we are confronted with a situation that demands a decision, it is *"only* love and reason" that "really count"; law, he maintains, must be kept "in a subservient place."[19]

According to Fletcher there are four presuppositions or working principles of situation ethics, namely pragmatism, relativism, positivism, and personalism. Fletcher frankly confesses his indebtedness to "American pragmatism" as propounded by Charles Peirce, William James, and John Dewey. He approves the Jamesian postulate of expediency as the criterion of right thinking and right conduct. What gives satisfaction (Dewey) or, in more unsophisticated language, what works, must be true and good. "Pragmatism is, to be plainspoken, a *practical* or *success* posture." Whatever does not work must be discarded not merely as unsatisfactory but also as false and bad. This implies that the end is more important than the means. It also implies that, though the means which leads to an end is necessarily prior to that end, yet the right means can be determined only after the right end has been achieved. Fletcher, of course, stresses the necessity of mixing in the ingredient of love as an absolute or a governing principle. "Christianly speaking,"

16. Fletcher, *Situation Ethics,* pp. 11–12.

17. Ibid., pp. 17ff.

18. Ibid., pp. 29–30. Fletcher's claim that St. Paul's dictum in II Corinthians 3:6—"The written code kills, but the Spirit gives life"—is a "guideline" which indicates the apostle's approval of situation ethics reveals a misconstruction of what St. Paul is teaching in this passage and also a misconception of Pauline theology *in toto.*

19. Fletcher, *Situation Ethics,* p. 31.

he says, "the norm or measure by which any thought or action is to be judged a success or failure, i.e., right or wrong, is *love.*"[20] But pragmatism and love, particularly Christian love, may not be treated as bedfellows, as a reading of the encomium of love in I Corinthians 13 shows. Love does not stop to ask, "Will it work?" nor does it look back to ask, "Did it work?" Practicality and success are not criteria of genuine love, no matter how much they may be applauded as expressions of "the genius and ethos or style of life of American culture and of the techno-scientific era."[21]

Secondly, situation ethics is defined as relativistic. As darkness is banished by light, so the absolute standards of law have been displaced by the relativistic perspective of modern man. The situation is a *fait accompli,* and a welcome one at that. We are advised by Fletcher that "our thought forms are relativistic to a degree that our forefathers never imagined" and that "we have become fully and irreversibly 'contingent.'" The liberating force of relativism has invaded and annexed the ethics of Christianity. The one fixed point around which all this relativism revolves is love: "Only love is a constant; everything else is a variable." The awkwardness of this position—that to insist on this tenet is to insist on a dogma that is not relative but absolute—seems to have escaped Fletcher's notice. He doggedly proclaims that "the shift to relativism carries contemporary Christians away from code ethics, away from stern, iron-bound do's and don'ts, away from prescribed conduct and legalistic morality"[22]—but always with the exception of the situational requirements dictated by the absolute of love.

Thirdly, situation ethics is defined as positivistic. Theological positivism, Fletcher explains, presupposes that "faith propositions are 'posited' or affirmed voluntaristically rather than rationalistically." They are, he says, "a-rational but not irrational, outside reason but not against it." Like many other principles, love, he maintains, is not provable; it is axiomatic. "Thus Christian ethics 'posits' faith in God and *reasons* out what obedience to his commandment to love requires in any situation." On the basis of this definition of positivism we are advised that any moral or value judgment in ethics is "a *decision*—not a conclusion . . . a choice, not a result reached by force of logic." These statements, however, are contradictory: Fletcher wishes at the same time to be independent of reason and yet dependent on it. To reason out the line of action required by love in a particular situation is to arrive at a conclusion reached by the force of logic. Clearly enough, Fletcher is intent on setting reason free from predetermined codes and systems of conduct (what he describes as "theological naturalism"), but in reality the new morality for which he pleads has not one but two governing principles, love and reason. Indeed, as we have already seen, he has committed himself to the categorical affirmation that in the moment of situational decision *"only* love and reason really count."[23]

---

20. Ibid., pp. 40ff.
21. Ibid., p. 42.
22. Ibid., pp. 43, 45.
23. See p. 70.

In describing situation ethics as, fourthly, personalistic because "it puts people at the center of concern, not things," Fletcher is not postulating anything strikingly original, any more than when he asserts the centrality of love in Christian morality. Yet although he strongly disapproves of pharisaic legalism, so severely censured in Scripture, he is unwilling to acknowledge that biblical teaching brings law and love together without obliterating the former. We have shown earlier[24] that law and love are not at odds with each other. On the contrary, far from being abrogated by it, the law is fulfilled in love; indeed, its sum is the twofold command to love God with all one's being and one's neighbor as oneself. What Fletcher does, in effect, despite the God language he uses, is to leave God out of the ethical picture by limiting his perspective to the human dimension. Thus he insists that "good derives from the needs of people," whereas the biblical position is that good derives from the character and the will of God. Ethical values are presented by him in a relativistic and humanistic light: *"Value is relative to persons and persons are relative to society, to neighbors."*[25] The most important relationship of all, the relationship to God, is missing! If love is restricted to the love of neighbors—"Love is of people, by people, and for people"—it is not surprising that he insists that "values are only extrinsically, never intrinsically, 'valuable.'" Love is then elevated to saving grace, without respect to evangelical belief and witness; it is reduced to the human level and then given the label "God":

> The Christian situationist says to the non-Christian situationist who is also neighbor . . . : *"Your* love is like mine, like everybody's; it is the Holy Spirit. Love is not the work of the Holy Spirit, it *is* the Holy Spirit—working in us. God *is* love, he doesn't merely *have* it or *give* it; he gives himself—to all men, to all sorts and conditions: to believers and unbelievers, high and low, dark and pale, learned and ignorant, Marxists and Christians and Hottentots."
>
> This is what is meant by "uncovenanted" grace. This is the "saving" truth about themselves which the faithless, alas, do not grasp! It is not the unbelieving who invite "damnation" but the unloving.[26]

In answer to the question, "Can a truly contemporary person *not* be an atheist?" Bishop Robinson, after approvingly quoting the dictum of Julian Huxley that "the god hypothesis is no longer of any pragmatic value," answers for himself and presumably for other situational ethicists in the following terms:

> Most of us today are practical atheists. The "god-hypothesis" is as irrelevant for running an economy or coping with the population explosion as it was for Laplace's system [which attempted to describe the universe's origin]. As a factor you must take into account that in the practical business of living, God is "out"—and no amount of religious manipulation can force him back in. He is peripheral, redundant,

24. See pp. 50ff.
25. The emphasis is Fletcher's.
26. Fletcher, *Situation Ethics,* pp. 40–52.

incredible—and therefore *as God* displaced: in Julian Huxley's words, "not a ruler, but the last fading smile of a cosmic Cheshire Cat."[27]

Robinson welcomes what he calls "the three thrusts of modern atheism": that God is intellectually superfluous, emotionally dispensable, and morally intolerable. "Atheism," he contends, "has done its purifying work," with the supposedly beneficial result that now "people rightly look for natural rather than supernatural causes." This means farewell to the creating, redeeming, and judging God of biblical revelation and the historic Christian faith. Robinson offers, however, the astonishing assurance that "though it looks as if everything is taken away—even the body of the Lord—yet this is not the destruction of Christianity but its liberation," for "with all metaphysical security shattered, with even the word 'God' of doubtful currency," God is still around: "After his death he is still disturbingly alive!"

Who or what is this "God"? Once again, it is a "God" who has been thoroughly secularized and humanized. God as the Supreme Being other than and over man has been completely eliminated. The Christian may discern the "intangible, ineffable reality of 'God'" supremely in the "genuinely human existence" of Jesus Christ, but the scriptural God who is the Father of our Lord Jesus Christ is altogether dispensable. God has been redefined and attached as an identity disk to meaningful interpersonal relationships.

> The man who finds himself compelled to acknowledge the reality of *God,* whatever he may call him or however he may image him, is the man who, through the mathematical regularities and through the functional values, is met by the same grace and the same claim that he recognizes in the I-Thou relation with another person. It may come to him through nature, through the claims of artistic integrity or scientific truth, through the engagements of social justice or of personal communion.

But "as a factor introduced to make the system work God is redundant," and "secularization must be gladly accepted."[28] It is important to realize, therefore, that the new morality has dispensed with metaphysics, dogmatics, and every element of the supernatural, and, to the extent that it may find it convenient to speak of God, has refashioned Him in the image of man with contours impressed on Him by the mold of an ethical concept.

For the situationist, then, love is in and law is out; as Fletcher puts it, "Only the Summary of the Law is the law!"[29] But it is juggling with words to suggest that by summarizing the law it ceases to exist or is miraculously transformed into what situationists regard as its opposite (love). To understand "the Summary" as "a successor to the commandments, and not a compressor," is to change the meaning

27. Robinson, *The New Reformation?* (1965), pp. 108–109.
28. Ibid., pp. 107–119.
29. Fletcher, *Situation Ethics,* p. 77.

of the term. Evidently the laws of language need be no more binding than the laws of conduct. As for the commandments of the Decalogue, we are informed that "situation ethics has good reason to hold it as a *duty* in some situations to break them, *any or all of them,*" with the assurance that we should be "better advised and better off to drop the legalist's love of law and accept only the law of love."[30] At one stroke law is both rejected and conflated with love; by the same waving of the wand justice is made one with love. Fletcher asserts "very positively" that "love *is* justice or that justice loves" and that "they are one and the same."[31]

Although love and justice may be the same for God, whom the situationist wishes man to be, it is sadly not the case with our fallen humanity. Love being, by Fletcher's reckoning, intangible and indefinable, it is useful for covering a multitude of sins; indeed, if his premise is granted, to plead love (which, being internal and solipsistic, cannot be questioned or disproved) should suffice to suspend the administration of justice because, love being equated with justice, to assert the claims of justice against the plea of love would be a reversion to legalism. We are being offered a prescription for confusion: the "loving" criminal could protest that to be punished is to be unlovingly and therefore unjustly treated; the oppression of a tyrannical regime could be defended as a display of just and therefore loving government.[32]

Utilitarianism

The situationist, as we have seen, yokes love "in partnership with reason."[33] Reason, moreover, is harnessed with pragmatism.[34] When seeking "a social policy," Fletcher explains, "the love ethic," as he calls it, "must form a coalition with utilitarianism. It takes over from Bentham and Mill the strategic principle of 'the greatest good of the greatest number.'"[35] This position, oddly enough, justifies being unloving to some in order to be loving to others. We are instructed, for example, that "even the radical principle of enemy-love has to be qualified in the calculations of the situation," and accordingly that "it is right to deal lovingly with the enemy *unless to do so hurts too many friends.*"[36] But then the question inevitably arises: how many is too many? The answer that "we choose what is most 'useful' for the most people" is not particularly helpful, because it is precisely the degree of hurt and usefulness that is frequently impossible to calculate at the

---

30. Ibid., p. 74. Here Fletcher is referring to the six commandments of the second table (the emphasis is his), but he has previously given the same ruling concerning the first table. Of the first commandment, for example, he has said that "like other laws" it "can be broken for love's sake" (p. 72).

31. Ibid., p. 93.

32. See the discussion of crime and punishment on pp. 113–118.

33. Fletcher, *Situation Ethics,* p. 69.

34. See pp. 70–71.

35. Fletcher, *Situation Ethics,* p. 95.

36. Ibid., p. 115.

time when the choice has to be made. In rationally calculating which course of action will bring about the most good or usefulness for the most people one has to focus one's attention on the end without regard to the means leading to that end; recognizing this, Fletcher formulates what he regards as one of the important principles of situation ethics: "Only the end justifies the means; nothing else." And here he joins hands with the Jesuits: "What has often been quoted as a proof of the Jesuits' double-dealing and evasion of the 'moral law' is, in fact, to their credit," he writes; "we embrace their maxim wholeheartedly: *Finis sanctificat media* (The end justifies or sanctifies or validates the means). This is precisely what our principle of extrinsic or contingent value leads to."[37] Absolutely nothing is wrong if it is calculated that the end to which it leads is a good end. This is the new law, and the situationist demands that it be obeyed.

> Every little book and manual on "Problems of conscience" is legalistic. "Is it right to . . ." have premarital intercourse, gamble, steal, euthanase, abort, lie, defraud, break contracts, *et cetera, ad nauseam?* This kind of intrinsicalist morass must be left behind us as irrelevant, incompetent, and immaterial. The new morality, situation ethics, declares that anything and everything is right or wrong, according to the situation.[38]

To tell a lie, for example, is not necessarily wrong; it all depends how and to what end it is told: "If a lie is told unlovingly it is wrong; if it is told in love it is good, right." It is startling to find St. Paul, of all people, invoked as a supporter of this doctrine. "Paul's 'speaking the truth in love' (Eph. 4:15) illuminates the point," Fletcher tells us; "we are to tell the truth for love's sake, not for its own sake. If love vetoes the truth, so be it."[39] There is something incongruous, indeed unscrupulous (but the end sanctifies the means!) about Fletcher's willingness to find a proof text for his position in so legalistic a document as the Bible and to lay claim to the approval of the apostle Paul for his new morality. Why call it new if it is as old as all that? The fact of the matter is that St. Paul in Ephesians 4:15 says nothing about speaking a lie—or vetoing the truth—in love. On the contrary, his admonition to speak the truth is in direct contrast to the immediately preceding warning (4:14) against "the cunning of men" and "their craftiness in deceitful wiles." It is quite specific that the Christian must not tell lies; he must tell the truth, but he should do so in love. Moreover, that St. Paul prohibits lying is plainly confirmed in verse 25 of this same passage (not to mention many other places) where he writes, "Therefore, putting away falsehood, let every one speak the truth with his neighbor."

Only by devising a route that is vain and rationally shabby can one achieve the end of presenting St. Paul—or Jesus, for that matter—as an exponent of situation

---

37. Ibid., pp. 121, 131.
38. Ibid., p. 124.
39. Ibid., p. 65.

ethics.[40] As we have seen,[41] the New Testament, and not least St. Paul, maintains that the law and its commandments are holy and just and good (Rom. 7:12). The apostle, indeed, categorically denounces as absolutely contrary to sound teaching and the Christian gospel the very practices that Fletcher's "love ethic" allows. What could be more explicit than the following instruction given to Timothy?

> Now we know that the law is good, if any one uses it lawfully, understanding this, that the law is not laid down for the just but for the lawless and disobedient, for the ungodly and sinners, for the unholy and profane, for murderers of fathers and murderers of mothers, for manslayers, immoral persons, sodomites, kidnappers, liars, perjurers, and whatever else is contrary to sound doctrine, in accordance with the glorious gospel of the blessed God with which I have been entrusted (I Tim. 1:8–11).

Fletcher gives a number of examples to illustrate the way in which the principles he has posited should be applied in different situations—what he calls "this contextual, situational, clinical case method" or "neocasuistry." We propose now to examine some of these briefly. When the woman in the incident in the Gospels poured the expensive ointment over Jesus' head this was, according to Fletcher, a display of "impetuous, uncalculating, unenlightened sentimental love," and those who were present were right to protest that this was a wasteful act and that the money for which the ointment could have been sold would better have been given to the poor. Their spirit was that of "calculating, enlightened love," and Jesus was wrong to defend the woman and to disregard their concern for "utilitarian distribution."[42] But how on earth does Fletcher know that this woman's love was uncalculating and unenlightened or that she did not achieve a laudable end in doing what she did? The world will be a poorer place if the impulse of devotion is eliminated and spontaneous generosity is disallowed. Jesus, after all, was the poorest of the poor, with no place to call His own; if anyone had a right to object it was He, not those who were well able to afford the cost of entertaining Him at dinner. But He perceived the true worth of this deed as an openhearted expression of dedication to and trust in Him.

If a physician has to choose between saving the life of "a young mother of three" and "an old skid row drunk," calculating, pragmatic love requires him to save the mother.[43] In World War II, when the British authorities "let a number of women agents return to Germany to certain arrest and death in order to keep secret the fact that they had broken the German code," we are assured that "situational casuistry [but not 'legalistic casuistry'] could easily approve their decision."[44] If a man has to decide whether to carry his own father or "a medical genius who has discovered a cure for a common fatal disease" out of a burning building, he will leave his father

40. See, for example, ibid., pp. 69, 139.
41. See p. 47.
42. Fletcher, *Situation Ethics,* p. 97.
43. Ibid., pp. 97–98.
44. Ibid., p. 98.

to burn to death if he is a situationist.[45] If a mother with an infant child realizes that her baby's crying is likely to betray to the enemy the presence of the whole company of which she is a member and thus lead to capture and death, it is right for her to kill her child with her own hand and wrong for her to allow it to go on living.[46] Situation ethics says that an officer's act of forcing men out of an over-crowded lifeboat to certain death in a rough sea was "bravely sinful, . . . a good thing"[47]—the calculation being that it was better for some to be saved than for all to perish—though the officer could not have been certain that all could not have been saved, which would have been a better and more utilitarian (because benefiting a greater number) and therefore a more loving end. Yet we are told that on his Antarctic expedition Captain Scott was right not to have abandoned one of the party who had to be carried on a stretcher, even though this decision meant that he and the others perished. This, if anything, is a reversal of the pragmatic, calculating love praised in the preceding incidents, and therefore an illustration that is inconsistent with Fletcher's principles. If it is retorted that Scott calculated that there was a chance of their all surviving, the same argument must be applicable to the officer in the lifeboat. Fletcher can do no better than to "assume Scott was not simply legalistic in his decision"—why not allow the woman who anointed Jesus the benefit of the same assumption?—and to offer us the observation that "we can't always guess the future, even though we are always being forced to try."[48]

As for sex, the situationist makes it plain that there are "no holds barred." The whore who by the services she provides helps a man to shed his sexual inhibitions is to be commended for her contribution to the "love ethic."[49] "Are we not entitled to say," Fletcher asks, "that, depending on the situation, those who break the Seventh Commandment of the old law, even whores, *could* be doing a good thing—*if* it is for love's sake, for the neighbor's sake? In short, is there any real 'law' of universal weight?" And to this he answers, "The situationist thinks not."[50] Accordingly, he issues an ethical *carte blanche* permitting any and every kind of sexual indulgence, with the usual proviso regarding the preservation of the love motive: "Whether any form of sex (hetero, homo, or auto) is good or evil depends on whether love is fully served."[51]

The ethical philosophy of this new morality is, despite all the high-sounding talk about love, a prescription for chaos. Its thoroughgoing subjectivism, the consequence of the repudiation of all external norms and standards, coupled with the infinite variety of intention and temperament among the individuals of the human race, means that (short of their first consulting with Fletcher as their father confessor,

45. Ibid., p. 115.
46. Ibid., p. 125.
47. Ibid., p. 136.
48. Ibid.
49. Ibid., pp. 126–127.
50. Ibid., p. 146.
51. Ibid., p. 139.

since he seems as ready to pontificate on which line of action is right and which wrong in a given situation as were the Jesuits of old) different persons may arrive at opposite conclusions in the same situation. Even the situationist's sole absolute—love—is subjectively presented, inescapably relativized by human finiteness and degraded by human fallenness. This, however, the situationist fails to take into account because he refuses to see man as a fallen creature in need of grace, assuming, on the contrary, that people are essentially good and capable—if only they make up their minds to it—of loving self-motivation in any situation. In fact, there seems to be a strongly Pelagian element in situationism.

If it were not for the fallenness of society there would be no call for the devising of situation ethics. If only every person was genuinely loving, unselfish, and of one mind with every other person, ethics would not even need to be discussed. But also precisely because of the pervasiveness of human fallenness, an unstructured, subjective theory like situation ethics can be expected to lead only to a state of chaos and to be destructive of human society. There is abundant evidence through-out history, and more than ever at the present time, that persons and communities are more readily motivated by selfishness than by love. Most people unfortunately have little difficulty in persuading themselves that what they want to do is loving and that the ends to which their actions lead are laudable. Action motivated by self-centered subjectivism and dressed up to appear beneficial to the greatest number is proving destructive of lives and families and whole communities. Society cannot survive without structure—especially the divinely ordered structure of law and decency. The contemptuous dismissal of God's law as a legalistic straitjacket is an expression of pretension to human autonomy and self-sufficiency on the part of those who imagine they can effect the death of God by reducing Him to merely human dimensions and then identifying Him with themselves. They then assume for themselves an authoritarian role as givers of the "new law" and formulators of the "new morality."

It is hardly a matter of dispute that all ethical action is situational and that every ethical decision has to be made with reference to a unique situation. Having no standard but that of subjective human love, the new morality lacks the objectivity that a fixed (though not legalistic) order provides. With no stabilizing reference point outside of itself, it becomes hopelessly unbalanced. Like a balloon that has slipped from its moorings, its course is unpredictable and it is fated to crash. Certainly the Christian ethic demands that each situation be approached and assessed with love and compassion, but it is the love of God that comes first and gives form and significance to the love of the neighbor, our fellow creature under God. To eliminate the love of God or—what amounts to the same thing—to conflate or equate it with the love of one's neighbor is to lose hold of the properly objective focus of the Christian ethic. Apart from divine objectivity human subjec-tivity cannot fail to be lopsided and ultimately meaningless, because it is from the objectivity of the Creator that the subjectivity of the creature derives its true purpose and significance. The ethical behavior of the Christian, then, is not only situational but also structured in accordance with the objective standard of orderliness, the revealed will of God, from which we learn that God's law and God's love, far from being mutually exclusive, are one and indissoluble.[52] The supreme manifestation of this truth is seen in Jesus Christ, who Himself as the incarnate Son was the expression of the perfect harmony between the law and the love of God, for in His living and His dying He freely and lovingly satisfied the perfect standard of divine holiness for our eternal redemption. It is Jesus Christ the righteous who is the propitiation for our sins (I John 2:1–2).

"New morality" and "situation ethics" are in fact only new names for old theories and attitudes. They denote an ethical mentality that was well known to Dietrich Bonhoeffer (though not yet by these designations) before midcentury, and he was not slow to contest its claim to represent the essence of Christian morality. Thus he wrote,

> There is a way of basing ethics upon the concept of reality which differs entirely from the Christian way. This is the positive and empirical approach, which aims at the entire elimination from ethics of the concept of norms and standards because it regards this concept as being merely the idealization of factual and practically expedient attitudes. Fundamentally, according to this view, the good is no more than what is expedient, useful, and advantageous to reality. From this it follows that there is no universal good but only an infinitely varying good which is determined in each case on the basis of "reality." . . . Reality, understood in this inadequate sense, cannot be the source of good, because all it demands is complete surrender to the contingent, the casual, the adventitious and the momentarily expedient, because it fails to recognize the ultimate reality and because in this way it destroys and abandons the unity of good.[53]

Bonhoeffer insists that "the Christian ethic speaks in a quite different sense of the reality which is the origin of good, for it speaks of the reality of God as the ultimate reality without and within everything that is."[54] It is certainly a strange development that advocates of the new morality tend to speak of and to quote Bonhoeffer as though he were one of them. The explanation seems to be that his striking and often paradoxical modes of expression tend to be detached from their context and then misconstrued and misapplied. Bonhoeffer's ethical position, however, is strictly conservative rather than startlingly radical.

52. See pp. 50ff.
53. Dietrich Bonhoeffer, *Ethics,* pp. 60–61.
54. Ibid., p. 61.

5

The New Confessional

I t is no wild exaggeration to say that for great numbers of people in our Western world the psychiatrist's couch has taken the place of the Catholic confessional booth and the Protestant counseling pew. Even within the ranks of organized Christianity many clergymen now seem to regard their primary task as that of psychotherapy rather than evangelistic outreach, biblical instruction, and pastoral visitation. Thus it is hardly surprising that there is a steady stream of clerics who are relinquishing their parochial and congregational charges, and some even their ministerial orders, in order to devote their time and energy entirely to the practice of psychotherapy. For those who no longer feel a strong attachment to the distinctive doctrines of the Christian faith this transition is understandable. No one would wish to deny that many persons afflicted with mental illness or psychopathic complaints need the expert treatment of a specialist. However, it cannot be emphasized too strongly that the healing power of the Christian gospel is of immense therapeutic value to the whole person, psychological and physical as well as spiritual, and indeed that the gospel alone deals with the problem of alienation and meaningless existence which is at the root of the predicament of unregenerate human personality.

Freudian Psychoanalysis

The father of modern psychoanalysis, Sigmund Freud (1856–1939), sought an explanation of the neuroses so prevalent in society by delving into the subconscious experiences of infancy. Freud theorized that the repression of instinctive, and in particular libidinal, desires is the radical cause of neurotic personality. Indeed, sexuality is central to the system he developed. The infant, he taught, apart from passing through the stages of the so-called Oedipus complex, derives erotic pleasure orally through the act of sucking its mother's breast and anally through the act of defecation. This childish fascination with the orifices at either end of the alimentary tract indicates, it was held, that the infant is erotically a pervert in its earliest days before there is an awareness of sexuality in the genital organs. "All the perverse tendencies," Freud wrote, "have their roots in childhood," and "children are disposed towards them all and practise them all to a degree conforming with their immaturity; in short, *perverted sexuality* is nothing else but *infantile sexuality,* magnified and separated into its component parts."[1] There is no need to stress here the immense influence that Freudian theory has wielded and continues to wield in psychotherapy.

Freud, who of course was persuaded that his psychoanalytical description was purely scientific, recognized three forces which might dispute the position of science, namely religion, art, and philosophy. Of these he viewed religion alone as "a really serious enemy." Art he dismissed as "almost always harmless and beneficent" in that "it does not seek to be anything else but an illusion."[2] As for philosophy, he regarded it without alarm as unopposed to science, though parting company with science "in that it clings to the illusion that it can produce a complete and coherent picture of the universe, though in fact that picture must needs fall to pieces with every new advance in our knowledge." Even though philosophy was guilty, in his judgment, of the "methodological error" of "over-estimating the epistemological value of our logical operations," its threat to science was negligible because it "has no immediate influence on the great majority of mankind," and "interests only a small number even of the thin upper stratum of intellectuals, while all the rest find it beyond them." Religion, however, he acknowledged to be "a tremendous force, which exerts its power over the strongest emotions of human beings," purporting as it does to give men knowledge of the source and origin of all things, to assure the faithful of the unclouded happiness that awaits them in the future, and meanwhile to provide guidance and comfort as they face present dangers and misfortunes. Freud admitted that this is something with which science cannot compete. It remains, then, for science to explain religion away. And this, as might be expected, is done with reference to the experiences of early childhood.

God becomes the projection and magnification of man into the figure of an idealized superman, a psychological relic of the exaggerated manner in which the infant views the parent. Thus when religion calls the Creator God "Father," "psychoanalysis concludes that he really is the father, clothed in the grandeur in which he once appeared to the small child." From this same notion the further concepts of the providence and the law or ethical will of God follow supposedly:

> The same father (the parental function) who gave the child his life, and preserved it from the dangers which that life involves, also taught it what it may or may not do. . . . This whole state of affairs is carried over by the grown man unaltered into his religion. The prohibitions and commands of his parents live on in his breast as his moral conscience; God rules the world of men with the help of the same system of rewards and punishments, and the degree of protection and happiness which each individual enjoys depends on his fulfilment of the demands of morality.

1. Sigmund Freud, *Introductory Lectures on Psycho-Analysis,* 2d ed. (1929), p. 261.

2. The quotations in this and the following paragraph are from Freud, *New Introductory Lectures on Psycho-Analysis* (1933), pp. 203ff.

Thus, Freud claims, psychoanalysis "has traced the origin of religion to the help-lessness of childhood, and its content to the persistence of the wishes and needs of childhood into maturity." While agreeing that human society cannot do without "the ethical commands to which religion seeks to lend its weight," he warns that "it is dangerous to link up obedience to them with religious belief"; indeed, he brushes religion aside as a neurotic phase (a tiresomely persistent one!) in the upward progress of mankind, describing it as "a parallel to the neurosis which the civilized individual must pass through on his way from childhood to maturity." Freud maintains that prohibitions, and especially religious prohibitions, give rise to severe inhibitions in people's lives; yet the only encouragement that he can give us—or rather mankind in general, for the individual in this scheme has no future but death—in our desire for a better world is that "our best hope for the future is that the intellect—the scientific spirit, reason—should in time establish a dictator-ship over the human mind."

This seems like a nebulous piece of wishful thinking hardly justified by Freud's own scientific disclosures. Given his premises it would have been more rational for him to advocate keeping the child's mouth away from its mother's breast, screening it from its excretory processes and products, and banishing the father from its entourage. Measured criticism came from another famous psychotherapist, Carl Jung (1875–1961), who perceived that Freud's perspective left little room for present or future idealism. Jung described "the end-product of the Freudian method of explanation" not only as "a detailed elaboration of man's shadow-side such as had never been carried out before," but also as "the most effective antidote imagin-able to all idealistic illusions about the nature of man."[3] Jung was unsympathetic to "a biassed portrayal of man from the shadow-side alone," though he held that "the horror which we feel for Freudian interpretations is entirely due to our own barbaric or childish naïveté, which believes that there can be heights without corresponding depths."[4] Jung's penchant for offsetting the troughs of human baseness with the crests of human achievement may be somewhat realistic for man in his fallenness but, contrary to the Christian conception of the beginning and the end, apparently envisages the coexistence of good and evil as a permanent state of affairs.

It will be of interest to take brief notice of Jung's comments comparing Freud with Alfred Adler (1870–1937), who, at first closely associated with Freud, subsequently broke away from him and formed his own school (it is not necessary for our present purpose to enter into a separate discussion of Adler's theories). Finding Freud's explanation of neuroses "in terms of pleasure and its satisfaction . . . one-sided and therefore insufficient," Jung asserts that "it is precisely here that his former pupil, Adler, comes forward to fill the gap" by demonstrating "convincingly that many cases of neurosis can be more satisfactorily explained on the ground of

3. Carl G. Jung, *Modern Man in Search of a Soul* (1933), p. 46.
4. Ibid., p. 47.

an urge to power than by the pleasure principle." Jung sees the "neglect of the unconscious" on Adler's part as "an inevitable reaction to Freud's emphasis on the unconscious," and expresses the judgment that "psychology, if it is to develop further," must "renounce so essentially negative an approach to the unconscious as Freud's."[5] While professing to be "no opponent of Freud's," Jung maintains that Adler's system is "at least as convincing" as that of Freud; and he critically affirms that both schools "deserve reproach for over-emphasizing the pathological aspect of life and for interpreting man too exclusively in the light of his defects." He is particularly unhappy with Freud's obsession with sexuality and declares that "Freud's is not a psychology of the healthy mind."[6]

> I do not mean to deny the importance of sexuality in psychic life, though Freud stubbornly maintains that I do deny it. What I seek is to set bounds to the rampant terminology of sex which threatens to vitiate all discussion of the human psyche; I wish to put sexuality itself in its proper place.[7]

As we saw above, Freud treats art and the esthetic as a harmless illusion which offers no real threat to his doctrine; this dismissive attitude is itself a consequence of his preoccupation with sexuality. Jung speaks of Freud's sexual theory as being "enormously important to him, both personally and philosophically."

> Above all, Freud's attitude towards the spirit seemed to me highly questionable. Whenever, in a person or in a work of art, an expression of spirituality (in the intellectual, not the supernatural sense) came to light, he suspected it. Anything that could not be directly interpreted as sexuality he referred to as "psychosexuality." I protested that this hypothesis, carried to its logical conclusion, would lead to an annihilating judgment upon culture. Culture would then appear as a mere farce, the morbid consequence of repressed sexuality. "Yes," he assented, "so it is, and that is just a curse of fate against which we are powerless to contend."[8]

There is no doubt that Jung actually regarded Freud as being psychotically obsessed with this belief. Thus he wrote,

> There was no mistaking the fact that Freud was emotionally involved in his sexual theory to an extraordinary degree. When he spoke of it, his tone became urgent, almost anxious, and all signs of his normally critical and sceptical manner vanished. A strange, deeply moved expression came over his face, the cause of which I was at a loss to understand. I had a strong intuition that for him sexuality was a sort of *numinosum.*

5. Ibid., pp. 50–51.
6. Ibid., pp. 134–135.
7. Ibid., p. 138.
8. This and the following extracts in this section are drawn from Jung's autobiographical *Memories, Dreams, Reflections* (1977), pp. 172–176.

In 1910, some three years after the incident referred to in the preceding quotation, there came an illuminating moment during the course of a conversation in Vienna, which Jung describes as follows:

> I can still recall vividly how Freud said to me, "My dear Jung, promise me never to abandon the sexual theory. That is the most essential thing of all. You see, we must make a dogma of it, an unshakable bulwark." He said it to me with great emotion, in the tone of a father saying, "And promise me this one thing, my dear son: that you will go to church every Sunday."

Jung narrates how he was astonished and alarmed by Freud's use of the terms *bulwark* and *dogma:*

> For a dogma, that is to say, an indisputable confession of faith, is set up only when the aim is to suppress doubts once and for all. But that no longer has anything to do with scientific judgment; only with a personal power drive. . . . Freud, who had always made much of his irreligiosity, had now constructed a dogma; or rather, in the place of a jealous God whom he had lost, he had substituted another compelling image, that of sexuality.

Jung states that this encounter struck at the heart of his friendship with Freud, and he mentions the bitterness that was characteristic of the latter:

> There is, after all, no harsher bitterness than that of a person who is his own worst enemy. In his own words, he felt himself menaced by a "black tide of mud"—he who more than anyone else had tried to let down his bucket into those black depths. . . . There was nothing to be done about this one-sidedness of Freud's. Perhaps some inner experience of his own might have opened his eyes; but then his intellect would have reduced any such experience to "mere sexuality" or "psychosexuality."

Jung and Psychotherapy

The doctrines of Freud, with their emphasis on the necessity for depth analysis and the removal of moralistic repressions and inhibitions (especially those related to sexuality), provided the theoretical mainspring of the so-called sexual revolution and the cult of amorality which have now burst like a flood on Western society, threatening to submerge all ethical values and standards. The warning signals given by Jung have not succeeded in stemming this tide. Jung himself, the son of a Christian pastor, could hardly be described as a Christian, for he certainly did not hold to the central tenets of the Christian faith. It is true that he defined his position as being "on the extreme left wing of the congress of Protestant opinion,"[9] but his religious outlook was thoroughly relativistic—"I attribute a positive value to all religions," he wrote.[10] Though appreciative of what he regarded as the positive

9. Jung, *Modern Man,* p. 281.
10. Ibid., p. 137.

worth of Christianity, he had little sympathy for its claim to uniqueness. Nonetheless, his advocacy of the basic importance of the spiritual for psychotherapy reveals a more profound perception of the nature of human personality and its problems than is found in Freud. Man does indeed yearn for happiness and dignity, but it is not in pleasure (Freud) or power (Adler) that he finds self-fulfillment. He needs to discover, as Jung recognized, the purpose and the meaning of his existence. "A psycho-neurosis," Jung affirmed, "must be understood as the suffering of a human being who has not discovered what life means for him. . . . The patient is looking for something that will take possession of him and give meaning and form to the confusion of his neurotic mind."[11]

Jung, then, was strongly critical of Freudian psychology because, having no place for the spiritual dimension, "it points no way that leads beyond the inexorable cycle of biological events." He was convinced that man needs to learn that God is his Father, which is "what Freud would never learn, and what all those who share his outlook forbid themselves to learn," bound as they are to the theory that God is no more than an immature projection of the human father-figure. "We moderns," Jung affirmed, "are faced with the necessity of rediscovering the life of the spirit; we must experience it anew for ourselves. It is the only way in which we can break the spell that binds us to the cycle of biological events."[12] He even charged that Freud's idea of the superego was "a furtive attempt to smuggle in his time-honoured image of Jehovah in the dress of psychological theory."[13] This accusation must have been highly displeasing to Freud.

It is not our purpose to discuss the Freudian and Jungian systems in depth. What is of immediate interest is Jung's insistence on the importance of the spiritual dimension and his interest in a remarkable phenomenon in the Europe of his day, namely the psychiatrist's usurpation of the place of the pastor. This is happening today to an even greater degree, especially on the American scene, with which Jung was familiar. His cautionary counsel is now needed more than ever:

> The fact that many clergymen seek support or practical help from Freud's theory of sexuality or Adler's theory of power is astonishing, inasmuch as both these theories are hostile to spiritual values, being, as I have said, psychology without the psyche. They are rational methods of treatment which actually hinder the realization of meaningful experience. By far the larger number of psychotherapists are disciples of Freud or Adler. This means that the great majority of patients are necessarily alienated from a spiritual standpoint—a fact which cannot be a matter of indifference to one who has the realization of spiritual values much at heart.[14]

Jung observed that "the wave of interest in psychology" was "coincident with the general exodus from the Church," and quoted the remark of a Protestant minister

11. Ibid., p. 260.
12. Ibid., pp. 139–140.
13. Ibid., p. 141.
14. Ibid., p. 263.

that "nowadays people go to the psychiatrist rather than to the clergyman." He declared, further, that of all his patients above the age of thirty-five "there has not been one whose problem in the last resort was not that of finding a religious outlook on life,"[15] and he urged that it was "high time for the clergyman and the psychotherapist to join forces to meet this great spiritual task."[16]

Jung admitted that to "that most ordinary and frequent of questions: What is the meaning of my life, or of life in general?" the psychotherapist "does not know what to say"; but it is not at all clear why Jung should have expected a confession of this kind to be "the beginning of the patient's confidence in him," especially when, as Jung asserted, the patient no longer has confidence in the clergyman or the philosopher who also has failed to offer a satisfactory answer to this question.[17] Why should the ignorance of the psychiatrist arouse more confidence than the failure of the clergyman and the philosopher? While Jung correctly diagnosed neurosis as "an inner cleavage—a state of being at war with oneself," and perceived that "healing may be called a religious problem," the Christian can only hold that he was seriously wrong in his opinion that "modern man has heard enough about sin and guilt." Modern man, Jung declared, "is sorely enough beset by his own bad conscience, and wants rather to learn how he is to reconcile himself with his own nature—how he is to love the enemy in his own heart and call the wolf his brother."[18] In Jung's view self-reconciliation, together with such help as religion may afford, is the cure. Freudian psychoanalysis does not go beyond bringing to the surface of our consciousness the evil that is within us: "Freud has unfortunately overlooked the fact that man has never yet been able single-handed to hold his own against the powers of darkness—that is, of the unconscious," Jung complained. Then he added that "man has always stood in need of the spiritual help which each individual's own religion held out to him," whatever that religion may be.[19]

We may readily agree that great numbers of people in the Western world today are "forcing the psychotherapist into the rôle of a priest,"[20] and that the therapeutic need of the neurotically afflicted person is spiritual as well as psychological—indeed, above all it is spiritual. We concur also with Jung's diagnosis of an inner crisis of disharmony and disintegration which is inseparable from the loss of both self-identity and the meaning of one's existence, and that this is essentially a *religious* crisis. But to call in religion, as understood in the widest sense, to help man reconcile himself to the coexistence of light and darkness within him and somehow to bring these opposites symbiotically together can never be the solution to the problem. What is needed and sought is not an uncertain twilight but the conquest of darkness by light. The catharsis of the couch may bring relief, but by

15. Ibid., pp. 263–264.
16. Ibid., p. 265.
17. Ibid., p. 267.
18. Ibid., pp. 273–274.
19. Ibid., p. 277.
20. Ibid., p. 278.

itself it can be only temporary (hence the regularity with which so many people visit their psychiatrists). Psychological analysis may remove misconceptions and contribute to self-understanding, but it does not put an end to the warfare within. Indeed, to clean out a person's psyche and to put nothing positive in place of what has been removed is to render that person open to a possession worse than that of which he has been relieved—precisely as Christ Himself taught:

> When the unclean spirit has gone out of a man, he passes through waterless places seeking rest; and finding none he says, "I will return to my house from which I came." And when he comes he finds it swept and put in order. Then he goes and brings seven other spirits more evil than himself, and they enter and dwell there; and the last state of that man becomes worse than the first (Luke 11:24–26).

The reason, moreover, why man is (to quote Jung again) "sorely beset by his own bad conscience" is not just the unresolved conflict in the depth of his being, but the rupture of his relationship with his Creator. The psychiatrist is quite right in recognizing that the cause of the neurotic sense of alienation that is so shattering to personal peace and fulfillment must be sought in the core of the personality. But psychiatry alone does not go deep enough. Only the gospel does that. Man's bad conscience comes not from a failure of self-acceptance or of adjustment to the warring elements of his nature—as though these were inescapably part of his constitution—but from his rebellion against God: it is first and foremost a bad conscience before God. Thus man's great need is not self-reconciliation, whether religiously assisted or not, but reconciliation between himself and God. The appeal of the Christian evangelist is, "We beseech you on behalf of Christ, *be reconciled to God"* (II Cor. 5:20). There is no other route to reconciliation with oneself, with one's fellow men, and with the rest of creation.

Christian catharsis is not self-purging, getting things off one's chest or out of one's system—though confession of sin is a necessity—but purging by Christ's atoning blood, which "cleanses us from all sin" (I John 1:7). Confession of sin must be accompanied by repentance of sin and faith in Christ as Redeemer and Lord. This brings the peace of forgiveness of sin (Col. 1:14, 20), the conquest of darkness by light, and the renewal of all things through the entry of the victorious Christ into one's being: the house swept clean is not left unoccupied, but is filled with the grace of God's presence and power. And because all this is entirely the work of God it cannot fail or come to nothing. It is the renewal of creation, the restoration of all that was lost in the fall, the bringing of redeemed humanity to its glorious destiny in Christ. "All this is from God," the apostle writes, "who through Christ reconciled us to himself and gave us the ministry of reconciliation; that is, God was in Christ reconciling the world to himself, not counting their trespasses against them" (II Cor. 5:18–19). It is precisely the blood of Christ, shed for sinners on the cross of Calvary, that purifies "your conscience from dead works to serve the living God" (Heb. 9:14).

In the end the relief that may be found through psychiatry is superficial, no matter how deeply it may delve into the dark regions of the subconscious, simply because apart from the gospel it is incompetent to penetrate to and cure the human problem at its true root. As Herbert Waddams says,

> The trouble about the method which dismisses guilt feelings as unnecessary is that it cures the symptoms without touching the underlying disease, which is a disease of the personality cut off from God. Since God has made man for himself, the conclusion that guilt feelings are false and that there is no such thing as sin will merely leave an aching and unfilled void in the personality. It is only by filling this void with God, and therefore by coming to him through forgiveness, that fulfilment and integration can be found.[21]

It is by the way of the gospel alone that the lifeline linking the creature to his Creator is reconnected, thereby enabling each person to find his true identity, to fulfill the wonderful potential of his human nature, and to recover the genuine meaning of existence. The war within is over: victory and harmony are achieved through Jesus Christ our Lord (Rom. 7:21–25). The true dignity of man is restored. There is no place for religious relativism: the claim of the Christian gospel is absolute. No one comes to the Father but by Christ (John 14:6; Acts 4:12).

21. Herbert Waddams, *A New Introduction to Moral Theology* (1965), p. 91.

The Ethics
of Humanism

Freudian theory has become a dominant force in both clinical and popular psychology and has been a major factor not merely in promoting the abandonment of traditional standards of morality but also in giving a stamp of scientific respectability to the current cult of amorality. Amorality is the denial of moral standards, and its acceptance therefore removes the age-old distinction between morality and immorality. As psychoanalysis is concerned with the individual self and its neuroses, it was perhaps only to be expected that its conquests in society would lead to preoccupation with the individual self and to the preaching of self-liberation, self-acceptance, and self-affirmation. The obsessive concentration of Freudianism on sex and the removal of sexual inhibitions opened the way for the sexual license and explicitness now purveyed on stage and screen and in literature. The insistence that, if man is to achieve self-realization and mature personhood, he must repudiate the ties of authority that bind him to his parents has contributed to the disruption of family life, which now so widely permeates the social structure of Western culture. The abolition of the family does not lack determined advocates and campaigners who wish to persuade us that it is a development much to be desired. But the scene today is one of ethical deterioration, and the goal of social and international harmony and the betterment of mankind seems as remote as it has ever been. This state of affairs even the humanist cannot realistically ignore; yet he is unwilling, and on his principles unable, to turn away from his belief that man, perhaps helped by some luck in the evolutionistic lottery, is the master of his destiny and that his future lies in his hands alone.

Man for Himself

Erich Fromm, in his book *Man for Himself: An Inquiry into the Psychology of Ethics,* asserts that "man's pride has been justified," since "by virtue of his reason he has built a material world the reality of which surpasses even the dreams and visions of fairy tales and utopias." Yet Fromm makes the admission that, despite this, "modern man feels uneasy and more and more bewildered" because he experiences "a sense of futility with regard to all his activities," with the result that

91

"while his power over matter grows, he feels powerless in his individual life and society."[1]

In a later book Fromm defines the human predicament still more graphically: "Never before has man come so close to the fulfilment of his most cherished hopes as today. Our scientific discoveries and technical achievements," he writes, "enable us to visualize the day when the human race will form a unified community and no longer live as separate entities." He assures us that "man has created a new world with its own laws and destiny," and that, "looking at his creation, he can say, truly, it is good."[2] Strangely, however, he who is praised as god over "his creation" fails to be god over himself. "But looking at himself what can he say?" Fromm asks. "Has he come closer to the realization of another dream of mankind, that of the perfection of *man?* Of man loving his neighbor, doing justice, speaking truth, and realizing that which he potentially is, an image of God?" Such questioning is admitted to be "embarrassing since the answer is so painfully clear," for "while we have created wonderful things we have failed to make of ourselves beings for whom this tremendous effort would seem worthwhile." Thus Fromm concedes that "ours is a life not of brotherliness, happiness, contentment but of spiritual chaos and bewilderment close to a state of madness."[3]

This commendably realistic recognition of the human predicament inevitably arouses concern for the future of mankind. Is there any bright prospect that we can offer for the generations to come? "We cling to the belief that we are happy," Fromm says; "we teach our children that we are more advanced than any generation before us, that eventually no wish will remain unfulfilled and nothing will be out of our reach." But what guidance are we able to give them? "Somehow they feel, as all human beings do, that life must have a meaning—but what is it? . . . They long for happiness, for truth, for justice, for love, for an object of devotion; are we able to satisfy their longing?" Fromm replies that "we are as helpless as they are," observing that "we pretend that our life is based upon a solid foundation and ignore the shadows of uneasiness, anxiety, and confusion which never leave us."[4] Although this sounds deeply pessimistic, Fromm wishes to convince us that he has the remedy for the sickness of society—and it is an explicitly humanistic remedy. He certainly does not encourage a return to traditional religion with its call to trust in God and its standards for ethical conduct. He counsels, rather, a return to the rationalistic presuppositions of the Enlightenment which, he affirms, "taught man that he could trust his own reason as a guide to establishing valid ethical norms and that he could rely on himself, needing neither revelation nor the authority of the church in order to know good and evil."[5]

1. Erich Fromm, *Man for Himself: An Inquiry into the Psychology of Ethics* (1947), p. 4.
2. Fromm, *Psychoanalysis and Religion* (1950), p. 1.
3. Ibid.
4. Ibid., p. 3.
5. Fromm, *Man for Himself,* p. 5.

Fromm postulates that human reason is by itself sufficient to guide man to proper standards of ethical behavior, and he holds that man's autonomy or self-mastery will enable him to follow the guidance of reason. Thus he insists that "valid ethical norms can be formed by man's reason and by it alone," and that "the great tradition of humanistic ethical thought has laid the foundation for value systems based on man's autonomy and reason." However, the expectation that modern psychological research, and especially psychoanalysis, would prove to be "one of the most potent stimuli for the development of humanistic ethics" has not been realized, as Fromm grants:

> While psychoanalysis has tremendously increased our knowledge of man, it has not increased our knowledge of how man ought to live and what he ought to do. Its main function has been that of "debunking," of demonstrating that value judgments and ethical norms are the rationalized expressions of irrational—and often unconscious—desires and fears, and that they therefore have no claim to objective validity.[6]

He charges psychoanalysis with having "made the mistake of divorcing psychology from the problems of philosophy and ethics," and with having "ignored the fact that human personality cannot be understood unless we look at man in his totality, which includes his need to find an answer to the question of the meaning of his existence and to discover the norms according to which he ought to live."[7]

This conclusion has a distinctly Jungian ring to it. But Fromm has not buried Freud. Fromm observes that when psychology needed to be rescued from this situation in which it had become "a science lacking its main subject matter, the soul," Freud came as a rescuer.[8] The claim that Freud's psychoanalytical method "made possible the most minute and intimate study of the soul" may be acceptable from the humanistic point of view; but the Christian knows, as we have shown earlier, that no humanistic procedure or theory which banishes God from the picture can possibly penetrate to the root of man's psychological disharmony. The most psychoanalysis can do is to lead to the diagnosis of the origins of particular neurotic states of mind. Such diagnosis can of course be very beneficial to the afflicted individual, but apart from the gospel with its power to heal the whole person it will never reach down to the true heart of the human predicament. At least Fromm acknowledges that the analyst has found that "mental sickness cannot be discovered apart from moral problems," and that "his patient is sick because he has neglected his soul's demands."[9]

Fromm allows the solution to man's moral problems to be religious, but only on the basis of his own man-centered definition of religion. Assigning to the psycho-

6. Ibid., p. 6.
7. Ibid.
8. Fromm, *Psychoanalysis and Religion,* pp. 5–6.
9. Ibid., p. 7.

analyst the role of "physician of the soul," he explains that "the psychoanalytical cure of the soul aims at helping the patient to achieve an attitude which can be called religious in the humanistic though not in the authoritarian sense of the word."[10] In line with this he expresses his "conviction that the problem of religion is not the problem of God but the problem of man," and that "religious formulations and religious symbols are attempts to give expression to certain kinds of human experience."[11] Seen within this perspective, the alienation which man experiences and needs to overcome is not alienation from God but alienation from himself. Fromm dismisses God, as does Freud, as a harmful human "projection," which, as the focus of the "authoritarian" brand of religion, deprives man of his powers and thus of self-fulfillment. This, of course, is the reversal of the Christian position, which sees God as the source and giver of the powers and qualities by which our humanity is dignified—certainly not as the one who takes them from us.

Fromm, however, wishes to persuade us that the man who is religious in the Christian sense is robbing himself and thus diminishing his humanity by attributing his own perfections and potentialities to a God who does not even exist. God, then, is an hallucination that must be got rid of for man's sake. Fromm reasons as follows:

> The more perfect God becomes, the more imperfect becomes man. He *projects* the best he has onto God and thus impoverishes himself. Now God has all love, all wisdom, all justice—and man is deprived of these qualities, he is empty and poor.[12]

The teaching of the New Testament and the history of Christian philanthropy and service to others expose such theorizing as the most transparent kind of wishful thinking. Yet we are advised that "this mechanism of projection," which is supposedly responsible for the formulation of the concept of God, "is the very same which can be observed in interpersonal relationships of a masochistic, submissive character, where one person is awed by another and attributes his powers and aspirations to the other person," with deplorable consequences for himself. In response to the question, "When man has thus projected his own most valuable powers onto God, what of his relationship to his own powers?" the answer is given: "They have become separated from him and in this process he has become *alienated* from himself. Everything he has is now God's and nothing is left to him. *His only access to himself is through God.*" Hence the assertion that "in worshipping God he tries to get in touch with that part of himself which he has lost through projection."

This unhealthy self-squandering is unwelcome, according to Fromm's strange logic, not only because it necessarily makes man feel like a sinner who is "slavishly

10. Ibid., p. 93.
11. Ibid., p. 113.
12. The quotations in this and the following paragraph are from Fromm, *Psychoanalysis and Religion*, pp. 50–51. The emphasis is Fromm's.

dependent on God," but also because it actually "makes him bad." Having signed over all that is good to God, he is left with nothing that is good for himself. Placing his faith in God, he loses faith in himself. And he is caught in "a painful dilemma": "The more he praises God, the emptier he becomes. The emptier he becomes, the more sinful he feels. The more sinful he feels, the more he praises God—and the less able he is to regain himself." Christians would certainly wish to protest that his kind of recital is a grotesque, though perhaps naive, caricature of evangelical faith and experience, which bear massive testimony to the dynamic and revitalizing power of the grace of the gospel to deliver people from the radical alienation and the "spiritual chaos and bewilderment close to a state of madness" to which Fromm has drawn attention.

The failure to attain self-fulfillment and the neuroses of adult life were explained by Freud as the entail not only of the child's exaggeration of the authoritarian father-figure into the supreme being of almighty God, but also of the so-called Oedipus complex, which, he held, manifested itself in the incestuous attraction of every child in infancy to the parent of the opposite sex; this deep-seated infantile fixation also had to be overcome if a person was to achieve maturity. This is a thesis that Fromm approves, but he places it in a wider setting, with the explanation that "this craving, in so far as it is to be found, is only one expression of the much more profound desire to remain a child attached to those protecting figures of whom the mother is the earliest and the most influential." It is a way, he says, for a man to remain a child and thus to "avoid the fundamental anxiety connected with the full awareness of one's self as a separate entity"; but this is done at the high cost of "failing to become a full human being." Fromm assures us, moreover, that when Jesus said, "I have come to set a man against his father, and a daughter against her mother, and a daughter-in-law against her mother-in-law" (Matt. 10:35), His intention was "to express in the most unequivocal and drastic form the principle that man must break incestuous ties and become free in order to become human"![13]

To interpret this saying in this manner shows a cavalier disregard not only of the context, which gives the saying its proper significance, but also of the entirety of Jesus' teaching, which plainly contradicts any such interpretation. It is forcing Jesus to be a Freudian before Freud. There is, besides, something extraordinarily bizarre about the willingness of a champion of humanism like Fromm (not to mention others who do the same thing) to produce a proof text from, of all books, the Bible, which is the source book of the "authoritarian" religion and ethics he abominates. He postulates an absolutely fundamental opposition or antithesis between authoritarian and humanistic ethics. By the former he means any ethical authority, like God, that transcends or is external to man; by the latter, rules and standards of conduct laid down by man for himself.

As human conduct, or rather misconduct, is precisely the problem, the primary question arises as to how misbehaving man can manage to prescribe norms of

13. Ibid., pp. 79ff.

behavior for himself. The solution propounded by Fromm is that of "rational authority" which "has its source in competence." If it is then asked who is to be the judge of rationality and competence, he replies that "the person whose authority is respected functions competently in the task with which he is entrusted by those who conferred it upon him"—which seems to imply that those who are ethically incompetent or recalcitrant are the judges of rational authority and ethical competence. This in turn raises a number of further questions. How, for example, are those whose conduct is marked by irrationality and incompetence to be made to conform to the ethical demands of "rational authority" except by the exercise of authoritarianism?

By contrast, "irrational authority," we are told, is the badge of authoritarian ethics; this implies, and is meant to imply, that there can be no rationality higher than that of man.[14] Accordingly it is affirmed that humanistic ethics, "based on the principle that only man himself can determine the criterion for virtue and sin," is "anthropocentric," that man is "the measure of all things," and that "there is nothing higher and nothing more dignified than human existence."[15] Fromm summarizes his ethical position as follows:

> Good in humanistic ethics is the affirmation of life, the unfolding of man's powers. Virtue is responsibility toward his own existence. Evil constitutes the crippling of man's powers; vice is irresponsibility toward himself.[16]

This is undoubtedly a declaration with a strong humanitarian appeal; but the question of what hope there is, if any, for the ethical improvement or redemption of mankind still remains to be answered.

Fromm perceives, in the manner of Jung again, that man has a need which lies deeper than his physical instincts and appetites. In this respect he complains that Freud's identification of the conscience with the superego and thus with the external authoritarianism of parents, state, or cultural tradition follows from an analysis of the "authoritarian conscience" only, in a way which apparently fails to envisage the possibility of a "humanistic conscience." Hence this mild criticism of Freud:

> Brilliant as his assumptions were they are not convincing in their denial of the fact that a large part of man's passionate strivings cannot be explained by the force of his instincts. Even if man's hunger and thirst and his sexual strivings are completely satisfied "he" is not satisfied. In contrast to the animal his most compelling problems are not solved then, they only begin. He strives for power, or for love, or for destruction, he risks his life for religious, for political, for humanistic ideals, and these strivings are what constitutes and characterizes the peculiarity of human life. Indeed, "man does not live by bread alone."[17]

14. Fromm, *Man for Himself,* pp. 8–9.
15. Ibid., p. 12.
16. Ibid., p. 20.
17. Ibid., p. 46.

Here he again borrows from the wisdom of the Bible, again wrenches a statement from its context, and conceals the main point of the truth that is being taught. The scriptural verse cited ("man does not live by bread alone") continues, "but . . . by everything that proceeds out of the mouth of the Lord" (Deut. 8:3; Matt. 4:4). No doubt it is not completed because it in fact propounds the "authoritarian" ethic and conscience which his humanistic presuppositions have led him to reject. As Fromm views things, the humanistic conscience, far from being the voice of God, "is our own voice, present in every human being and independent of external sanctions and rewards"[18]—something centered in ourselves and engendered by ourselves. Conscience, thus conceived, is *"a re-action of ourselves to ourselves"*; it is "the voice of our true selves which summons us back to ourselves, to live productively, to develop fully and harmoniously—that is, *to become what we potentially are."* Consequently, Fromm points out, "humanistic conscience can justly be called *the voice of our loving care for ourselves."*[19]

The solution that Fromm offers to the ethical problem of man involves the denial that man is inherently sinful and the affirmation that man possesses a natural ability to do what is ethically right for himself and for society. Obviously, the optimistic view of humanistic ethics "that man is able to know what is good and to act accordingly on the strength of his natural potentialities and of his reason would be untenable if the dogma of man's innate evilness were true."[20] Attributing the concept of man's evilness to "the crippling effect of the authoritarian spirit," Fromm declares that the aim of humanistic ethics is not the repression of man's evilness but rather "the productive use of man's inherent primary potentialities."[21]

But even the humanist must admit that the study of mankind affords little justification for ethical optimism. Thus Fromm, though asserting that man has reason to be proud of his progress and hopeful about his future, cautions that the triumph of good is neither automatic nor preordained. "The decision," he says, "rests with man. It rests upon his ability to take himself, his life and happiness seriously; on his willingness to face his and his society's moral problem. It rests upon his courage to be himself and to be for himself."[22] These are fine-sounding words, and they express a true longing of the human heart for a better world; but the hope that man can somehow pull himself together has a hollow ring when we take into consideration the testimony (both of the past centuries of human history and of the present state of our world) to the appalling and undiminishing perpetuation of "man's inhumanity to man." Moreover, as though this were not enough to persuade us of man's desperate need for help from a power beyond himself, we should also weigh the significance of the endless flow of distraught and neurotic

18. Ibid., p. 158.
19. Ibid., p. 159. The emphasis is Fromm's.
20. Ibid., p. 210.
21. Ibid., p. 229.
22. Ibid., p. 250.

clients, from what are regarded as the cultured and sophisticated strata of human society, to the consulting rooms of the psychiatrist. The flourishing of psychiatry is itself an unmistakable symptom of the sickness of mankind.

Humanistic Religion

Despite an avowed abhorrence of authoritarianism, it is impossible to escape the impression that many humanists who practice psychotherapy have to a remarkable degree subjected themselves to the authoritarian dogmatism of Sigmund Freud, whose appearance on the scene they seem to regard as the humanistic equivalent of a theophany. The structure of Freud's system broods like a numinous influence over modern psychological theory. Even when criticisms and qualifications are expressed they are generally not central but peripheral in significance. Fromm, as we have seen, feels that Freud put too much stress on sexuality, but he nonetheless insists that "his theory is a profound *symbolic* expression of the fact that man's failure to use and spend what he has is the cause of sickness and unhappiness."[23] Rollo May, who believes in humanism as the true religion of man, elevates Freud, together with Friedrich Nietzsche, to a position of honor in his pantheon as, prophet-like, he describes the religion of the future in his book *Man's Search for Himself:*

> In our own day the examples of those who attack existing religious institutions as opposed to ethical growth include Nietzsche, in his protest that Christian morality is motivated by resentment, and Freud, in his criticism of religion as ensconcing people in infantile dependency. Regardless of their theoretical beliefs, they represent the ethical concern for man's well-being and fulfilment. Though in some quarters their teachings are regarded as inimical to religion (as some of them are), I believe that in future generations the main insights of both Freud and Nietzsche will be absorbed into the ethical-religious tradition, and religion will become the richer and more effective for their contributions.[24]

While a measure of hopefulness for the future is revealed in this passage, there is also a strong existentialist element in May's appraisal of the human situation in which we now find ourselves. Frustration and anxiety are regarded as part and parcel of the existence of man; and man must accept, and indeed choose, himself as he is, achieving freedom and progress by self-responsibility and self-affirmation. The chief problem of people in our contemporary society May has diagnosed as *emptiness.* This judgment has been formed, he says, "on the basis of my own clinical practice as well as that of my psychological and psychiatric colleagues." He has observed that persons "feel swayed this way and that with painful feelings of powerlessness, because they feel vacuous, empty."[25] This malaise

23. Ibid., p. 219.
24. Rollo May, *Man's Search for Himself* (1953), pp. 191–192.
25. Ibid., p. 14.

is compounded, he states, by "another characteristic of modern people," *loneliness*. And emptiness and loneliness together lead to the "even more basic" problem of *anxiety;* for, as May sees things, "being 'hollow' and lonely would not bother us except that it makes us prey to that peculiar psychological pain and turmoil called anxiety."[26] The counsel he gives is "to strengthen our consciousness of ourselves, to find centers of strength within ourselves which will enable us to stand despite the confusion and bewilderment around us."[27]

May's counsel is just another variation of the humanistic gospel of self-adequacy. The potential of self-improvement is supposedly present in every person. "Freedom," we are assured, "is man's capacity to take a hand in his own development." It is "our capacity to mold ourselves."[28] And we are advised, further, that "the basic step in achieving inward freedom is 'choosing one's self.'" The expression "to choose one's self" is borrowed from Sören Kierkegaard (whom many revere, rightly or wrongly, as the progenitor of existentialism), and is explained by May as meaning "to affirm one's responsibility for one's self and one's existence."[29] Man, moreover, is portrayed as the "ethical animal" (though the stark realities of the human situation require the qualification that he is "ethical in potentiality even if, unfortunately, not in actuality"). The simple basis of his capacity for ethical judgment, as also for "freedom, reason, and the other unique characteristics of the human being," is described as "his consciousness of himself."[30] He gains ethical awareness, however, "only at the price of inner conflict and anxiety"—a conflict which is depicted, so we are told, in the biblical narrative of the fall of man, which is presented, surprisingly, as saying the same thing as the Freudian infancy narrative. "Like the story of Prometheus and other myths, this tale of Adam speaks a classic truth," says May, for it "is actually describing in the primitive way of the early Mesopotamian people what happens in every human being's development some time between the ages of one and three, namely, the emergence of self-awareness."[31]

Georg Hegel's description of the fall of man as a "fall upward" is of course cited with approval, and the opinion is offered that "the early Hebrew writers who put the myth into the book of Genesis might well have made it the occasion for celestial song and rejoicing, for this is the day—rather than the creation of Adam—when man the human being was born."[32] This idiosyncratic interpretation of the biblical account of the fall is popular with the theorists of psychopathology, who claim that it vindicates their dogma that knowledge, liberation, and self-fulfillment are attained by bursting the bonds of authoritarianism, despite the plain fact that

26. Ibid., pp. 26, 34.
27. Ibid., p. 45.
28. Ibid., p. 160.
29. Ibid., pp. 168–169.
30. Ibid., p. 175.
31. Ibid., p. 182.
32. Ibid.

their explanation of the passage is, as usual, contrary not only to the context but also to the Bible in its entirety. Fromm writes in a similar vein:

> In the myth of the Garden of Eden man's existence is described as one of complete security. He is lacking in knowledge of good and evil. Human history begins with man's act of disobedience which is at the same time the beginning of his freedom and the development of his reason.[33]

The Genesis account, in fact, clearly depicts man prior to the fall, not as being without knowledge, but as possessing knowledge. This knowledge, however, was entirely knowledge of good. In consequence of man's disobedience, knowledge of evil was added to his knowledge of good, with the result that his knowledge is now knowledge of good and evil. To add evil to good, or to exchange good for evil, is not something to celebrate. The humanistic rejoicing seems to imply either a dualistic view of the world or a denial of the primacy of good. But in the biblical perspective the fall is the root of every human problem, ethical and otherwise. The humanistic mentality shows little concern for consistency when at one and the same time it rejoices over the fall and its consequences and clings to the hope that man will succeed in raising himself, in falling upwards, to his prefallen state in which good prevails over evil. It is the presence of evil that makes ethics so crucial a discipline. For the ethicist to welcome evil and to suppose that the fall is the road that leads to unfallenness makes as little sense as to suggest that Satan is at war with himself. The humanistic exegesis of the story of the fall, however, now has an honored place in the canon of psychoanalytical wisdom; it is proposed as a paradigm of the necessity for every individual to break free from the security of maternal attachment, from the authoritarianism of paternal dominance, and from the derivative notions of God and religion, in order to achieve the dignity of self-freedom and self-affirmation. To use Freudian terms, we are asked to accept the doctrine that the development of mankind is "the development from incest to freedom"![34]

Carl Rogers is a psychotherapist who, at least theoretically, has almost unbounded confidence in human nature. In his book *On Becoming a Person* he propounds the doctrine that the experience of the individual self is the highest authority.[35] People need to learn to like themselves and to approve of themselves in a radically positive manner. It is not enough, he contends, to say that in successful psychotherapy "negative attitudes toward the self decrease and positive attitudes increase," for in fact "the client not only accepts himself—a phrase which may carry the connotation of a grudging and reluctant acceptance of the inevitable—he actually comes to *like* himself."[36] Rogers is another who, while venerating Freud,

33. Fromm, *Psychoanalysis and Religion,* p. 84.
34. Ibid., p. 81.
35. Carl R. Rogers, *On Becoming a Person: A Therapist's View of Psychotherapy* (1961), pp. 23–24.
36. Ibid., p. 87.

feels that the master's pronouncements about the human psyche were too gloomy and that a more genial view of the nature of man is justifiable. He speaks of his "growing recognition that the innermost core of man's nature, the deepest layers of his personality, the base of his 'animal nature,' is positive in nature—is basically socialized, forward-moving, rational and realistic." He berates religion, and particularly the Protestant Christian tradition of his upbringing, for having "permeated our culture with the concept that man is basically sinful" and that "only by something approaching a miracle can his sinful nature be negated." Although Rogers feels that Freud and his followers have presented "convincing arguments" that "man's basic and unconscious nature is primarily made up of instincts which would, if permitted expression, result in incest, murder, and other crimes," he is not satisfied with their conclusion, because he is now persuaded "that these untamed and unsocial feelings are neither the deepest nor the strongest, and that the inner core of man's personality is the organism itself, which is essentially both self-preserving and social."[37] Therapy reveals, Rogers maintains, that the individual "is realistically able to control himself" and "is incorrigibly socialized in his desires," that "there is no beast in man," but that "there is only man in man," and that the attainable goal of the person is simply "to become himself."[38] Therapy enables an individual "to *be* what he *is.*"[39]

This is the sort of comforting diagnosis which people like to hear, and no doubt therapy is capable of eliciting from clients what they would wish to be; but the equation that this is what they are able through self-realization to become does not necessarily follow. Despite the lofty claims of humanistic psychotherapy, the problems of human society remain unresolved and are multiplying rather than decreasing. In the humanistic perspective, of course, the future remains open and alone arouses the hope that there may yet be ethical improvement. But this hope, as we have seen, requires both the rejection of any notion of the radical sinfulness of man and the postulation of fundamental human goodness together with the ability of man to achieve the salvation of himself and society. Rogers, however, is not any more confident of the future than is Fromm. He, too, sees mankind as faced with a crucial choice:

We can choose to use our growing knowledge to enslave people in ways never dreamed of before, depersonalizing them, controlling them by means so carefully selected that they will perhaps never be aware of their loss of personhood. We can choose to utilize our scientific knowledge to make men necessarily happy, well-behaved, and productive, as Dr. Skinner suggests. We can, if we wish, choose to make men submissive, conforming, docile. Or at the other end of the spectrum of choice we can choose to use the behavioral sciences in ways which will free, not control; which will bring about constructive variability, not conformity; which will develop creativity, not contentment; which will facilitate each person in his self-

37. Ibid., pp. 91–92.
38. Ibid., pp. 105, 108.
39. Ibid., p. 113.

directed process of becoming; which will aid individuals, groups, and even the concept of science, to become self-transcending in freshly adaptive ways of meeting life and its problems.

"The choice," Rogers declares, "is up to us."[40] But he does not tell us whom he means by "us." Is it mankind in general—a thought which can leave us with only forebodings of deep despair? Is it the scientists and the therapists, who cannot even agree among themselves and are ethically as fallible as their fellow mortals? Is it the politicians, far too many of whom give proof, from generation to generation, that their position of responsibility does not render them immune to corruption and unscrupulous conduct? It is impossible, apart from wishful thinking, to escape the conclusion that the humanist is counseling man to pull himself up by his bootstraps.

Transactional Analysis

Another prescription that has been dispensed for the cure of man's ethical ills is transactional analysis, of which Thomas Harris is a leading exponent. Harris's therapy, like several others we have examined, is founded on the principles of Freudian analysis. He posits four possible transactional or interpersonal "life positions," using the following popular designations: "I'm not OK—You're OK," "I'm not OK—You're not OK," "I'm OK—You're not OK," and "I'm OK—You're OK." He defines three "states of being" in each person: "Parent," "Adult," and "Child." These three states of being can be seen as corresponding to the Freudian distinction between the authoritarian superego (parent), the irrational id (child), and the rational ego (adult). We are warned of the need to keep these three parts of each individual separate from each other. The trouble resulting from failure to do so Harris calls "contamination of the Adult."[41]

Harris, however, is dissatisfied with the ethical determinism of Freudian psychology.[42] He expresses his preference for the concept of "an objective moral order or a universal 'should'"; he also believes man is free to shape himself in accordance with the teaching of existentialist philosophy. He cites approvingly the view of Jean-Paul Sartre that "man creates his own human essence [indeed, 'his own definition of man'] through a series of choices," and that, on this basis, "man's existence precedes his human essence." Man, Harris explains, creates not only his own essential humanity, "but he simultaneously creates all human dignity"; this is so both because "he can only choose what is good for him" and because "what is good for him must be good for all men"[43]—two very questionable assumptions.

This reasoning appears to be a perilous leap from the particular to the universal.

40. Ibid., pp. 399–400.
41. Thomas A. Harris, *I'm OK—You're OK: A Practical Guide to Transactional Analysis* (1967), p. 98.
42. Ibid., p. 61.
43. Ibid., pp. 218–219.

But Harris's desire to bring together individual choice and universal objectivity is designed to dissolve a difficulty that would otherwise inconvenience him: to affirm that there is no universal "should" would lead to the conclusion that "there is no way of saying that Albert Schweitzer was a better man than Adolf Hitler," while to say that they were both right would be "an obvious contradiction." This consideration rightly leads Harris to ask the question, "But by what standard do we determine who was right?" And his answer is that the postulation of an "objective moral order or of ultimate truth" is justified by the recognition that *persons are important* in that they are all bound together in a universal relatedness which transcends their own personal existence."[44] The assertion that persons are important is unlikely to meet with disagreement, but it leaves unresolved the problem that in the corporate personhood of human society there still coexist individual members who may be described as ethically good and bad, right and wrong, like Schweitzer and like Hitler; there also remains the possibility, given the premises of humanism, that the bad may outweigh or at least be no less universal than the good.

Harris's scheme requires that in every member of human society the "Adult" be in complete control, without any encroachment from the "Parent" or the "Child." This visionary prescription for the redemption of mankind is expounded in the following manner:

> I am a person. You are a person. Without you I am not a person, for only through you is language made possible and only through language is thought made possible, and only through thought is humanness made possible. You have made me important. Therefore, I am important and you are important. If I devalue you, I devalue myself. This is the rationale of the position I'M OK—YOU'RE OK. Through this position only are we persons instead of things. Returning man to his rightful place of personhood is the theme of redemption, or reconciliation, or enlightenment, central to all the great world religions. The requirement of this position is that we are responsible to and for one another, and this responsibility is the ultimate claim imposed on all men alike.[45]

Yet this earnest homily amounts to little more than whistling in the dark to keep one's courage up, since the presence of evil or sin in human persons, both individually and collectively, cannot be ignored. Harris does not attempt to sidestep this awkward topic. He admits that "sin, or badness, or evil, or 'human nature,' whatever we call the flaw in our species, is apparent in every person," and that "we simply cannot argue with the endemic 'cussedness' of man." He affirms his belief that "the universal problem is that by nature every small infant, regardless of what culture he is born into, because of his situation (clearly *the* human situation), decides on the position I'M NOT OK—YOU'RE OK," or on some other partially or wholly negative position. This, says Harris, is "a tragedy," which, however, does not become "demonstrable evil" until "the first ulterior move is made toward another person to ease the burden of the NOT OK." It is "this first retaliatory effort," he continues,

44. Ibid., p. 220. The emphasis is Harris's.
45. Ibid., p. 223.

which demonstrates the individual's "'intrinsic badness'—or original sin—from which he is told he must repent." Harris affirms his conviction "that we must acknowledge that this state —the position I'M NOT OK—YOU'RE OK— is the primary problem in our lives and that it is the result of a decision made early in life under duress."[46] Thus once again the attempt is made to persuade us that the wickedness and perversion of human nature are rooted in the unremembered months of infancy, and that every infant born into the world is inescapably flawed by the relationship in which he is placed. Freud, though dead, yet speaks!

The humanist can hardly go further than that without trespassing on religious territory, which is beyond the human and the natural and, therefore for him, inadmissible. Yet he blithely takes over theological terminology such as "original sin" and "redemption," and presumes to impose on Christianity an interpretation that is as novel as it is outrageous. We are even invited to believe that the central message of humanistic psychology is after all no different from the central message of the Christian gospel. (The total incompatibility of humanism with supernaturalism is at this point quietly disregarded.) Thus Harris informs us that "the central message of Christ's ministry was *the concept of grace.*" He then appropriates for humanism the concept of grace, apparently undisturbed by the consideration that the grace at the center of Christ's message is always and solely the grace *of God,* the great taboo of humanism. "The concept of grace," Harris writes, "as interpreted by Paul Tillich, the father of all 'the new Christian theologians,' is a theological way of saying I'M OK—YOU'RE OK. It is not YOU CAN BE OK, IF, or YOU WILL BE ACCEPTED, IF, but rather YOU ARE ACCEPTED, unconditionally."[47] This interpretation, as anyone who is acquainted with the teaching of the New Testament knows, is an evisceration of the Christian doctrine of grace.

Despite Harris's brave advocacy of transactional analysis, however, his faith in his system is faltering and insecure—so much so that he expresses the tentative hope that things may take a turn for the better through the hypothetical occurrence of a random mutation! "Perhaps," he says, "we are approaching another significant point, where because of the necessity of self-preservation we shall undergo another mutation, we shall be able to leap again, to reflect—with new hope based on the enlightenment of how we are put together—I am important, you are important. I'M OK—YOU'RE OK."[48] Thus his tottering confidence in human self-adequacy disposes him to hand over the future to the lottery of blind chance, which, being beyond the control even of "omnicompetent" man, takes the place of the classical *deus ex machina* descending from midair. Meanwhile everything is left hanging.

Behaviorism

A more dogmatic theory concerning the relationship of mutations to ethical change is propounded by the behaviorist B. F. Skinner. Now that the notion of

46. Ibid., pp. 225–226.
47. Ibid., p. 227.
48. Ibid., p. 224.

purposeful and irreversible upward progress by natural selection has been generally abandoned by evolutionists, the role of luck in the occurrence of unpredictable mutations has become the focal point in the spotlight of evolutionary eschatology. Skinner links the advance of civilization to the haphazard appearance of advantageous cultural practices which human society then selectively appropriates for itself:

> The important thing about a culture so defined is that it evolves. A practice arises as a mutation, it affects the chances that a group will solve its problems, and if the group survives, the practice survives with it. It has been selected by its contribution to the effectiveness of those who practise it. Here is another example of that subtle process called selection, and it has the same familiar features. Mutations may be random. A culture need not have been designed, and its evolution does not show a purpose.[49]

But to theorize about ethical mutations in this way is a nebulous exercise. If selection is a human process, there can be no certainty that a harmful mutation may not be mistakenly selected, with destructive consequences for society— especially when it is remembered that virtually all biological mutations are deleterious. If selection is not a human process, but some undefined extrahuman power at work within history, it looks suspiciously like a pseudonym for God who, though unseen, is working His purposes out. The prospect offered us by Skinner is no more convincing or consistent than that offered us by Harris.

Discontented with the evident incompetence of what he calls "traditional views" to bring about improvement, Skinner affirms his belief that "the major problems facing the world today can be solved only if we improve our understanding of human behavior."[50] The position he holds denies independent validity to feelings and ideas (or what he calls "mentalism") and asserts the primacy of behavior, which, he maintains, is related to feelings and ideas as a cause is to its effects. The person who wishes to change society must start with the cause, not with the effects. Thus Skinner states that "when we are helping people to act more effectively, our first task may seem to be to change how they feel and thus how they will act, but a much more effective program is to change how they act and thus, incidentally, how they feel."[51] He insists, indeed, that "we gain nothing by turning to feelings": to say, for example, that "people comfort the distressed, heal the sick, and feed the hungry because they sympathize with them or share their feelings" misses the mark, since it is "the behavior with which such feelings are associated" that makes the difference.[52]

Skinner's theory of human conduct is strongly deterministic: it is a person's genes and his environment, rather than the person himself, that are responsible for

49. B. F. Skinner, *About Behaviorism* (1974), p. 203.
50. Ibid., p. 8.
51. Ibid., p. 175.
52. Ibid., p. 192.

his behavior. "A scientific analysis of behavior," Skinner says, "must, I believe, assume that a person's behavior is controlled by his genetic and environmental histories rather than by the person himself as an initiating, creative agent."[53] Skinner, then, cannot properly be described as a moralist, for from his standpoint it is no good telling people to conform to certain moral standards when their genes and their environment render this impracticable. "If we are asked, 'Is a person moral because he behaves morally, or does he behave morally because he is moral?' we must answer, 'Neither.' He behaves morally *and* we call him moral because he lives in a particular kind of environment."[54] To change people, accordingly, one must change their environment:

> One of the most tragic consequences of mentalism is dramatically illustrated by those who are earnestly concerned about the plight of the world today and who see no help except in a return to morality, ethics, or a sense of decency, as personal possessions. But what is needed is a restoration of social environments in which people behave in ways called moral.[55]

Skinner frankly admits that, "as the philosophy of a science of behavior, behaviorism calls for probably the most drastic change ever proposed in our way of thinking about man," since "it is almost literally a matter of turning the explanation of behavior inside out."[56]

This sweeping claim need not be discussed here, except to say that a far more drastic and radical change was the removal of God from the concept of man and thereby the denial of both the existence of God and the creatureliness of man. This was intended to leave man on his own. But Skinner's theory brings us face to face with an intractable problem: what is the sense in telling man, whose ethical conduct is controlled by his environment and not by himself as "an initiating, creative agent," that the solution to his troubles is for him to take the initiative and creatively to control his environment? It cannot be both ways, though Skinner evidently thinks it can. But in so thinking he does violence to his humanistic logic. Though he has postulated a determinism which defines man as the victim of his genes and his environment, he is altogether unwilling to abandon the contrary doctrine of the autonomous nature of man. The first article of the humanist creed is that man is the master of himself, his world, and his destiny, and, this being so, that the world of mankind is in a special sense the construction of man himself. "The essential issue is autonomy," Skinner declares; and he adds the rhetorical question, "Is man in control of his destiny or is he not?" Skinner's assurance that "man remains what he has always been," and that "his most conspicuous achievement

53. Ibid., p. 189.
54. Ibid., p. 194.
55. Ibid., pp. 195–196.
56. Ibid., p. 249.

has been the design and construction of a world which has freed him from constraints and vastly extended his range," invites us to give all the glory to man.

Such contradictoriness, instead of clarifying matters, leaves them more confused. The humanist mentality, in its various manifestations, shows signs of a characteristic schizophrenia which assigns to man all the credit for what is regarded as good and progressive in our world, but absolves him of responsibility for all that is evil and unattractive by placing the blame on the concept of God or religion or parents or genes or environment. If, however, this world of ours is indeed man's construction, then man must be held responsible for what is bad in it as well as for what is good. And this might at least be conducive to a much more realistic perception of the nature of the human predicament.

Sociobiology

Genes and environment are also assigned a role of primary importance in the ethical theory of Edward Wilson, which is even more radically deterministic than that of B. F. Skinner. It is Wilson's contention that ethics is the sphere of the biologist before the philosopher, because human conduct, including the will that directs it, is in his opinion wholly governed by genes and environment and must therefore be explained in terms of physics rather than philosophy. Accordingly, Wilson postulates a thorough knowledge of the physiological mechanism of the brain is essential to understanding sociological ethics. Motivated by an altruistic desire "to maintain the species indefinitely," he insists that "we are compelled to drive toward total knowledge, right down to the levels of the neuron and the gene," until we arrive at "a full neuronal explanation of the human brain."[57] This will make it possible for us to chart the cerebral mechanism analytically on the drawing board and to master the mental machine as an electronics engineer does the computer. "Stress," we are assured, "will be evaluated in terms of neurophysiological perturbations and their relaxation times. Cognition will be translated into circuitry."[58] And this will open up a glorious new era for ethics because, "having cannibalized psychology, the new neurobiology will yield an enduring set of first principles for sociology."[59]

In such a perspective it is not surprising to find that God is regarded as at best irrelevant, even though Wilson is prepared to concede that "God remains a viable hypothesis as the prime mover."[60] Wilson, whose thinking is controlled by evolutionistic presuppositions, certainly has no sympathy toward theism. Indeed, it is his opinion that religion is no more than a naturalistic phenomenon with a physiological basis, with the consequence that "religious practices can be mapped onto

---

57. Edward O. Wilson, *Sociobiology: The New Synthesis* (1975), pp. 562–563.
58. Ibid., p. 563.
59. Ibid., pp. 574–575.
60. Wilson, *On Human Nature* (1978), p. 205.

the two dimensions of genetic advantage and evolutionary change," which supposedly explain everything human.[61] It should be noticed that Wilson invests evolutionism with a religious character, regarding it as a dogma to be believed by faith (an effect, presumably, dictated by his genes). "The evolutionary epic is mythology," he writes, "in the sense that the laws it adduces here and now are believed but cannot be definitely proved to form a cause-and-effect continuum from physics to the social sciences." Perhaps that is one reason which disposes him to demand that the scientist should no longer exclude religious concepts as extraneous, but should recognize that they, like everything else, have a naturalistic origin. "Most importantly," he affirms, "we have come to the crucial stage in the history of biology when religion itself is subject to the explanations of the natural sciences"; this he sees as leading to the welcome result that "if this interpretation is correct [a rather inconvenient qualification, surely], the final decisive edge enjoyed by scientific naturalism will come from its capacity to explain traditional religion, its chief competitor, as a wholly material phenomenon."[62]

By "traditional religion," of course, Wilson means theism with its belief in God, not evolutionism with its belief in natural selection, as expressed in the following hypothesis: "If humankind evolved by Darwinian natural selection, genetic chance and environmental necessity, not God, made the species."[63] He holds an explanation of traditional religion "by the mechanistic models of evolutionary biology" to be "crucial," because to explain it in this way will also mean, he believes, to get rid of it. Thus he predicts that if religion "can be systematically analyzed and explained as a product of the brain's evolution, its power as an external source of morality will be gone for ever."[64] So hypothesis is built on hypothesis. Like his fellow humanists Wilson takes it as axiomatic that theistic religion has been morally harmful to the human race.

The sociobiological way forward for man, who, *ex hypothesi*, is determined by his genes, is for him to determine his genes in such a way that he will in the future be determined by them in the right way. But this confronts us once again with the old problem: how can man determine that by which he is determined? Wilson advises us that "the key phrase" is "genetic determinism" and that "on its interpretation depends the entire relation between biology and the social sciences."[65] What does he mean by this? The solution he envisages requires, as we have seen, "total knowledge"—knowledge derived from the study of human genetics, ecology (the study of the relationships of organisms to their environment), and ethology (the naturalistic study of whole patterns of behavior), which is the response to the involuntary cybernetic circuitry of the human brain. This involves a denial of the freedom

61. Ibid., pp. 172, 177.
62. Ibid., p. 192.
63. Ibid., p. 1.
64. Ibid., p. 201.
65. Ibid., p. 55.

of the will, which in turn seems to preclude the possibility of any purposeful planning to change things for the better. Wilson poses and answers the problem in a quite categorical manner:

> If our genes are inherited and our environment is a train of physical events set in motion before we were born, how can there be a truly independent agent within the brain? The agent itself is created by the interaction of the genes and the environment.

Finding himself obliged to draw the conclusion that "our freedom is only a self-delusion,"[6] he suggests that "the physical basis of the will" could be explained by a system of "feedback loops" in the brain which "control most of our automatic behavior." Granting that "there is no proof that the mind works just in this way," nonetheless he holds that "it is entirely possible that the will—the soul, if you wish—emerged through the evolution of physiological mechanisms," though, "clearly, such mechanisms are far more complex than anything else on earth."[67]

Having laid this speculative foundation, Wilson proceeds to state that "pure knowledge is the ultimate emancipator"—not, however, in the sense that knowledge will itself solve our ethical and social problems, but in the sense that "self-knowledge will reveal the elements of biological human nature from which modern social life proliferated in all its strange forms." Then, on the basis of this revelation or enlightenment, it will be possible to take stock of the situation and "to distinguish safe from dangerous future courses of action with greater precision." But on Wilson's premises the desirable ethical transformation will be achieved by altering, not the superstructure of human behavior, but "the hard biological substructure"—a possibility, perhaps, "many years from now, when our descendants may learn to change the genes themselves."[68]

The hope that man will some day learn to determine what determines him is not only hypothetical, it is in itself contradictory and scientifically disreputable. In fact, it flies in the face of reality, for if one thing is plain, it is that the vast, quite stupendous increase in man's knowledge has not brought about any improvement in his behavior. The study of mankind left to himself is not conducive to optimism, and the humanistic predication of a bright future that man himself can bring about by his own powers must of necessity leave out of account the abundant evidence of the fallenness of the human race. The fact that Wilson wistfully contemplates certain lower orders of life and holds them up as ideal examples or paradigms of social ethics is itself an implicit acknowledgment of man's inability to behave as he should. He considers, for example, the insect societies, whose members he sees to be "more cooperative and altruistic than people," and suggests that "if ants were to be endowed in addition with rationalizing brains equal to our own, they could be our peers" and paragons of a morality higher than ours. It was only by accident,

---

66. Ibid., p. 71.
67. Ibid., p. 77.
68. Ibid., pp. 96–97.

he asserts, that civilization became "linked to the anatomy of bare-skinned bipedal mammals and the peculiar qualities of human nature";[69] indeed, if only dinosaurs had grasped the concept of nobility "they might have been us" (something which perhaps they were fortunate to be spared!).[70] So unpromising is the prospect that Wilson's hope rests on the postulation that "the human species can change its own nature"—something it is not necessary to wish for the happily regulated insect communities.

To change man's own nature is a radical remedy indeed, even assuming it were a possibility. Wilson imagines that it might be done through "altering gene complexes by molecular engineering and rapid selection through cloning," thereby installing "new patterns of sociality" in bits and pieces. Again his thoughts turn wistfully to lower orders which man, in the evolutionary upsurge, is supposed to have long since left behind. "It might be possible," he says, "to imitate genetically the more nearly perfect nuclear family of the white-handed gibbon or the harmonious sisterhoods of the honeybees." But this is wishful thinking, and Wilson remembers that it is "the very essence of humanity" which constitutes the problem. The note on which he ends is one of doubt, if not despair, rather than of faith and hope: "Perhaps," he wonders, "there is something already present in our nature that will prevent us from ever making such changes."[71] He seems to be nearly ready for the Christian affirmation that if man is to be radically changed he needs a power other than his own.

The Cult of Selfism

The preceding discussion of some distinctive trends in modern ethical philosophy and psychological therapy has provided some evidence of the atheistic foundation on which the theory and practice of much contemporary psychiatry are constructed. The presupposition, which has the firmness of a religious dogma, that man is his own god and holds the solution to his problems in his own hands, if he will but free himself from his inhibitions, has brought in a tide of preoccupation with the individual self under such slogans as "self-acceptance" and "self-affirmation." *Selfism* is the term Paul Vitz uses to designate this obsessive self-centeredness. In his book *Psychology as Religion: The Cult of Self-Worship,* he effectively demonstrates that "psychology has become more a sentiment than a science and is now part of the problem of modern life rather than part of its resolution," being now "a form of secular humanism based on worship of the self."[72] Vitz knows of what he writes, for he is a professional academic psychologist who for years went with the current of irreligion fashionable in his discipline until his unforeseen conversion to

69. Ibid., p. 23.
70. Ibid., p. 197.
71. Ibid., p. 208.
72. Paul Vitz, *Psychology as Religion: The Cult of Self-Worship* (1977), p. 9.

the Christian faith, by which, he says, his life was turned around. "The noteworthy aspect about this," he writes, "is that it happened to a totally unprepared, recalcitrant, secularized psychologist who thought that the only natural direction of change was exactly in the opposite direction. There were certainly no available models for it in psychology."[73] Yet this dynamic and transforming experience is not limited to one particular class of persons or to one particular period of history, nor can its reality be denied by the psychologist.

"Change or perish," which was and to a large extent still is the slogan of evolutionism, is a creedal concept that like a ferment has penetrated to every level of society. For those who have not found the key to life's meaning change is undoubtedly a necessity; but it must be change of the right kind, or it will prove to be change for the worse. Today people have been encouraged to seek change of any kind and at any price as a road to self-discovery and self-fulfillment. As Vitz observes,

> Selfist psychology emphasizes the human capacity for change to the point of almost totally ignoring the idea that life has limits and that knowledge of them is the basis of wisdom. For selfists there seem to be no acceptable duties, denials, inhibitions, or restraints. Instead, there are only rights and opportunities for change. An overwhelming number of the selfists assume that there are no unvarying moral or interpersonal relationships, no permanent aspects to individuals. All is written in sand by a self in flux. The tendency to give a green light to any self-defined goal is undoubtedly one of the major appeals of selfism, particularly to young people in a culture in which change has long been seen as intrinsically good.[74]

Moreover, the doctrine of the essential goodness of the self and the emphasis on the benefits of self-acceptance to the individual can readily produce damaging consequences for society. "Exactly how extreme are the convictions of the selfists about the total intrinsic goodness of human nature?" Vitz suggests that they are "quite extreme."

> The popularizers whose books number sales in the millions almost unanimously assume the goodness of the self. They rarely even discuss the problem of that self-expression which leads to exploitation, narcissism, or sadism. The combination of passing over this unpleasant aspect and constantly articulating a clear message of "love and trust yourself and do your own thing" obviously accounts for a good deal of their popularity.[75]

It is only to be expected that the sinner will enjoy being assured that he is radically good and that the notion of sin and of a God who punishes sin, or who bestows grace and forgiveness, is a figment of the perverted psyche; but such assurances, which are as unscientific as they are untrue, do nothing to change or

73. Ibid., p. 12.
74. Ibid., p. 38.
75. Ibid., p. 45.

improve the human situation, for they leave man and the society of mankind still sinful and still in desperate need of redeeming grace. The self remains inwardly disrupted and alienated, existence continues to have no coherent purpose or meaning, and the person has still not found his true identity. Realization that this is indeed the correct view of man and of society caused the distinguished psychologist O. Hobart Mowrer to rethink his preconceptions in a quite radical manner:

> For several decades we psychologists looked upon the whole matter of sin and moral accountability as a great incubus and acclaimed our liberation from it as epoch-making. But at length we have discovered that to be "free" in this sense, i.e., to have the excuse of being "sick" rather than sinful, is to court the danger of also becoming lost.... In becoming amoral, ethically neutral, and "free," we have cut the very roots of our being; lost our deepest sense of selfhood and identity; and with neurotics themselves, find ourselves asking: "who *am* I?"[76]

In many respects existentialism may be described as the quintessential philosophy of selfism, for in it the individual self is held to be absolutely on its own and responsible for the formation of its own essence and its own ethic. "Man's destiny is within himself," Sartre has written.[77] "If God does not exist," he explains, "we find no values or commands to turn to which legitimize our conduct. So, in the bright realm of values, we have no excuse behind us, nor justification before us. We are alone, with no excuses."[78] Consequently, man must be his own creator: "Man makes himself. He isn't ready made at the start. In choosing his ethics, he makes himself."[79] By creating himself he creates value for his life: "If I've discarded God the Father, there has to be someone to invent values.... Moreover, to say that we invent values means nothing else but the meaning that you choose."[80] Sartre asserts, accordingly, that "ontology and existential analysis must reveal to the moral agent that he is *the being by whom values exist.*"[81] And it follows that in the existentialist creed "man makes himself man in order to be God."[82]

Selfism, precisely because of its obsession with the individual self, is actually depersonalizing; for personality is realized only in person-to-person relationships, primarily within the tripersonal being of God Himself, then in the bond between God as Creator and man as creature, and finally in the interaction between man and man in human society. Self-centeredness or psychological solipsism is inevitably antipersonal and therefore destructive of the person. In this as in its other effects humanistic dogma proves to be dehumanizing.

---

76. O. Hobart Mowrer, "Sin, the Lesser of Two Evils," *American Psychologist* 15 (1960): 301–304.

77. Jean-Paul Sartre, *Existentialism* (1947), p. 42.

78. Ibid., p. 26.

79. Ibid., p. 51.

80. Ibid., p. 58.

81. Sartre, *Being and Nothingness: An Essay on Phenomenological Ontology* (1956), p. 627.

82. Ibid., p. 626.

Crime and Punishment

It was only to be expected that the deterministic doctrines of the "mind physicians" would, as they gained control of the thinking of society in general, extend their influence beyond the psychiatrist's clinic to interpersonal relations of all kinds, especially as these doctrines were invested with an aura of scientific respectability. The persuasion that our behavior is determined by our genes, our environment, and the associations of infancy must affect and govern our attitude not only toward neurotic individuals but toward all persons. Parental correction of the misdemeanors of children in the home is denounced as harmful to the self-development of the younger generation. The exercise of discipline in schools likewise is widely deplored as an unwarrantable violation of the sacred rights of the pupil. The suing of parents by their children and of teachers by their students, or by the parents of their students, to claim redress for damages suffered from restrictive and authoritarian conduct is even sanctioned as acceptable practice. Undiscipline and the breakdown of authority in homes and schools, now so commonplace, are inevitable consequences of the prevalence of the theory of selfism. Nor is it surprising that these doctrines have deeply penetrated the thinking of legislators and of those who are appointed to administer justice in the courts, with the result that all too frequently the criminal is regarded not as an offender but as a victim of his circumstances who needs treatment rather than punishment.

This attitude to the criminal has every appearance of being benevolent and compassionate (as no doubt it is intended to be). But to deprive a person of responsibility is not a kindness, for responsibility is essential to human dignity. Created in the image of God, man is by constitution a responsible being: he is answerable for the way he lives and behaves. To remove responsibility is to depersonalize him, and thereby to dehumanize and brutalize him. If indeed he and his conduct are controlled by forces alien to himself, it is reasonable that he should be subjected to other forces for the purposes of improving his behavior and curing his "sickness"—in short, that like one of Pavlov's dogs he should undergo clinical experimentation in the laboratory. To repeat the warning of Mowrer: "To have the excuse of being 'sick' rather than sinful is to court the danger of also becoming lost." In our law courts today the plea is commonly offered (and accepted) that an individual who has committed a violent assault, or a rape, or a murder, was not responsible for his action at the time of the offense because he was driven by an impulse impossible to resist, or found himself in a situation beyond his control, or was simply suffering from temporary insanity. When such a plea, the equivalent of a denial of answerability, is accepted, it ceases to be a criminal case. The innocent defendant will then be detained in a place where he will receive psychotherapeutic treatment for the purpose of curing him of his psychopathological affliction. Little concern seems to be shown for the real victim who has suffered injury at his hands or for society, which is rendered increasingly vulnerable to the antisocial conduct of the violent and the unscrupulous.

One certainly does not wish to deny that a person's upbringing and environment can have an undesirable effect on his behavior. A child that grows up in a brutal and immoral household or community is at a serious disadvantage. Such factors should unquestionably be given the most serious consideration. Nor is it intended to deny that some crimes are committed by persons who are mentally unbalanced. Such persons should be sent to mental institutions, not prisons. Nor does one wish to deny that convicted criminals, while being justly punished for their offenses, should be encouraged to change their attitudes and given the opportunity to improve themselves by study and instruction in useful occupations. Punishment should not be dissociated from attempts at remedial treatment with the objective of rehabilitation. By the same token there is an urgent need to improve the appallingly degrading conditions of so many of our prisons, which are conducive to worse depths of degradation rather than to moral betterment and the recovery of a sense of social responsibility and personal dignity. Meanwhile public security is imperiled by the custom of turning loose untamed and unimproved ruffians after comparatively brief terms of incarceration.

Charles Colson, who himself has had the experience of being confined in prison and whose life is now dedicated to the reform not merely of prisons but also of their inmates, knows what he is speaking about when addressing the subject of crime and punishment. He fully admits the necessity of prisons for the detention of hardened and dangerous criminals, but has an abundance of evidence to support his judgment that they are far from being centers of rehabilitation and that to describe them euphemistically as "correctional institutions" is a misnomer. "There are some good theological reasons why crime should be soundly punished in some way," he says. "But the punishment backfires on society when offenders are degraded, sexually perverted, morally twisted, depersonalized, and have their families and futures shredded into a midden of rancid memories."[83] He deplores the perpetuation of imprisonment as the sole means of punishment, and advocates "the well-established biblical principle of restitution" as a more effective and beneficial way of dealing with many who have been convicted of felonies. Experiments along this line are already being made in a number of places with encouraging results. Restitution results in justice being done to the victim of crime as well as to the offender. Based on consent between the criminal and the victim, it results in a reduction in long and costly prosecutions which take up court time that should be devoted to dealing with crimes of a more serious nature and which distract police from more important duties; the offender is afforded a genuine opportunity to reinstate himself and recover his dignity as a useful member of society. Colson explains,

> Restitution simply means making up for the loss or damage caused. For example, a
> burglar might be sentenced to live in a halfway house and work to repay the person

83. Charles Colson, *Jubilee,* April/May 1979 (© Prison Fellowship).

he robbed. A doctor or business man convicted of dodging $20,000 in taxes might be fined $100,000 on an income-graduated fine schedule. A youth arrested for vagrancy and possession of marijuana might be put on tight parole and sentenced to learn a useful trade in evening classes. A hot check artist might be made to work weekends without pay for the firm he defrauded. Restitution guarantees that crime doesn't pay.[84]

It is plain that the degrading and overcrowded conditions of our prisons cannot reasonably be expected to reduce the criminal propensities of those who are a danger to society. But this consideration affords no justification for the idea that criminals are not responsible for their actions and should not be punished as evildoers, for this view is also destructive of human dignity, as we have said, and can easily lead to consequences of an even more serious nature. C. S. Lewis calls this view "the humanitarian theory of punishment"; insisting that "the 'Humanity' which it claims is a dangerous illusion and disguises the possibility of cruelty and injustice without end," he urges "a return to the traditional or Retributive theory not solely, not even primarily, in the interests of society, but in the interests of the criminal." Thus the belief that the humanitarian theory is "mild and merciful" is regarded by Lewis as "seriously mistaken." This judgment is based on the following considerations:

> According to the Humanitarian theory, to punish a man because he deserves it, and as much as he deserves, is mere revenge, and, therefore, barbarous and immoral. It is maintained that the only legitimate motives for punishing are the desire to deter others by example or to mend the criminal. When this theory is combined, as frequently happens, with the belief that all crime is more or less pathological, the idea of mending tails off into that of healing or curing, and punishment becomes therapeutic. Thus it appears at first sight that we have passed from the harsh and self-righteous notion of giving the wicked their deserts to the charitable and enlightened one of tending the psychologically sick. What could be more amiable? One little point which is taken for granted in this theory needs, however, to be made explicit. The things done to the criminal, even if they are called cures, will be just as compulsory as they were in the old days when we called them punishments.

Lewis contends that "this doctrine, merciful though it appears, really means that each one of us, from the moment he breaks the law, is deprived of the rights of a human being"; and the reason, he says, is this:

> The Humanitarian theory removes from punishment the concept of desert. But the concept of desert is the only connecting link between punishment and justice. It is only as deserved or undeserved that a sentence can be just or unjust. I do not here contend that the question "Is it deserved?" is the only one we can reasonably ask about a punishment. We may very properly ask whether it is likely to deter others and to reform the criminal. But neither of these two last questions is a question about justice. There is no sense in talking about a "just deterrent" or a "just cure." We

84. Ibid.

demand of a deterrent not whether it is just but whether it will deter. We demand of a cure not whether it is just but whether it succeeds. Thus when we cease to consider what the criminal deserves and consider only what will cure him or deter others, we have tacitly removed him from the sphere of justice altogether; instead of a person, a subject of rights, we now have a mere object, a patient, a "case."[85]

The prospect is one that Lewis finds alarming, because, once notions of retribution and punishment have been abandoned, the treatment prescribed by the experts ("the official straighteners," as Lewis calls them) will be administered to persons who are declared to be innocent victims instead of guilty offenders, without regard to the wishes of the supposedly blameless "patient." "To be taken without consent from my home and friends; to lose my liberty; to undergo all those assaults on my personality which modern psychotherapy knows how to deliver; to be re-made after some pattern of 'normality' hatched in a Viennese laboratory to which I never professed allegiance"—this is an eventuality that Lewis finds far from alluring.[86] The "kindness" of "those who torment us against our own good will" is something that "stings with intolerable insult."

> To be "cured" against one's will and cured of states which we may not regard as disease is to be put on a level with those who have not yet reached the age of reason or those who never will; to be classed with infants, imbeciles, and domestic animals. But to be punished, however severely, because we have deserved it . . . is to be treated as a human person made in God's image.[87]

The humanitarian theory, Lewis warns, will be most congenial to rulers who wish to incapacitate ideological opponents and nonconforming citizens with a show of benevolence, since it will put in their hands "a finer instrument of tyranny than wickedness ever had before." When crime and disease are held to be synonymous, "it follows that any state of mind which our masters choose to call 'disease' can be treated as crime."[88] Moreover, "if crime is only a disease which needs cure, not sin which deserves punishment, it cannot be pardoned. How can you pardon a man for having a gumboil or a club foot?" With the abolition of justice and the setting up of mercy in its place without regard to the personal rights and deserts of the individual, the enforced "kindnesses" of humanitarianism will prove in reality to be "abominable cruelties." Accordingly, the warning is given that "Mercy, detached from Justice, grows unmerciful."[89]

At the time C. S. Lewis published this essay (1949) the nature and extent of the tyrannical oppression of millions by the dictatorial rulers of the Soviet Union were

85. C. S. Lewis, "The Humanitarian Theory of Punishment," in *God in the Dock: Essays on Theology and Ethics* (1970), pp. 287ff.
86. Ibid., p. 290.
87. Ibid., p. 292.
88. Ibid., p. 293.
89. Ibid., p. 294.

not as widely publicized as they are now. His perceptive prognosis was in fact already a reality under the Russian totalitarian system which, bent on the enforcement of atheism, has placed multitudes behind the walls of concentration camps and in psychiatric wards—ostensibly for their own good and for the good of society as a whole—simply because they have refused to renounce their religious convictions and practices. They are put away as sufferers of neurotic disease from whom their fellow citizens must be protected. Lewis's admonitory words fit the Russian situation precisely:

> We know that one school of psychology already regards religion as a neurosis. When this particular neurosis becomes inconvenient to government, what is to hinder government from proceeding to "cure" it? Such "cure" will, of course, be compulsory; but under the Humanitarian theory it will not be called by the shocking name of Persecution. . . . The new Nero will approach us with the silky manners of a doctor, and though all will be in fact as compulsory as the *tunica molesta* or Smithfield or Tyburn, all will go on within the unemotional therapeutic sphere where words like "right" and "wrong" or "freedom" and "slavery" are never heard. And thus when the command is given, every prominent Christian in the land may vanish overnight into Institutions for the Treatment of the Ideologically Unsound.[90]

The alarming implications, then, of the humanitarian theory for the dignity of the individual and the health of society are abundantly plain, and the reality of the threat it poses is even now being experienced by those Christians and other "dissidents" who, though in fact mentally sound, have been consigned to madhouses for psychological and chemotherapeutic treatment by their atheistic overlords. But, as though this were not disturbing enough, we must go further and point out that the humanitarian theory, if allowed to prevail, must ultimately be destructive to the gospel itself, for the cross of Christ is meaningless if it is not seen against the background of the sinner's guilt and condemnation. The gospel is not for the innocent and the blameless but for the guilty who are in desperate need of forgiveness and restoration. The central assurance of the gospel is that the person who believes its message "does not come into judgment, but has passed from death to life" (John 5:24). The logic of the gospel is that the incarnate Son, in the perfection of His sinless life, offered up Himself in the stead of the guilty sinner, enduring the punishment of our sins so that through faith in Him we might bear the purity of His holiness and thus be acceptable to God, not in ourselves but in Him. In the words of the prophet, "The Lord has laid on him the iniquity of us all" (Isa. 53:6). "He himself bore our sins in his body on the tree," writes St. Peter, "that we might die to sin and live to righteousness. By his wounds you have been healed. . . . For Christ also died for sins once for all, the righteous for the unrighteous, that he might bring us to God" (I Peter 2:24; 3:18). And St. Paul declares that "for our sake [God] made him to be sin who knew no sin, so that in him we might become the righteousness of God" (II Cor. 5:21). Obviously, if there is no guilt and no

90. Ibid., p. 293.

punishment and we are not answerable to God, there is no need for the gospel, and the Christian message makes no sense. Moreover, if we do away with the justice of God we must dispense also with the mercy of God; then, as man is neither responsible before God nor in need of His forgiveness, we are well advised to eliminate God altogether from the picture, which is precisely what the humanists with their humanitarian theorizing have done. In doing so, however, they have at the same time dehumanized man, who, as we have seen, fulfills his creaturely potential only in a truly harmonious relationship with his Creator. So man does need the gospel after all, for the gospel is the unique means to the restoration of that relationship and thereby to the restoration of man's proper dignity. And the return to God starts with man's recognition of himself as a guilty sinner under divine condemnation and with his thankful and trusting reception of the grace of God freely offered him in and through Christ Jesus, who made full atonement for the sinner by His substitutionary death, Man for man.

Capital Punishment

The question of the retention or abolition of the death sentence continues to be strongly debated, even though (and no doubt also because) in the Western world the execution of murderers has either been discontinued, as in Great Britain, or is very seldom carried out, as in the United States. The central question is, Is it ever right or just to take the life of any person?[91] In some ecclesiastical circles the sixth commandment is interpreted as an absolute prohibition of killing of any kind, but the untenability of this interpretation is evident from the explicit prescription of the death penalty in the Mosaic legislation which decrees that "the murderer shall be put to death" (Num. 35:16–21). The killing which is forbidden, then, is murder, not capital punishment.

Another argument against capital punishment is that in the Mosaic system it was not only murderers who were executed but also persons guilty of other offenses, such as adultery and sodomy, which are not treated as capital offenses in the New Testament. The example is cited of the woman caught in adultery, whom the scribes and Pharisees rightly said should be stoned to death according to the law of Moses, but whom Jesus dismissed with the words, "Go, and do not sin again" (John 8:1–11).[92] This narrative may certainly be taken to show that adultery is no longer punishable by death, but it does not tell us that this applies also to murder or that there has been a total abrogation of capital punishment. Some, indeed, have wished to maintain, on the strength of St. Paul's assertion that "Christ is the end of the law" (Rom. 10:4), that in Christ the whole Mosaic legislation

91. The related question of killing in warfare is discussed on pp. 199ff.

92. There is manuscript evidence that raises the question whether this story is an authentic part of the Fourth Gospel, but scholars generally agree that the narrative is primitive and convincingly recounts an event in Jesus' ministry.

together with its death sentences has been abolished. But to tear St. Paul's statement from its context and misconstrue it in this way is to do violence to Scripture,[93] for Christ came to fulfill the law, not to abolish it (Matt. 5:17–20). In any case the invalidation of the law would involve the abrogation not only of the capital punishment it enjoins, but also of the prohibition of the sixth commandment against killing; thus by the same logic it might be concluded that people are now free to kill but not to be put to death for killing.

Death for the murderer, however, is a penalty which is prescribed not only in the Mosaic law. Long before Moses it was clearly defined as a principle of just retribution in the time of Noah following the destruction of the flood; in Genesis 9:5–6 it is recorded that God said,

> For your lifeblood I will surely require a reckoning; of every beast I will require it and of man; of every man's brother I will require the life of man. Whoever sheds the blood of man, by man shall his blood be shed; for God made man in his own image.

In the verses which precede this passage there is a reaffirmation of the supremacy of man over the rest of the animal creation ("into your hand they are delivered") and the use of animal flesh for food is sanctioned—and therefore also the killing of animals for food. This dominance of man as a result of the special character which radically distinguishes him from all other creatures is explained by the reminder that "God made man in his own image." Man alone is endowed with the godlike capacities of rationality and will and purposefulness; he alone is answerable to God for his life and action; he alone can enjoy fellowship with his Creator through worship and praise. Thus there is an especially sacred bond between God and man, and the life of each human person is invested with distinctive sanctity and dignity.

The preciousness of human life is evident in the requirement not only that an animal which causes a man's death (and thereby overturns the proper order of creation) should be deprived of life, but also that the man who murders his brother is to be put to death, because in doing so he has despised the image of God with which his being is imprinted and has treated his fellow man as though he were a brute beast whose life can be taken without compunction. As Franz Delitzsch has observed, "The murderer is to suffer that which he has inflicted; for murder is not only the extreme of unbrotherliness, but also a crime against the inviolable majesty of the divine image."[94] Abolitionists have advanced the argument that it is barbaric and savagely vindictive to punish the person found guilty of homicide with the same crime for which he has had to answer—in other words, to punish the murderer by murdering him. This argument, however, is doubly vulnerable. Firstly, it is not uncommon in cases other than murder for the punishment to correspond to the crime—for example, for the kidnapper who has seized and held

---

93. See the discussion of Romans 10:4 on pp. 51–52.
94. Franz Delitzsch, *A New Commentary on Genesis,* trans. Sophia Taylor (1888), vol. 1, p. 287.

his victim in solitary confinement himself to be arrested and incarcerated in a prison cell. Secondly, the argument leaves out of account the distinction between injustice and justice, between crime and retribution. The punishment must be demonstrably commensurate with the offense. There would quite rightly be an outcry if murderers were regularly sentenced to seven days' imprisonment and persons guilty of parking offenses were executed, or if the penalty were the same for both. The distinction has been explained by Ernest van den Haag:

> Punishments—fines, incarcerations, or executions—although often physically identical to the crimes punished, are neither crimes, nor their moral equivalent. The difference between crimes and lawful acts, including punishments, is not physical, but legal: crimes differ from other acts by being unlawful.[95]

It has been further argued that the death penalty is ineffective as a deterrent to the commission of murder. This, however, is something which, in the nature of the case, it is impossible to prove one way or the other. To demonstrate experimentally whether the death penalty actually deters murder would require statistical comparison of two parallel situations which are identical except that the threat of capital punishment exists in one but not in the other. But, human nature being what it is, and so many unseen factors (mental, psychological, and circumstantial) being involved, the arrangement of a controlled experiment is clearly an impossibility. All too frequently, moreover, the abolitionist's concern seems to be for the murderer rather than for the murderer's victims. And here it is a consideration of the utmost importance that the death penalty is an absolutely effective deterrent against the perpetration of more murders by the same person. Unfortunately, it is not at all uncommon for convicted murderers to be set free because of some minor legal technicality or to be released on parole after a short period of imprisonment, and then to vent their homicidal passion on more innocent victims who would have been spared the horror of a bloody death had their assailants been executed in the first place. Van den Haag is forced to conclude that advocates of the abolition of the death penalty "think the lives of convicted murderers . . . are more worth preserving than the lives of an indefinite number of innocent victims." He perceives that such persons are not interested in deterrence so much as they are obsessed with the campaign for the abolition of capital punishment.

> The intransigence of these committed humanitarians is puzzling as well as inhumane. Passionate ideological commitments have been known to have such effects. These otherwise kind and occasionally reasonable persons do not want to see murderers executed ever—however many innocent lives can be saved thereby. *Fiat injustitia, pereat humanitas.*[96]

95. Ernest van den Haag, "The Collapse of the Case Against Capital Punishment," *National Review* 30 (1978): 404. See also his *Punishing Criminals* (1975).
96. Van den Haag, "Collapse," p. 403.

Furthermore, the death penalty for murder certainly deters the generally decent and respectable citizen from resorting to homicide at those moments when anger or envy makes him wish to be rid of someone, even though it remains debatable whether it deters the hardened criminal. Without the death penalty the unique and inviolable character of the human person is in effect denied, murder is reduced to the level of lesser crimes, and the life of man becomes cheap. It is not surprising that the ideology of humanism, which denies the existence of the Creator and therefore also the constitution of man in the divine image, and which proclaims man to be merely a product of animal evolution, takes an indulgent view of murder, and actually prepares the way for the heartless and indiscriminate slaughter of literally millions of innocent victims under the tyrannies of, for example, godless Communism, as the annals of our age testify only too plainly. In the Western world, the leniency which is now customarily accorded murderers has increased the insecurity of society as a whole, with the result that there is an insistent majority demand for the enforcement of the death penalty for homicide of the first degree. Legislators and politicians would be well advised to give heed to this demand and to take steps to reassure society that the life of the human person is sacrosanct in the eyes of the state. To quote van den Haag again:

> The irrevocability of a verdict of death is contrary to the modern spirit that likes to pretend that nothing is ever definitive, that everything is open-minded, that doubts must always be entertained and revisions must always remain possible. Such an attitude may be helpful to the reflections of inquiring philosophers and scientists; but it is not proper for courts. They must make final judgments beyond a reasonable doubt. They must decide. They can evade decisions on life and death only by giving up their paramount duties: to do justice, to secure the lives of the citizens, and to vindicate the norms society holds inviolable.[97]

In theory different governments have the liberty as secular institutions to pass legislation in accordance with what they see to be the needs of the time or the situation. Christians should remember that they too are citizens and that they have a responsibility to speak up for the safeguarding of the proper standards of human dignity and justice. There is agreement that capital punishment is not appropriate for every case of homicide and that extenuating circumstances must be taken into account. But the retention of the death penalty for willful and ruthless murder is important if the sacredness of the individual is to be guaranteed and protected. Otherwise the ignoring of the divine image in which each person is created, and which is central to the inherent worth of the individual, betokens the decline of society into ungodliness and its concomitant evil of inhumanity.

Dietrich Bonhoeffer, while condemning "all deliberate killing of innocent life" as arbitrary, affirmed that "of course there is nothing arbitrary about the killing of a

97. Ibid., p. 407.

criminal who has done injury to the life of another."[98] Such plain speaking based on biblical principles is always necessary. Perhaps we too easily forget that every unrepentant sinner is, before God, under sentence of death; indeed, that death entered our world as a consequence of sin, which is willful self-estrangement from God who is life and the source of all life; and, further, that God's justice and mercy met together in the redeeming death of Christ at Calvary, where He endured our death sentence. The justice of the secular kingdom which is designed for the commonweal of fallen society should reflect the justice of the transcendental realm of the kingdom of God—with, however, this significant qualification: that even the guilty murderer as he faces execution and the eternity beyond may be assured that, through faith in Another who died for him, "the free gift of God is eternal life in Christ Jesus our Lord" (Rom. 6:23; cf. 5:12; Heb. 2:14–15).

98. Dietrich Bonhoeffer, *Ethics,* p. 116.

7

Eugenic Utopianism

Technology and Modern Maladies

The society of mankind is bedeviled by physical, psychological, and ethical problems. It is generally agreed that there is an urgent need to change human nature, or at least to improve the lot and the conduct of the race. The modern era has witnessed the most phenomenal advances in science and technology, especially in the Western world; but the increase in wealth and health has not brought with it any increase in human happiness or human kindness. Notwithstanding all the scientific triumphs of contemporary man, humanity seems to be trapped in a revolving spiral that is going nowhere. "For some three centuries," René Dubos has observed, "western man has believed that he would find his salvation in technology," but "despite the spectacular progress in prophylactic and therapeutic medicine, . . . we are still a disease ridden society." For one thing, there is an "increase in the prevalence of degenerative and other forms of chronic ailments," which is "due in part to the fact that more people escape death from nutritional and infectious diseases." For another, the effluvia of our technological age—noxious fumes, noise, radioactivity, and waste products—contribute to the pollution of our environment and at the same time to the sickness of our sophisticated society. Add to this the frenetic manner of living in the modern megalopolis, and it is hardly surprising that malignancies, vascular disorders, allergic conditions, and mental illnesses are on the increase, and that great numbers of people are dependent in their day-to-day existence on cigarettes, drugs, and sedatives. Dubos draws attention to the startling fact that chronic pulmonary disease has become the greatest and most costly single medical problem in Northern Europe, and may be expected to spread to all areas undergoing industrialization.[1]

We may be thankful that modern medicine and hygiene have virtually eliminated some diseases such as smallpox, diphtheria, and the plague, which formerly afflicted society often to a disastrous degree. Ironically, however, these very advances have laid man open to other complaints, as we are now becoming increasingly aware. Dubos, for example, has warned that "it can no longer be taken for granted that a further increase in living standards will result in health improvement," but that "the

1. René Dubos, "Adaptation to the Environment and Man's Future," in *The Control of Environment* (discussion at the Nobel Conference, Minnesota, 1966), pp. 62ff.

123

more probable situation is that it will result in a new pattern of diseases."[2] We are faced with the unwelcome conclusion that old problems solved mean new problems created. To cite Dubos again:

> It had been assumed a few years ago, that, as medical care becomes more widely available, the demand for it would decrease because the population would become healthier. Unfortunately, the opposite has happened. The pattern of diseases is constantly changing and new and more exacting kinds of demands for medical care are constantly arising. In fact, it is to be feared that the medical burden will become so heavy in the future that medical ethics will have to be recast in the harsh light of economics.[3]

This picture is further complicated, and darkened, by the fact that numbers of disorders which previously caused death before the age of reproduction was reached are now treated in such a way that, without actually being cured, they are held in check, with the result that those afflicted with them can now enjoy a normal life span and the pleasures of parenthood. But this means that these disorders are passed on to the children, with the undesirable consequence that, instead of remaining static or even being phased out, the incidence of these disorders is multiplying at a constantly increasing rate. And this creates a whole new dilemma, for it means that the medical and therapeutic advances of our time are in this respect responsible for the genetic deterioration or entropy of the human species.[4]

It is to be feared that this genetic dystrophy is further promoted by the harmful pollutants which pervade the environment, themselves the products of our technological age, and by the artificial additives now used in the processing of food (not to mention the good things that are removed, ostensibly for our benefit). Life is becoming more and more unnatural, so that now it is almost impossible to breathe in clean air, to drink pure water, or (for those of us who have food to eat) to enjoy food that has not been "improved."

Certainly people now live longer than they did a hundred years ago, but longer life has not meant greater happiness and self-fulfillment. It has become common practice to "care for" the elderly by segregating them in homes for the aged or (for those who can afford it) in retirement communities, always of course with the best of good will. This practice, however, has the effect of cutting them off from fellowship with younger persons, and fosters the feeling—which readily develops into a psychosis in many cases—that being old they are now useless and unwanted.

This "explosion in death control," as William Shockley calls it, is yet another development that is "due to the advances in medical technology";[5] its effect on

---

2. Ibid., p. 71.

3. Ibid., pp. 72–73.

4. See, for example, Paul Ramsey, "Moral and Religious Implications of Genetic Control," in *Genetics and the Future of Man* (discussion at the Nobel Conference, Minnesota, 1965), p. 112.

5. William Shockley, "Population Control of Eugenics," in *Genetics and the Future of Man*, pp. 79–80.

society must be seen in combination with the modern mania for birth control not only by contraception but also by abortion, which is shaping society in such a way that the balance between age and youth is being destroyed. Western society, in consequence, is becoming increasingly an elderly society. This has caused some sociologists to suggest that the balance should be restored by sanctioning the termination of life that is no longer of value to the community. If it is permissible to terminate life before birth, why not also before death, that is, before death would otherwise take place in the course of nature? Birth control in fact, particularly by means of abortion, can lead by a logical line to death control (in the sense of terminating the life of the elderly, not in the sense in which it is used in the quotation from Shockley above).

Death Control

Edmund Leach, in his BBC Reith Lectures for 1967, although professing to have no solution for this problem, nonetheless implied that if it is ethically justifiable to stop life at the beginning it is less than logical to be shocked at the idea of stopping life later on when a person has ceased to function usefully in society. He maintained that men, offered by science the total mastery over their environment and their destiny, have become like gods; and he reminded his hearers that it is the function of gods not only to create but also to destroy. "We too," he said, "must accept our dual responsibility and come to terms with the fact that the total elimination of disease would be an entirely intolerable blessing."[6]

The paradoxical assertion that "the total elimination of disease would be an entirely intolerable blessing" accurately reflects the intractable dilemma in which modern man continually finds himself, despite all the enlightenment of his scientific knowledge. It may be true, according to popular notions, that gods destroy as well as create, but it is a strangely novel conception that gods should destroy themselves. The conquest of disease is the primary incentive for medical research. But Leach perceives that even if a stage were reached where disease was overcome and eliminated, this would not signal the achievement of utopia, because there would still remain the most baffling and intractable problem of all: that of aging, decrepitude, and death. The slaughter of the senile, like the abortion of unborn life, far from being a godlike act (the slaughterers themselves would in due course come to the moment appointed for their own elimination), would be an admission of incompetence to act like gods. Just as logical, and altogether more expeditious, would be the slaughter of all persons who, even before reaching the agreed age limit, become incapacitated by disease or who for some other reason are judged to be unprofitable to the human species—an ideology which has all too recently justified the liquidation of Jews, cripples, and other "undesirables."

6. Edmund Leach, The BBC Reith Lectures, in *The Listener* 78 (1967): 751.

In every generation aging and death bear irrefutable witness to the imperma-
nence of man and the disintegration of his powers; they constitute the ultimate
frustration, the final surd, the irreversible destiny which makes nonsense of every
pretension of man to be his own god. Faced with this witness, humanistic confidence collapses. It is pathetically imagined that it will be possible to get rid of the
problem of aging and dying by killing people before they grow old and thus
conserving the vigor of society. But there are more important things than vigor:
wisdom and affection, for instance. And in any case the one thing that death
control will certainly not eliminate is death. Yet, given the evolutionist presupposition that the species is of far more consequence than the individual, that Man
matters rather than man, it is far from fantastic to envisage the enactment of a law
which, in the interests of mankind, would prescribe that on reaching, say, the age of
sixty, persons should be "put to sleep"—painlessly of course—by means of a pill, a
potion, or an injection.

But this humanistic "solution" to the problem of an elderly society would be
certain to create more problems than it solves. Far tougher than arbitrarily ridding
society of the aged will be the problem of ridding society of the psychoses developed
as people approach the date of their elimination or as they are forced to see the last
of proscribed loved ones. Indeed, as we have already seen, our modern society, for
all its science, is fast becoming psychotic, and the psychologist is faced with a
baffling task as he seeks to understand and deal with all the frightening ailments
and aberrations afflicting the human psyche. The elimination neither of disease nor
of the elderly can be expected to dispel the neurotic mentality; on the contrary, the
more human society is controlled from birth to death, the more neurotic it is likely
to become and the worse afflicted with psychosomatic illnesses.

In his discussion of whether it is "permissible to destroy painlessly an innocent
life which is no longer worth living," Dietrich Bonhoeffer sanctions the taking of
human life only when there is no possible alternative course of action. "The
destruction of the life of another," he says, "may be undertaken only on the basis of
an unconditional necessity; when this necessity is present, then the killing must be
performed." It was this principle which impelled him to associate himself with the
plot to kill Hitler, whose removal he saw as an unconditional necessity for Germany
and the civilized world. "But the taking of the life of another," he warns, "must
never be merely one possibility among other possibilities, even though it may be an
extremely well-founded possibility":

> If there is even the slightest responsible possibility of allowing others to remain alive,
> then the destruction of their lives would be arbitrary killing, murder. Killing and
> keeping alive are never of equal value in the taking of this decision; the sparing of life
> has an incomparably higher claim than killing can have. Life may invoke all possible
> reasons in its cause; but only one single reason can be a valid reason for killing. To
> fail to bear this in mind is to undo the work of the Creator and Preserver of life
> himself. It follows from this that to support the rightfulness of euthanasia with a

number of essentially different arguments is to put oneself in the wrong from the outset by admitting indirectly that no single absolutely cogent argument exists.[7]

This argument is sound and should be heeded; but the problem, as always in our fallen society, is that those who are in a position to take lives and who wish to do so will all too readily persuade themselves that they are compelled by unconditional necessity, even when it is innocent lives that they are intent on destroying.

We cannot disregard the lesson taught by history that those who by one means or another exercise control over their fellow men have a propensity to exempt themselves from the restrictions and regulations which they impose on others. They above all wish to play the role of gods—issuing decrees, but not themselves submitting to the decrees they enforce. In controlling the lives of others they will themselves be uncontrolled. But not ultimately, for they will not really be gods but men; and however impregnable their tyranny may seem to be, it will at last be subject to death and judgment before the presence of the one true God. Meanwhile the urge of the ungodly tyrant is to be as God and to exercise godlike authority over his fellow creatures, as though he were creator and lord of all. The corruption of his nature guarantees the corruption of the power he seizes. Hence the nemesis by which his footsteps are hounded. The utopia he promised becomes instead a place of torment and brutality. Hitler the redeemer becomes Hitler the monster. The Nazi paradise, originally so alluring, is stamped not with the image of God but with the mark of the beast. Its incense is the stench of corpses.

Of all people the most psychotic are those with the mania for power. The façade of their own infallibility has to be propped up by the control not merely of the bodies but also of the minds of those whom they wish to dominate. Mental manipulation, brainwashing, and savagely enforced conformity, which reduce persons to puppets, and the insecurity stemming from the knowledge that everybody—even and perhaps especially the person nearest to one—is trained to be an informer have already become commonplaces in the totalitarian regimes of our day. The philosophy of *1984* has ceased to have a futuristic ring:

> Power is tearing human minds to pieces and putting them together again in new shapes of your own choosing. Do you begin to see, then, what kind of world we are creating? It is the exact opposite of the stupid hedonistic Utopias that the old reformers imagined. A world of fear and treachery and torment, a world of trampling and being trampled upon, a world which will grow not less but *more* merciless as it refines itself. . . . Already we are breaking down the habits of thought which have survived from before the Revolution. We have cut the links between child and parent, and between man and woman. No one dare trust a wife or a child or a friend any longer. But in the future there will be no wives and no friends.[8]

7. Dietrich Bonhoeffer, *Ethics,* pp. 116–117.
8. George Orwell, *1984* (1961), p. 220.

1984 is a dramatic and by no means unrealistic portrayal of the potential for inhumanity that is inherent in human nature. The Christian deplores this potential no less than does the idealistic humanist, but, recognizing man's flawed nature as the entail of his fallenness, insists that the solution to the human predicament lies in the restoration of the Creator-creature relationship by the grace of the gospel, which effects the renewal of man's true nature. The humanistic sociologist, as we have seen, also acknowledges the need for a change in man's nature, but affirms his faith that this can and must be done by man on his own, by the reorganization of his genes or by any other method that will make him a socially responsible and productive being.

Frustrated by the failure of modern concepts and techniques to produce a change for the better in human behavior, some sociologists are in effect bowing before the intractable realities of the present situation and in desperation are hoping that some huge catastrophe will provide a last chance for the human race to reconstruct itself in an ethically acceptable manner. Looked at in this perspective, the mass destruction brought about by a thermonuclear war might be regarded as, in the long run, a blessing rather than a curse, though a more drastic remedy for the ills of mankind could not be imagined. Certainly the rapid incineration of millions would at one stroke solve the much-publicized problem of the population explosion; the hope is that it would at the same time afford a new and otherwise unavailable opportunity for the eugenic control of society by enabling the small remnant of the human race to make a fresh start. At any rate Kingsley Davis seems to regard this as the main hope for a better future:

> Under the circumstances, we shall probably struggle along with small measures at a time, with the remote possibility that these may eventually evolve into a genetic control system. We shall doubtless increasingly seek to restrain reproduction in those cases in which there is patently a large risk of grossly defective offspring. . . . The morality of specific techniques of applied genetics—artificial insemination, selective sterilization, ovular transplantation, eugenic abortion, genetic record-keeping, genetic testing—will be thunderously debated in theological and Marxian terms dating from past ages. . . . It seems more likely, however, that the change will be precipitated more suddenly by something new in human history, a genetic crisis. The survivors of a nuclear holocaust might prove willing to adopt a thorough system of genetic control in order to minimize the horrifying effects of radiation on the next generations. Once the barriers inherent in the existing social organization of human life were thus broken, genetic control would probably persist because of the competitive power it would give to the societies that maintain it.[9]

William Shockley also seems to discern a ray of hope piercing through the mushroom-shaped cloud. Speaking of "the threat of enormous genetic damage from a nuclear war," he finds a promise beyond the threat: "Eugenics would then

9. Kingsley Davis, "Sociological Aspects of Genetic Control," in *Genetics and the Future of Man,* pp. 203–204.

be forced upon the human race," he asserts, "in much the same way as infanticide was in more primitive times, as a necessary step in the struggle for existence."[10] This tenuous hope, however, depends on the supposition that there will be a residue of persons whose genetic mechanism has not been irreparably damaged by the nuclear holocaust, and that this residue will behave more sensibly and with greater competence than people do now and have done in the past.

Plato's Utopian State

Genetics is a modern science and genetic engineering a novel notion, but the concept of eugenics is almost as ancient as man himself. It has always been the custom of the stock farmer, for instance, to select his best cattle for breeding, and that is in essence the practice of eugenics. In the ancient world the most celebrated blueprint for a eugenic utopia was propounded in Plato's *Republic*, written in the fourth century B.C. Just as the animal breeder selects only the best specimens for reproduction and rejects those that are weak and inferior, so it was advocated that marriage, or more accurately mating, should come under the control of the state so that a choice might be made of those citizens who were regarded as fit to become parents. Those approved for propagation were to live together, but without the privilege of private possessions. Matings were to take place at prescribed times which would coincide propitiously with certain religious festivals. Inferior persons would be discouraged from mating, but should any do so the offspring from their union would not be permitted to survive. Moreover, the approved matings would be regulated by the rulers with a view to maintaining the optimum size of the state. Family life and the attendant responsibilities of parenthood were to be abolished. Parents would not know who were their children nor children who were their parents, and the upbringing of the children would be entirely in the hands of the state. Substandard infants were to be "put away." Abortion was to be practiced in the case of women who conceived as the result of illicit intercourse. Age limits were fixed within which parenthood was permissible, namely, twenty to forty for women and twenty-five to fifty-five for men.[11]

This scheme for the elimination of the family, the rigidly enforced control of population growth, and the ruthless practice of abortion or, should that fail, infanticide in every case of conception not sanctioned by the government, must have seemed startlingly radical, not to say abhorrent, to the Athenians, who regarded family life as belonging vitally and integrally to the structure of society. As has often been pointed out, Plato was influenced by the pattern of society so carefully developed by the city-state of Sparta, where everyone from infancy to old age pursued physical culture and civic virtue with singleness of purpose. Benjamin

10. Shockley, "Population Control," p. 100.
11. Plato, *The Republic of Plato,* trans. Benjamin Jowett (1888), 5.458ff.

Jowett has commented pointedly on Plato's mistake in looking to Sparta for the inspiration of his ideal commonwealth:

> Least of all did he observe that Sparta did not really produce the finest specimens of the Greek race. The genius, the political inspiration of Athens, the love of liberty—all that has made Greece famous with posterity, were wanting among the Spartans. They had no Themistocles, or Pericles, or Aeschylus, or Sophocles, or Socrates, or Plato. The individual was not allowed to appear above the state; the laws were fixed, and he had no business to alter or reform them. Yet whence has the progress of cities and nations arisen, if not from remarkable individuals, coming into the world we know not how, and from causes over which we have no control? Something too much may have been said in modern times of the value of individuality. But we can hardly condemn too strongly a system which, instead of fostering the scattered seeds or sparks of genius and character, tends to smother and extinguish them.[12]

There was indeed an element of callousness and inhumanity in the Spartan system. Society loses something essential to its humanity when its members are manipulated like a herd of prize cattle. The physical result may be impressive—and the physical side is not unimportant—but it is only a part, and not the noblest part, of the essence of humanity. To quote Jowett again:

> Many of the noblest specimens of the human race have been among the weakest physically. Tyrtaeus or Aesop, or our own Newton, would have been exposed at Sparta; and some of the fairest and strongest men and women have been among the wickedest and worst.[13]

This consideration shows that any program for eugenics involving the selection of those types which are regarded as most fit to survive and most likely to benefit posterity is confronted with a fundamental problem: the difficulty, as William Shockley admits, of reaching "agreement as to what does constitute the ideal type of man."[14] The perfect man is an abstraction that does not belong to the world of real experience. Even the greatest personages in the world's history have had their areas of vulnerability; all have suffered from defects of character or physique which, in the eyes of the eugenist, would have disqualified them from being accepted as ideal types. Some had parents who would not have been permitted to reproduce; indeed, the ancestry of some geniuses could hardly have been more unpromising. There is no denying that the noblest figures in human history are men and women who have achieved distinction by rising above their disabilities. The improvement of the human race is a legitimate concern, but one of the first principles of eugenic planning should be the realistic renunciation of the kind of idealism which looks on man as perfectible to a limitless degree. Man is sinful, and because he is sinful he is a creature of contradictions. Discoveries and advances that promise well for the

---

12. Benjamin Jowett, introduction to Plato's *Republic* (1888), p. cxc.
13. Ibid., p. clxxxviii.
14. Shockley, "Population Control," p. 98.

betterment of mankind he invariably perverts to unworthy and inhuman purposes. The sinfulness of human nature is the ever-present barrier which blocks progress to higher and nobler goals. That is why one of the great fallacies of our day is to confuse scientific progress with human progress. The failure of human nature is obvious on every side in the horrifying mess that man has made of this world—in the inequity, the misery, the cruelty, the bloodshed, the futility, and the purposelessness which blight the lives of multitudes.

Eugenists, driven by a desire to improve the human race, advocate the imposition of certain controls which, according to their reckoning, will in the course of time produce beneficial effects. These controls will work negatively by progressively eliminating deleterious elements which at present threaten the well-being of future generations, and positively by raising the human stock to hitherto unreached heights (of character as well as of physique) through a selective and thorough limitation of procreation to only the best types. Immediately, however, the old problem arises: how and by whom are these controls to be enforced? Plato's answer is that their enforcement should be in the hands of the highest authorities of the state, whose decrees may not be questioned or disregarded. Werner Jaeger has commented on Plato's eugenic scheme:

> None of his regulations shows more bluntly, and for us more shockingly, how he demanded that his ruling class should surrender all personal interests to those of the state. This destroys the last relic of individuality, the right which no other state has ever ventured to challenge, the individual's right to his own body.[15]

It is ironic that these words were written at a time when the totalitarian regimes of German Nazism and Russian Communism were ruthlessly exacting their claim to possess the bodies and determine the destinies of many millions of human beings. The promise of liberty and plenty for all, which sounded out so clearly at the beginnings of these movements, has a hollow mocking ring now, since never before in history have the dignity of the person and the sanctity of the individual been assaulted on such a scale. The world had to wait till the dawn of our much-vaunted twentieth century for the appearance of these monstrous tyrannies, under which not only politicians and economists, but authors, musicians, and artists, and even scientific researchers have been forced to prostitute their gifts and skills by conforming to the ideological restrictions prescribed by the state. And the theoretical principles of contemporary totalitarianism have been professedly humanistic!

Needless to say, things are very different now from what they were in Plato's day. Plato's vision was of an ideal city-state with a citizenship limited by means of abortion, infanticide, and restriction of parenthood to 5,040 persons; we are faced with population problems of vastly greater proportions. When Plato was writing there was no such thing as a science of genetics; in our time genetics, though still a

---

15. Werner Jaeger, *Paideia: The Ideals of Greek Culture* (1944), vol. 2, p. 248.

young branch of investigation, is a discipline in which a great deal of important knowledge concerning the mechanics of heredity is being built up. The question is how—if at all—that knowledge should be applied in attempts to improve the human stock. Many sociologists share the judgment of Kingsley Davis that "delib- erate genetic control certainly appears to be the 'absolute weapon,' the most powerful means for survival yet contemplated." This expression of hopefulness is qualified, however, by uncertainty; for Davis grants that "genetic regulation, like any other human effort, runs the risk of failure," and acknowledges the possibility that "the artificially created thoroughbreds of the species might prove less viable than the mongrels."[16] Some consider this a virtual certainty rather than a mere possibility.

Davis's delineation of a eugenic utopia demands, as a first step, the decision whether the entire population or (as in Plato) merely an elite is to be involved. Once that decision is made, a "social adjustment" would then be necessary, by which couples would be required no longer to desire children genetically their own, but "to welcome a child which comes from artificial insemination or, better, from an implanted fertilized ovum" derived from donors of superior quality. He offers the assurance that "the parents would thus regard the child as their own— much as a purchased house or car becomes a source of pride to its new owners, regardless of the fact that they themselves did not manufacture it"; he adds the provision that "the nation could maintain a board of geneticists to determine who should furnish the sperm and the ova and what crosses should be made in the artificial mating." The males in the population not selected to contribute to the official "sperm-banks" would be sterilized and the females disqualified from sup- plying ova would have their ovulation suppressed or diverted. Ethical as well as physical qualities would be taken into account:

> The board of supervising geneticists would have confidential records on the pedigree of all persons born in the population, as well as records of their traits and achieve- ments. On this basis it would determine who is to be sterilized and who is to furnish sperm or ova.[17]

The assertion that "such a scheme would keep marriage and the family as a means of rearing children, and so would do minimum violence to traditional social structure," sounds extraordinarily naive, and possibly somewhat disingenuous in the light of Davis's description of the family as "a very primitive mode of social organization" and of its retention as "a curious fact." Much more curious is the fact that a humanist should plan to sweep aside what is naturally human in favor of the practice of humanistic supernaturalism. Under this plan the "father" would be divested of any genuine paternity, a spectator without a role to play in bringing additions to his "family" into the world; the "mother" would be a mere lodging-

16. Davis, "Sociological Aspects," pp. 202–203.
17. Ibid., pp. 195ff.

house proprietress for the reception of somebody else's fertilized ovum. The instinct for one's own flesh and blood would be suppressed and relegated to the museum of quaint quiddities of the past. There are some, indeed, who display a militant antipathy to the concept of the family and speak of it as something inherently and dangerously evil. Edmund Leach, for example, deprecates "so much soppy propaganda about the virtue of a united family life" emanating from "psychologists, doctors, schoolmasters, and clergymen," and wishes to persuade us that "far from being the basis of the good society, the family, with its narrow privacy and tawdry secrets, is the source of all our discontents."[18]

If a hostile attitude to the family is implicit in Freudian theory, it is explicit in the philosophy of Marxism. The *Manifesto of the Communist Party,* composed by Karl Marx and Friedrich Engels in 1848, demanded the abolition of the family as a bourgeois phenomenon founded on the principle of capital and private property, since, it was maintained, the wife and children were treated as virtually the slaves of the husband. The utopian prediction was made that the disappearance of capital would be accompanied by the disappearance of the family. Meanwhile "the bourgeois clap-trap about the family and education, about the hallowed co-relation of parent and child," was denounced as "disgusting."[19] The collectivization of all property and possessions included, accordingly, the collectivization of children. This proved in practice, however, to be a policy which because of its harmful social and ethical consequences the Soviet Union found expedient to abandon; and the leaders in Red China similarly were forced to turn away from party dogma in this respect. To extol, as Leach does, the Chinese commune as an example to be followed in the phasing out of the family betrays an extraordinary unwillingness to admit the chaotic and disastrous state of affairs engendered by the experiment of communizing the children of that country. Children that belong to the state belong nowhere. They are rootless; deprived of the intimate center of security and affection that the family affords, they seek acceptance and identity by the formation of mobs of their own tender age which, as the course of events has demonstrated, become a fearsome and uncontrollable menace to society.

Programs for the Control of Behavior

Over and over again, the replacement of the natural by the artificial has led to consequences that are anything but beneficial—monstrosities, deformities, deficiencies. But modern scientism, with its pretensions to omniscience and omnipotence, shows an unwillingness to learn this lesson. Yet even if, for the sake of argument, one were to grant that problems of this kind could be overcome by eugenic techniques, there would remain one deep-seated obstacle to perfection

18. Leach, Reith Lectures, p. 695.
19. *The Marx-Engels Reader,* ed. R. C. Tucker (1972), p. 349; cf. pp. 115, 123; also see Friedrich Engels, *The Origin of the Family, Private Property, and the State* (1884).

with which science is incapable of dealing, namely the impossibility of breeding sin out of the species. The careful choice of men and women who are not only fine physical specimens but also persons of moral integrity, emotional stability, and intellectual distinction, as donors of spermatozoa and ova for the projected eugenic "banks," will not begin to scratch the surface of this fundamental problem of the human race. Genetic surgery for the correction of faults or undesirable combinations in the units of heredity is already in the experimental stages, but the geneticist cannot extend his operations to the surgery of the human soul. As already suggested, the thoroughbred society that he hopes to produce might well turn out to be a generation of vipers, capable of wickedness hitherto unknown, for there is no denying that the increase in scientific knowledge in our age has not led to a decrease in human depravity; on the contrary, the benefits it has provided have been more than counterbalanced by the invention of new techniques of oppression, falsehood, and destruction.

It will not do for the humanist, whether he be scientist, philosopher, or churchman, to assure us that ours is an era of enlightenment in which man has at last come of age and is fully capable of doing for himself whatever needs to be done, nor to deplore the concept of human sinfulness as evidence of a defeatist mentality and the relic of a discredited religious past. All his planning for the improvement of the human species is based on the recognition that man and society are not what they should be. Even if he refuses to speak of sin, he is confronted on all sides with the abject depravity of mankind, displayed in an almost endless variety of forms of selfishness, dishonesty, perversity, and violence. The evidence of human sinfulness is plentiful both within oneself and throughout society, and to close one's eyes to it is not only unrealistic but also unscientific.

The achievement of a situation in which babies are produced and reared under scientifically controlled laboratory conditions would presumably be the *ultima thule,* the garden of paradise, for those who clamor for the complete equality of the sexes. Once the stage was reached at which all babies were brought into being through the culture of an approved ovum fertilized by an approved spermatozoon selected from a refrigerated "bank," the donors of which could have lived and died decades or centuries earlier, any social differentiation between the sexes would become meaningless. If, as some hope, the fetal period from "conception" to the conclusion of "gestation" could be so completely controlled that it would take place outside the female womb, sexuality itself would become an anachronism, except as a means to genital pleasure and stimulation. Margaret Mead has predicted that

> responsiveness to the world situation may take the form of a new willingness to assume responsibility for supporting massive dependence on modern scientific methods for the control of conception and the use of such inventions as artificial insemination, artificial lactation, and perhaps extra-uterine gestation.

She depicts the sexual equality that could be expected from such a sociological transformation:

> There would be a growing disregard for sex as a basic mode of differentiation. Boys and girls would be given a similar education and like demands would be made on them for citizenship, economic contribution, and creativity. . . . The two-sex exclusive pair model of human relationships would lose its power. Instead, companionship for work, play, and stable living would come to be based on many different combinations, within and across sex lines.[20]

The enforcement, by one method or another, of universal neutering or sterilization for the purpose of safeguarding eugenic excellence would open the way for "safe" and unrestricted promiscuity, both heterosexual and homosexual. This in turn would lead to both an alarming proliferation of neurotic ailments and an appalling increase in the incidence of venereal disease. This is the unprotected Achilles' heel of the program for the neutralization of the sexes.

The most unpredictable thing about man as a social being is his behavior, and this must be a major concern for the eugenist. The variety of patterns of behavior and temperament in human society is virtually limitless. This complexity, which is characteristic of the individual as well as the group, is compounded by the factor of contradiction. While it is possible to classify people in accordance with certain character types, it is a matter of everyday experience that persons can and do act out of character. There is general agreement, too, that certain kinds of behavior and temperament are undesirable because they are harmful or antisocial, and that their elimination would be requisite before an ideal society could be achieved. The hope of some utopian planners that this elimination will in time become possible by genetic recombination has been dismissed by Gardner Quarton as "rather wild speculation," especially as the contributions of the genes to behavior and personality are exceedingly complex and all related experiments have so far been unproductive.[21]

In any case, however much the cast of our temperament may be genetically determined, it would be foolish and undignified to blame our misdemeanors on our chromosomes. The distinctive worth of man is apparent in the fact that he is a responsible creature, able to distinguish between good and evil and to respect the rights of his fellow men, and that he is endowed with will power for determining his own conduct. There are, of course, other factors which may influence a person's behavior, such as environment, upbringing, and abnormal functioning of the endocrine glands. But it is a fundamental element in the structure of society that ordinarily men are answerable for their conduct. And it must be emphasized again that behind all human misbehavior is the deep-seated factor of sin, with the

---

20. Margaret Mead, "The Life Cycle and Its Variations," in *Daedalus* 96, no. 3 (1967): 872–873.

21. Gardner C. Quarton, "Deliberate Efforts to Control Human Behavior and Modify Personality," in *Daedalus* 96, no. 3 (1967): 840–841.

profound implication that what the sophisticated sociologist describes neutrally as an "undesirable behavior trait" is not only inimical to the good of society but also a violation of one's own being and an affront to one's Creator.

There is very little indication, however, that the eugenic visionary is deterred by considerations of this order. For what he foresees is a utopia in which the solution to the problem of aberrant human behavior will be sought by removing responsibility from the individual and placing it in the hands of society, or, more accurately, in the hands of those who wield the power over society. To suggest the techniques by which it is hoped to accomplish this transformation is not difficult, for at least some of these techniques are already commonplace in totalitarian states: massive indoctrination and brainwashing, additives to the diet and the drinking supply, administration of hormones and drugs (Quarton expresses the judgment that "it is certainly reasonable to guess that control of mood in man may be possible by pharmacological means in the next fifty years"),[22] the conditioning of reflexes along Pavlovian lines, neurosurgery, stimulation of the brain by remote electronic instruments, and protracted surveillance of a person's actions and reactions by means of computerized monitoring devices. Quarton in fact envisages the automatic control of behavior by the use of sophisticated technological inventions:

> The most efficient utilization of behavior-control technology would involve mixing techniques. If, for instance, a human subject had electrodes implanted in such a way that any ongoing action could be rewarded, punished, or prevented, and if microtransmitters and receivers made external wires and apparatus unnecessary, he could be placed in a learning situation, and selected patterns of behavior could be encouraged or discouraged automatically. With effective monitoring and computing equipment, much of the process could be controlled automatically.[23]

We shall undoubtedly be assured that manipulations of this kind are justified on the grounds of humanitarianism and the improvement of the species. But as every person has undesirable tendencies in his make-up, where is it all going to stop? The utopia could not be attained except by the comprehensive control of society. We should all then be like experimental mice in a laboratory labyrinth, stimulated—painfully if necessary—to learn the prescribed route, or like automata without minds or wills of our own, programmed to follow a predetermined pattern of behavior. This means, once again, that the humanistic process designed for the upgrading of humanity would lead to dehumanization. As a being completely controlled from his conception in a test tube to his euthanasia at a fixed age, man will have been deprived of his freedom, his individuality, his responsibility, his dignity. And there is the ever-recurring question: Who will control the controllers? For those who superintend the achievement of this utopia will themselves have become monstrous and inhuman, guilty of the appalling sin of the dehumanization of their fellow men.

A further question concerns the organization of society for the performance of the various tasks that are necessary for the balanced functioning of the community. The projected utopia will presumably have educators and industrialists, businessmen and technologists, writers and mechanics, artisans and laborers. To allow each person free choice respecting the function he is to fulfill in society would be untidy and disorderly. Accordingly, a further provision in the eugenic program is the bringing of the diverse duties and aptitudes of man under the control of genetic manipulation. Every individual born in the utopian community will possess a genetically predestined function or "vocation" within society. The blueprint for the megalopolis of the future is that of a human ant heap. We have already noticed Edward Wilson's envious admiration of the insect societies with their clear-cut caste systems and their built-in division of labor, and his praise of their denizens as "more cooperative and altruistic than people."[24] Kingsley Davis is one who sees this as more than an evolutionistic might-have-been for man, but he admonishes us that the enforcement of the eugenic system will require "tight control," especially "if human breeding were used to produce diverse types in the population for special tasks, somewhat analogous to the division of labor in insect societies."[25]

The prospect of predestination by genetic selection is, however, no more alluring than the other features of the eugenic paradise envisioned by would-be benefactors of the human species. The regimentation of society along fixed tracks of routine may seem to promise superefficiency, but it also promises monotony and frustration which could rapidly give rise to devastating psychopathic effects. Man cannot be reduced to the functional level of an insect that operates by instinct and still remain man. Such a program, moreover, would amount to little more than a development, on a more sophisticated scale, of the social pattern of Plato's ideal republic with its arbitrary stratification of the populace into a hierarchical structure: at the top the privileged class of the guardians, below them the militia, then the artisans, and, lowest of all, the substratum of unprivileged slaves. There really is not a great step from Plato to *1984!*

Davis concedes that in the ordinary sequence of events "human beings are a long way from such self control"; but, as we noticed earlier, he imagines that the process might be speeded up by a nuclear holocaust which would challenge the survivors to plan a responsible eugenics program for the future. He observes that social change may be "saltatory" as well as gradual.[26] By "self control" Davis evidently means control by society of itself or, put in another way, the willingness of society to submit to the imposition of strict genetic control through the official enactment of specific laws designed for this purpose. Shockley, who shares Davis's

24. See pp. 109–110.
25. Davis, "Sociological Aspects," p. 197.
26. Ibid., p. 201.

perspective, affirms that "it is clear that man's destiny will be shaped by the acts of man";[27] and Leach emphasizes the total ability of man to shape his own destiny:

> It is not vanity to say that man has become like a god, it is essential to say it and also to understand what it means. Since, god-like, we can now alter nature, including that part of nature which is man himself, we can no longer console ourselves with the thought that a search for scientific knowledge is its own justification. It has ceased to be true that nature is governed by immutable laws external to ourselves. We ourselves have become responsible.[28]

Mind over Matter

Such statements indicate a shift that now seems to be taking place in the ranks of humanism. Although unwilling to abandon their dedication to the governing concept of evolutionism, humanistic scholars are becoming disposed to take mankind out of the hands of evolution and to place evolution in the hands of mankind. The evolutionary force, if there is such a thing, and if it is still working, is working too slowly. The evolutionist is facing a crisis of faith, for he is now troubled with nagging doubts about the dogma that evolution is sovereignly working its purpose out as age succeeds to age. It is not natural selection but human selection and self-control on which everything now depends. There is an air of disillusionment in the way that no less a luminary than Julian Huxley has spoken of "the restricted nature of biological progress"—restricted, indeed, in his reassessment of the situation, to man and his future in a world where otherwise evolution has grown tired and given up the struggle.[29] Mind must now take over from matter—that is, the human mind as distinct from natural selection, that conveniently imagined and indemonstrable *tertium quid* which as the holy spirit of evolutionism has superintended all things hitherto. Henceforth, we are told, things must proceed at a new and higher level, that of human psychology and rationality. Thus Huxley has written,

> The appearance of the human type of mind, the latest step in evolutionary progress, has introduced both new methods and new standards. By means of his conscious reason and its chief offspring, science, man has the power of substituting less dilatory, less wasteful, and less cruel methods of effective progressive change than those of natural selection, which alone are available to lower organisms.[30]

What Huxley and others have postulated is a new stage of evolution, a transition from the old and now obsolescent mechanisms to a new plateau affording a new and more elevated prospect of human utopianism. It has been a long climb. We are informed that the first major transition, taking place in the lowland of matter, was

27. Shockley, "Population Control," p. 104.
28. Leach, Reith Lectures, p. 624.
29. Julian Huxley, *Evolution: The Modern Synthesis* (1942), pp. 546ff.
30. Huxley, *The Uniqueness of Man* (1941), p. 32.

from the inanimate to the animate, from the inorganic to the organic; and that the second was from biological irrationality to the sovereign mind of man. This new evolutionistic perspective we shall call neoevolution. It is strange indeed that so many scientists should put their faith in so unscientific a concept as that of evolutionary development from matter to mind, for nothing is better established scientifically than that inorganic matter is lifeless and mindless and that all life comes from previous life of the same kind. The transition from matter to mind can be postulated only as something that must, because the hypothesis demands it, have taken place in the remote and unrecoverable past; this requires a colossal leap of blind faith.

The chief prophet and first mystic of neoevolution was the French Jesuit philosopher Pierre Teilhard de Chardin, who died, little known, in New York in 1955. The visionary quality of his thought has captivated the minds of intellectuals seeking a new seer to such an extent that societies called by his name have sprung into being on both sides of the Atlantic; they have a curiously mixed but devoted membership of theologians, atheists, scientists, and academic dabblers of many varieties. As is true of others for whom the human species rather than the individual is of importance, he writes reverentially of Man with a capital M; he has also invented a brand-new terminology to describe the new era on which we have now entered: the era of the *noösphere* (the sphere of *nous* or mind), conceived as a sort of magnetic field or power zone which somehow is active in bringing the psychic and social forces of humanity to the point of unification. Teilhard admits that "to spirits said to possess 'common sense' the idea of a general trend of Man towards some state of superhumanity appears improbable, almost laughable," but points out that slow and imperceptible change is ceaselessly taking place in the universe, and asks why "the most essential current of Life" should, unlike everything else, be fixed. He draws attention to the great difference between primitive and modern man, and asks further,

> A Humanity which has become capable of taking its place consciously in cosmic evolution and of vibrating in unison (I would even say with its own wavelength) under the influence of a common emotion—is not such a Humanity, whatever its residual imperfections and the crises associated with its metamorphosis, already, when compared with the neolithic world, organically a veritable superhumanity?[31]

But this exalted "Humanity" to which even at this moment we belong—let alone the far more exalted goal or consummation to which it is supposed to be moving—is a mystical and indeed a mythical rather than a scientific conception. Unwelcome realities which in the psychological and social spheres of human life have remained constant throughout history cannot be so easily disregarded. Teilhard, however, passionately preaches the gospel of "the continuation of the evolutionary movement at the heart of Humanity," even though his eschatological perspective is

31. Pierre Teilhard de Chardin, *L'Energie Humaine* (1962), pp. 153ff. The translations from this work are my own.

somewhat ill-defined. His creed is that "around us and within us the Energy of Humanity sustains itself by the Energy of the Universe of which it is the crown, and ever pursues its mysterious progress towards the superior states of thought and liberty." This creed, though scientifically unfounded, he presents as scientific fact, not whimsical fancy. And he interprets this faith as a call to action:

> A single way remains open before us: to entrust ourselves to the infallibility and the worth now finally beatifying the operation to which we belong. In us the evolution of the world towards spirit is becoming conscious. Our perfection, our interest, our preservation of essentials cannot henceforth consist in anything else than in pushing precisely this evolution further forward with all our powers. We cannot yet understand exactly where this is leading us, but it would be absurd for us to doubt that it will conduct us to a goal of supreme worth.[32]

What is "of fundamental importance," according to Teilhard, is "to ensure, rationally, the progress of the World of which we are a part," and to do so "not only, as hitherto, for our little individual life, for our little family, for our little country, no longer even only for the entire earth, but for the salvation and the success of the Universe itself."[33]

Two things are becoming apparent: firstly, that for the good of the whole we must be prepared for the individual or the particular to be swallowed up by the universal; secondly, that the purpose of this is our cooperation in "the evolution of the world towards spirit." This means, as we shall soon see more fully, that the transition from the "biosphere" or world of physical life to the "noösphere" or world of mind, now supposedly in process, is not the final transition in Teilhard's scheme. For he envisages as the ultimate refinement the transition or spiritualization of the universe into the "theosphere" or world of divine spirit. There is, Teilhard maintains, "no essential difference" between physical energy and moral force. This follows from his premise that the stuff of the cosmos is spiritual. The present domain therefore of the Energy of Humanity is that of the "physico-moral," and the "immense task" which confronts the "technician of the Energy of Humanity" is

> not only to overcome scientifically the maladies and the phenomena of counter-evolution (sterility, physical enfeeblement) which threaten the increase of the Noösphere, but also by various means (selection, control of the sexes, administration of hormones, hygiene, etc.) to set free a superior type of man.[34]

The "profound metamorphosis" which Teilhard presages will come about, he explains, through the development in our modern consciousness of "a special sense for laying hold of the Totality in which alone the marvel of our mutual liberation and compenetration (or transparence) can operate." He stresses the importance of

32. Ibid., pp. 155–156.
33. Ibid., p. 158.
34. Ibid., pp. 159–160.

the cultivation of a "cosmic sense," so that people will "cease to be individuals shut off in separation" and will prepare themselves for "integration into the Total Energy of the Noösphere."[35] He envisions the totality of mankind acting as a single organism motivated by a united consciousness and a collective emotion. He believes that there will be no limit to the spiritual expansion, penetration, and fusion resulting from such coherence of the mass of humanity.

> To conquer and harness the forces of the ether and the sea is fine. But what is this triumph compared with the global mastery of human thought and love? Truly, never has an opportunity more magnificent than this been presented to the hopes and endeavors of the Earth.[36]

Turning to the theme of eugenics, Teilhard complains that "we are incredibly slow in promoting (and even in conceiving) the realization of a 'body' of humanity"; he deplores "the anomaly of a society which concerns itself with everything except organizing the recruitment of its own elements." It seems that he would have concurred with Leach's judgment that man, now godlike, must destroy as well as create. Eugenics, Teilhard points out, "is not confined to a simple selection of births." Because the earth's surface is confined and limited, we have to decide what attitude should be adopted towards unprogressive ethnic groups. "To what degree, racially or nationally," he asks, "should areas of inferior activity be tolerated?" Moreover, what justification is there for effort expended in the preservation of what is often no more than the fag end of life?

> Something profoundly fine and true (I would say faith in the irreplaceable worth and the incalculable resources contained in each personal element) is apparently concealed beneath this obstinate determination to sacrifice everything in order to preserve a human existence. But ought not this solicitude of Man for his individual neighbor to be balanced by a higher passion, engendered by faith in this other superior personality which is anticipated, as we shall see, from the terrestrial success of our evolution? To what extent ought the development of the strong (insofar as this may be clearly defined) to take precedence over the preservation of the feeble?[37]

Thus Teilhard signals his approval of compulsory euthanasia and the removal of those who are regarded as feeble and inferior so that the progress of the strong may not be impeded.

The organization of the human race advocated by Teilhard will be, first, international, and then, as the ultimate goal is approached, "totalitarian."[38] Moreover, the way ahead demands not the limitation of force, which in any case Teilhard regards

---

35. Ibid., pp. 163–164.
36. Ibid., p. 165.
37. Ibid., p. 166.
38. Ibid., p. 167. "Totalitarian" (*totalitaire*) does not have here the pejorative connotation now commonly attached to it.

as both impossible and immoral, but its controlled direction into channels which will be for the benefit of all. "The cure for our ills," he affirms, lies in the discovery of a natural and fruitful cause into which "the superabundance which oppresses us" can be channeled: "An ever greater excess of free energy, made available for ever vaster conquests: this is what the world is waiting for from us and this is what will save us."[39]

But the development of the external solidarity of mankind is no more than the pointer to something far more profound which is going on, the inner and psychical organization of the noösphere. The mingling and fusion of the races are leading directly, says Teilhard, to a community and equality not only of language but of morality and idealism.

> Beneath the combined effect of the material needs and spiritual affinities of life Humanity is beginning to emerge all around us from the impersonal in order to take on, as it were, a heart and a form. . . . The organization of the Energy of Humanity, taken in its totality, is directed, and urges us, towards the ultimate formation, over and above each personal element, of a *common human soul.*[40]

This is stated as a fact, not a theory. No proof, scientific or otherwise, is adduced. Indeed, the mass of evidence that points to a contrary conclusion is completely ignored.

The predicted end-product of "a common human soul" is something more than good will among men and worldwide brotherhood. What is portended is a single human, or rather superhuman, organism, for Teilhard posits as a necessity the consummation of evolution in a universal Personality which is attained by the "ultraconcentration" of all personal human elements in a higher consciousness. "The world would not function," he asserts, "were it not for the existence, somewhat in advance of time and space, of a 'cosmic Point Omega' of total synthesis." The appearance of man marked a great step forward on the road of evolutionary progress towards this goal of total synthesis: "Through hominization," Teilhard writes, "the Universe has reached a more exalted level where its physico-moral powers are taking the form little by little of a fundamental affinity binding individuals to each other and to what we have called the 'Point Omega.'" The force that is bringing this to pass is "the essential Energy of the World—that which, after having in chaos agitated the cosmic mass, emerges to form the Noösphere"; the name of this dynamic force is, simply, Love.[41] The command to "love one another" is the fundamental principle and the key to the future of man and the world. We are assured that "there is no obstacle which will be able to prevent the Energy of

39. Ibid., p. 168.
40. Ibid., p. 171.
41. Ibid., pp. 178ff.

Humanity from freely achieving the natural objective of its evolution"—the objective of "the totalization, in a total love, of the total Energy of Humanity."[42]

"The essential message of Christ," according to Teilhard, "is not to be sought in the Sermon on the Mount nor even in what took place on the cross: it consists in its entirety in the proclamation of a 'divine Fatherhood'"—in other words, "in the affirmation that God, personal being, is presented to Man as the goal of a personal *union.*"[43] And just as the Energy of Humanity has been responsible for "the appearance first of Life, from which the Biosphere arose, and then of Thought, introducing the Noösphere," so also there awaits us a further and ultimate metamorphosis, springing from "the Christian birth of love," namely "the recognition of an 'Omega' at the heart of the Noösphere—the passage of the circles to their common center: *the appearance of the 'Theosphere.'*"[44]

Teilhard denies, of course, that he is living in a land of dream and fantasy. In his view ascent on the evolutionary ladder from matter to mind and then to spirit leads to an eschaton, a future of perfection, where there is room for "Man" or for "the Energy of Humanity" but not for men, not for you and me as individual personalities. The picture he holds before us is beautifully painted in visionary and idealistic colors, but his gospel of salvation is demonstrably alien to that of the New Testament. The terminus of the long process he depicts is, it seems, a sort of Pythagorean paradise in which matter and individuality have disappeared and all has become mind and spirit. It is the consummation of what he has called "the general 'drift' of matter towards spirit." "This movement," he explains, "must have its term: one day the whole divinizable substance of matter will have passed into the souls of men; all the chosen dynamisms will have been recovered: and then our world will be ready for the Parousia."[45] Everything, the universe in its totality, will in the end be divinized. There is a striking similarity between this purview and the description of the cosmic pilgrimage of Man and Woman given by Lilith in George Bernard Shaw's play *Back to Methuselah:*

> After passing a million goals they press on to the goal of redemption from the flesh, to the vortex freed from matter, to the whirlpool in pure intelligence that, when the world began, was a whirlpool in pure force.[46]

It all looks suspiciously like dehominization!

The Christian Perspective

In the midst of all this largely humanistic planning, prediction, and speculation with reference to the ethical future of man, it remains for us to say something about the perspective of the Christian as he faces the problems of the human situation.

42. Ibid., pp. 189ff.
43. Ibid., p. 193.
44. Ibid., pp. 197–198.
45. Teilhard de Chardin, *Le Milieu Divin* (1960), p. 94.
46. George Bernard Shaw, *The Complete Plays* (n.d.), p. 962.

In the first place, it must be insisted that the view of man as the master of his own destiny and the sole controller of his future is entirely alien to the Christian understanding of the state of man and society. Certainly no Christian would wish to deny that man is a responsible being and that there is a logical sequence of cause and effect in the sphere of human conduct. A man reaps what he sows; evil pays its own wages; and the sinner has only himself to blame when he comes under judgment. The Christian is strongly motivated to plan and work for the establishment of morality, justice, and dignity in the community of mankind. But he does not see man as the center and sum of things. In the biblical perspective God and God alone is the sovereign Lord of the whole universe: sovereign in creation, in providence, in judgment, and in redemption; and sovereign therefore over all human history. The staggering problems which so darkly threaten man and his future are quite definitely not problems to God. The frustration of man is not the frustration of God. The Christian knows that in its ultimate outcome the future rests securely in God's hands. The God who brings everything into existence is also the God who brings everything to completion. This means that, no matter how menacing appearances may be, the Christian's very proper concern for the progress and well-being of his fellow men is tempered by a calm confidence which springs from his knowledge that God is in control. This is not pietistic escapism; it is getting the overall picture into true focus—and that surely is the first essential for the person who wishes to take life and humanity and the world seriously.

Secondly, the Christian has no reason to deny that, though in the ultimate issue all will be conformed to the will and purpose of God, there is a sense in which the future does rest with man. In his fallenness man has terribly abused his God-given mandate to govern the rest of creation; but that mandate has not been abrogated, and its social, cultural, and scientific responsibilities still rest squarely on man's shoulders. Created in the divine image and endowed with unique powers, man is answerable not only for his own self but also for the state of the world over which he has been placed and to which he belongs. He has a duty to promote decency and order in himself and in society, to ensure as far as he possibly can in this fallen situation that human affairs are controlled in such a manner as to benefit and ennoble the commonwealth, and to safeguard the rights and freedoms of all people. It is within this setting that respect for one's fellow man and the environment, concern for a better future, and care for the weak, the hungry, the oppressed, and the underprivileged assume their real importance. Since the second of the two great commandments is that we love our fellow men as ourselves, the Christian is the last person who should shrug off such matters as though they were no concern of his. Disease, poverty, unemployment, and tyranny he recognizes as evils which he must strive to remedy and remove. Injustice and brutality are abhorrent to him. The dignity of the person, each person, is precious to him, as it is precious also to God, who has sealed each person with His likeness.

Thirdly, the Christian is the only true realist. He is this precisely because he brings God as well as man into the picture. To leave God out means that any assessment of the human situation must inevitably vacillate between optimism and despair. Some will stake all on optimism, expressing an invincible confidence in the ultimate indefectibility of natural selection or fortuitous mutation or eugenic wisdom. Others, unable to close their eyes to the depressing evidence of the depravity of human nature, will conclude that only a pessimistic or even nihilistic view of the future of mankind is justified. And still others will attempt to temper pessimism with optimism by issuing admonitions to the effect that mankind will be overtaken by irretrievable disaster if steps are not taken forthwith to ensure the ennoblement of the species.

The Christian is the true realist because he recognizes that man, by reason of the fallenness of his nature, is incapable of producing by his own planning and effort the utopia for which he longs. He knows that human endeavor to this end, admirable though it may be in many respects, is doomed to frustration. That is why he points man away from himself to God, from whom alone salvation and reintegration can come. In particular he points to Christ, the incarnate, crucified, risen, and glorified Son of God, as the One in whom God reconciles the world to Himself. Furthermore, the Christian future does indeed include a "utopian" consummation, but it is not something induced by man's self-mastery, or evolutionary impulse, or some other kind of mystical energy. Christian optimism rests on the sovereign purpose of God in Christ for the establishment of the new heaven and the new earth, in which all God's purposes in creation will be brought to their eternal fulfillment. The citizens of this everlasting kingdom will be those who have been regenerated by the grace of God through faith in Jesus Christ. They are new and true persons recreated in the image of God in which they were first created, and rejoicing in the fulfillment of their reintegrated manhood. And they are full persons, redeemed in body as well as soul, exulting in the dignity of their being as they do everything to the glory of God; they are drawn from every age of human history, not just from some ultimate eugenic community. They are not dehumanized automata or brutalized serfs, nor are they some kind of dematerialized humanity whose identity has been dissolved in a nebulous sphere of numinosity. Through union with Christ they become the heirs of all things, and the enjoyment of their heritage will not be spoiled by illness or disease; it will not be clouded by sorrow; it will not be frustrated and lost through death. For all these things which now are enemies to our self-fulfillment and our delight in others will then have passed away; in the unending summer of the divine love redeemed humanity will blossom into the full fruition of its innate potential in the joyful service and praise of God. This is the resplendent hope of the Christian, a hope whose realization is assured in Christ.

The Christian perspective, then, is one of confident optimism; but at the same time there is a Christian pessimism regarding the world and society in their present fallen state. Every merely human claim to be able to shape and control the destiny of mankind is seen to be stamped with futility, and every utopian dream is known to be a mirage without substance. The constant lesson of history is that every achievement of man is overtaken by a perverting and deforming nemesis. The

phenomenal technological advance of our own age has brought with it not only
new benefits but also a phenomenal increase in suffering and destruction. The evil
seems to be outpacing the good. And the reason for this is in man himself, not
outside of him. It is the inevitable consequence of his willful alienation from his
Creator and his attempt to invert the fundamental order of things by suppressing
the truth about God and foolishly presuming to behave as though it is he who
sovereignly controls the course of history. The problem is essentially a human
problem, and it is essentially no different today from what it was in Plato's day or
in any other period of the history of man.

Christian optimism, then, flows from the knowledge of the sovereignty and
goodness of God and the indefectibility of His purposes. Christian pessimism flows
from the knowledge of the fallenness of human nature and its incapacity to achieve
the perfect society. As Paul Ramsey has said, "We have to contrast biblical or
Christian eschatology with genetic eschatology."[47] The outlook for society in terms
of biblical eschatology was described by the apostle Paul in the following words,
which, though written nineteen hundred years ago, apply in every detail to the
human situation of our own time:

> The final age of this world is to be a time of troubles. Men will love nothing but
> money and self; they will be arrogant, boastful, and abusive; with no respect for
> parents, no gratitude, no piety, no natural affection; they will be implacable in their
> hatreds, scandal-mongers, intemperate and fierce, strangers to all goodness, traitors,
> adventurers, swollen with self-importance. They will be men who put pleasure in the
> place of God, men who preserve the outward form of religion, but are a standing
> denial of its reality (II Tim. 3:1–5, NEB).

In a measure unknown before in human history the twentieth century has experienced fulfillment of Christ's eschatological prediction that "even your parents and
brothers, your relations and friends, will betray you," and that "on earth nations
will stand helpless, not knowing which way to turn," while "men will faint with
terror at the thought of all that is coming upon the world" (Luke 21:16, 25–26,
NEB). Christian eschatology foresees this age as ending not in a man-devised utopia
but in the sudden breaking of the day of the Lord, when Christ appears to execute
judgment on the ungodly and to set up the unending perfection of His kingdom
from which all evil will be eliminated.

In the meantime the Christian has to live in the world as it exists between the
two comings of Christ, knowing that the redeeming grace of God is freely available
to the repentant sinner, and also that the aspirations of unregenerate man for a
perfect world, even if he be scientist or philanthropist, will meet with frustration
because of the contradictions at the root of fallen human nature. Commanded to
love and serve his fellow man, the Christian shares in the longings of others for an
ideal society. He too yearns for the time when evil and imperfection will be banished

47. Ramsey, "Moral and Religious Implications," p. 132.

from the human scene. He cannot approve, however, of the employment of means which will have the effect of dehumanizing and depersonalizing the individual components of society, and which for that very reason will be ineluctably self-defeating. He perceives that the end product, far from being utopian, will be as inhumane as it is inhuman.

As for the ethics of genetic intervention, Dwight J. Ingle has warned that "the idea of forcing a program of eugenics on any population is a threat to basic freedoms." He continues,

> Some governmental interventions in basic freedoms at the social level are even now models of injustice. Guided by social scientists, theologians, and jurists without competence in testing claims to knowledge, with little information and too little wisdom, governments are already fostering social malignancy, and without the general consent of the populations. Biologists are not enlightened by a greater wisdom; those asking for large-scale programs now, and especially for forced intervention through eugenics, should be rebuffed.[48]

But the extreme of doing nothing is as unacceptable as the extreme of doing everything. To do nothing is irresponsible; to do everything is to enforce what man alone cannot achieve, to act *ultra vires*. Ingle argues for the reasonableness of steering a course between laissez faire and the use of totalitarian methods for dealing with the social and biomedical problems of mankind.

Aware of his responsibilities, the Christian does not deny the importance of genetic research or the beneficial contribution that the study of genetics has to make to our understanding of homo sapiens. Nor does he belittle the necessity of an ethics of genetic duty which should be respected and fulfilled by all.[49] This is an ethics of self-control not imposed arbitrarily on society, but self-imposed by the individual. A person who knows that he or she carries a defect or a disease which is transmissible to children should be prepared to forgo, in the interests of both the family and the race, the privilege and pleasure of marriage and parenthood—or at least the latter. Married couples who discover that they will pass on to their progeny seriously harmful or degenerate characteristics should refrain from having children of their own. Adoption would be a reasonable procedure for them. There are some cases in which voluntary sterilization may be the right course to follow. Advance in genetic knowledge will certainly mean the opportunity for advance in genetic responsibility. In this as in other matters which affect the welfare of the community, Christians should be prepared to lead the way in honoring their duty.

48. Dwight J. Ingle, "Ethics of Genetic Intervention," in *Medical Opinion and Review* 3, no. 9 (1967): 61.
49. Ramsey, "Moral and Religious Implications," p. 166.

8

Sexual Ethics

Mankind is differentiated into two sexes, male and female. This is a fact of creation (Gen. 1:27); and it is precisely this differentiation which makes it possible to fulfill the mandate to be fruitful and multiply (Gen. 1:28), which is added to the statement of man's creation. The differentiation is anatomical, certainly; but the anatomical contrast between man and woman is evident not only in the difference between the distinctive male and female sexual organs but also more generally in the difference between man's and woman's physique and temperament. The distinction is thoroughly constitutional. The man is physically strong and muscular in a way that the woman is not. He can run faster, throw farther, and lift heavier weights than she can. The comparative softness of the woman's physical constitution belongs with the particular warmth and gentleness of her psychological attitudes and relationships as the counterpart of man and the mother of children. That is why terms like *wifely* and *motherly* carry a sense that is more than merely anatomical or relational. It follows also that of the two sexes the woman is physically the more vulnerable. This provides the basis for the time-honored practice of chivalry: the man is the champion of the woman; he treats her with courtesy and consideration; he attends to her needs before he attends to his own; and he is her protector.

Sexuality and the Image of God

It was Karl Barth's contention that the image of God in which man was created consisted simply in the sexual differentiation of man into male and female—a differentiation, however, which also involves a relationship. Barth admits that "this plurality, the differentiation of sex, is something which formally man has in common with the beasts," but argues that since man, unlike the rest of the animal creation, was originally one and undivided into groups, species, and races, "the only real differentiation and relationship is that of man to man, and in its original and most concrete form of man to woman and woman to man." This leads him to draw the conclusion that "as God is One, and He alone is God, so man as man is one and alone, and two only in the duality of his kind, i.e., in the duality of man and woman," and that "in this way he is a copy and imitation of God."[1] There is no

---

1. Karl Barth, *Church Dogmatics* (1958), vol. 3, part 1, pp. 185–186.

denying that man's creation as male and female is something he has in common with the beasts and therefore a mark of his creatureliness. Barth's argument, however, is based on the statement (concerning man's formation), "male and female he created them," which he interprets as a statement distinguishing man from the rest of creation and therefore as signifying the proper content of the image of God in which man was made.

But this is a thoroughly unsatisfactory argument because it could be applied, if one were so disposed, to any of the animal species, each of which was created "according to its kind" (or species) with the power and the command to "be fruitful and multiply" (Gen. 1:21–22). This power and this command rest precisely on the fact, even though it receives no special mention, that the birds and the beasts were created male and female. In this respect it can equally well be said that each animal species is one and alone, and that man in terms of his animal sexuality is but one species among many. Of course, from the evolutionary point of view, which Barth does not question, his thesis is impossible to sustain, since man's animality and sexuality are then held to be derived solely from the lower orders of creation, with the consequence that it would be sounder to argue that these qualities constitute (no doubt in a benign sense) the mark of the beast rather than the image of God.

In discussing the two sexes Barth very rightly draws attention to the two aspects of differentiation and relationship. Perhaps he does not make it sufficiently clear (though this is surely his understanding) that in the society of mankind this difference and this relation between male and female are, apart from mere considerations of anatomy, categorically superior to those between male and female beasts because man and woman enjoy an association with each other that is profoundly personal in character. Human personality, as we have earlier observed, is an important manifestation of the image of God in which man has been created. It reflects at the human level something of the distinction and communion of the three persons, Father, Son, and Holy Spirit, in the trinitarian being of God.

But though the person-to-person relationship is fundamental in human sexuality, we cannot accept sexuality as constitutive of the image of God in which man was created—even granting that it may and should be expressive of that image, as should be the case with man's every action and relationship. For human personality is not dependent on human sexuality or on associations between the sexes. Indeed, the interpersonal relationship of the Holy Trinity is definitely not sexual. This consideration alone should be sufficient to refute the notion that man's sexual differentiation is constitutive of or in some sense central to his being made in the image of God. If interpersonal relationships were inseparable from sexual relationships, there would be no opportunity for associations between persons of the same sex, between man and man or between woman and woman or between adult and child—a situation that is manifestly false and contrary to common experience. This becomes absolutely clear when we consider the Person-to-person relationship between God and man, which is completely unrelated to sexuality, and in particular when we consider the perfect actualization of this relationship in the communion between God and the incarnate Son, who was truly and fully man and our fellow, yet without the need to experience the sexual union of marriage. We should bear in mind, too, the teaching of the incarnate Son that in the heavenly state, in which there will be a perfect relationship between God and man and between man and man, and in which the image of God will be totally restored and fulfilled in our humanity, sexuality as a function will be a thing of the past: "In the resurrection," Jesus declared, "they neither marry nor are given in marriage" (Matt. 22:30). The sexual distinction, then, between male and female cannot belong to the definition of the divine image.

The image in which man was created, moreover, is specifically that of the Second Person of the Trinity rather than that of the tripersonal Godhead; for the Son is Himself the image of the invisible God (Col. 1:15), and His personhood exists within and by virtue of the interpersonal reality of the divine being as three in one and one in three. That is why it is in likeness to Christ that man truly conforms to the image in which he was created; Christians, says St. Paul, "are being changed into his likeness from one degree of glory to another" (II Cor. 3:18); indeed, they are "predestined to be conformed to the image of [God's] Son" (Rom. 8:29). This is a further indication of the inappropriateness of taking man's creation as male and female to be the key which unlocks the mystery of his being made in the image of God.

The Scope and Purpose of Sexuality

Since man was created male and female, sexuality belongs to man's creaturehood and is a factor which is both integral and indispensable in the structure of human society. The biblical teaching concerning the scope and purpose of sexuality is clear and consistent.

1. The primary function served by the creation of two sexes is the *procreation* of children and the propagation of the race. The design of the sexual organs is obviously for this purpose, enabling the man to contribute and the woman to receive the male sperm for the impregnation of the ova in her womb, where during gestation the new human being is formed and grows; her breasts are intended for the suckling of the newborn child. The difference between male and female physical and anatomical structure plainly points to procreation as the primary purpose of sexuality. Erotic stimulation is meant to serve this end, not to be an end in itself. Hence God's command to man, whom He created male and female, to "be fruitful and multiply, and fill the earth" (Gen. 1:28). Before all else, then, human sexuality is designed for the increase and perpetuation of mankind.

2. Further, the differentiation of mankind into two sexes is designed for *companionship.* For man to be an isolated, egocentric individual would be tragic and destructive to his personhood. Self-fulfillment is impossible apart from relationship with and especially love for others—God first and then one's fellow man, as the

summary of the law shows. In the biblical perspective those who are solitary are regarded with special pity and concern, and the companionship of spouse and family is seen as a remedy for loneliness: "God setteth the solitary in families," says the psalmist (Ps. 68:6, KJV).[2] Those who have lost the companionship of spouse and family are objects of loving care. As St. James writes, "to visit orphans and widows in their affliction" is a mark of "religion that is pure and undefiled before God" (James 1:27). It is recorded that the Creator said, "It is not good that the man should be alone; I will make him a helper fit for him" (Gen. 2:18). The marriage union is human companionship at its most intimate level.

3. Inseparably associated with the first two purposes of sexuality, namely procreation and companionship, is the recognition of marriage as a *one-flesh union,* in which a man and his wife are so intimately and lovingly identified with each other that "they become one flesh" (Gen. 2:24). The consummation of the marriage bond enables the husband to speak of his wife as "bone of my bones and flesh of my flesh" (Gen. 2:23) because their love for each other is truly a unifying experience and something of deep sacredness.

4. It follows that sexuality receives its full and proper expression in *monogamous* union. The one-flesh principle implies that as sexual partners husband and wife belong to each other and to no one else. And that monogamy is a principle of creation is evident from the same passage, where this conclusion is drawn: "Therefore a man leaves his father and his mother and cleaves to his wife" (Gen. 2:24). The later sanctioning of divorce and remarriage was a departure from the original ordinance of God. Hence the comment of Jesus, when questioned about the practice of divorce, that "from the beginning it was not so," and His insistence on the continuing validity of the standard of monogamous faithfulness, since husband and wife "are no longer two but one." The plain logic of this is then forthrightly affirmed in the declaration, "What therefore God has joined together, let no man put asunder" (Matt. 19:3–9).

5. The understanding of marriage as a monogamous union involving lifelong fidelity is confirmed and enhanced by the apostolic teaching that the one-flesh union of husband and wife is itself a *mystery,* because, in a manner which transcends the merely physical relationship, it reflects or points to the intimate spiritual union in which Christ, the supreme Bridegroom, is joined forever to His body and bride, the church. The sanctity of the marriage bond could have no clearer emphasis than this. The mystical union of Christ and His beloved so far surpasses all simply human experiences of union that human language is incapable of encompassing it; consequently it is expressed by Christ in an apparently paradoxical manner: "You in me, and I in you." This mystical union, however, is well understood because it is even now being experienced by the Christian believer (John 14:20; cf. 15:4). Moreover, the love which unites Christ as Bridegroom to His church as bride provides a perfect pattern for the love bond which should prevail in human

---

2. NEB: "God gives the friendless a home."

marriage. Thus husbands are exhorted to love their wives "as Christ loved the church and gave himself up for her, that he might sanctify her," and "that she might be holy and without blemish" (Eph. 5:22–33). And the Corinthian believers are told by the apostle, "I betrothed you to Christ to present you as a pure bride to her one husband" (II Cor. 11:2). Passages such as these indicate that marriage is not free from ethical demands: just as the love which unites Christ and His church is a pure and holy love, so also the marriage union between husband and wife should be a relationship of pureness and sanctity, not an excuse for licentiousness.

6. Since sexuality is designed for procreation, it produces *children* as the fruit of marital love. Accordingly, it leads to the phenomenon of the *family,* which is itself a sort of trinity of father, mother, and children, for children may realistically be described as bone of their parents' bone and flesh of their parents' flesh. Children and grandchildren ("children's children") can justifiably be regarded as an extension of the family, but the nucleus is the one-flesh union of husband and wife. Thus when children have reached adulthood, they may leave their parents without disrupting the ties of the family and may themselves enter into marriage for the establishment of their own families, which at the same time extend and perpetuate the families from which they came. But while they may leave their parents, they are not free to abandon them. Hence the abiding force of the fifth commandment, which requires that parents be honored. The responsibility to love and care for parents continues even after children have left them to marry and set up their own homes.

The Structure of the Family

The family was never intended to be structureless and disordered; indeed, there is nothing more disruptive of the family than the absence of structure and order. Properly understood, the family is itself a structure whose own due order belongs to and partakes of the order of creation and as such reflects the orderliness of God and His creative purpose. Due order is essential for the right functioning of things. Because of the amazing orderliness of its structure the universe is called the cosmos (*cosmos* being simply the Greek word for order), and this orderliness permeates the universe in its entirety. It characterizes not merely the macrocosm of the solar system but also the microcosm of the atom and the tissue cell and the complex functioning of the body. So remarkable is this cosmic precision that the scientist Sir James Jeans likened it to that of mathematical thought, though he realized that the analogy suffered from the limitations of our human comprehension: "The universe," he wrote, "can be best pictured, although still very imperfectly and inadequately, as consisting of pure thought, the thought of what, for want of a wider word, we must describe as a mathematical thinker."[3] It is hardly surprising, then, that within this ordered universe (and we should notice that even the term *universe* derives from

3. James Jeans, *The Mysterious Universe* (1930), p. 136.

recognition of the unity and harmony of the ordered whole) mankind is designed to function in an orderly manner.

The disorder of human society gives rise to disastrous disharmony at the very point where there should be the most perfect accord, since man's true destiny is to serve as God's viceroy in the created realm. But although there is disorder, there is not total chaos, which would be an altogether insufferable situation of meaningless insanity. Because the divine image in which man is created has not been totally defaced, the intolerability of total chaos is instinctively recognized; hence, as we have seen earlier, the restraints that are commonly placed on the disorderly conduct of our race. There is not a nation on earth that does not have some form of government for the control of public behavior and courts of law and a police force for the protection of the innocent and the punishment of the disorderly. Such measures at least place some curb on the ungodly and chaotic propensities of our fallen human nature. Families are the social units or cells which together constitute the human community and the body politic. They too come under government control to the extent that marriages must be legally contracted and registered, and that it is the duty of the husband to provide for his wife and the father for his children.

The relationship between Christ and the church provides the schematic prototype for the structural order of the family. The actual basis of this scheme is the formation of man in the divine image at creation. As we have said, the image to which man was designed to conform is that of the Second Person of the Trinity. Since the fall of man and the incarnation of the Second Person of the Trinity, the scheme has been one of redemption. This is plain when it is remembered that the purpose of redemption in Christ is precisely the restoration and fulfillment of the divine purpose in creation. Thus the relationship between the Second Person of the Trinity and mankind as created is inseparably connected with the relationship between Christ the incarnate Son and the church, which is humanity redeemed and re-created; the family is intended to be a reflection of that divine-human relationship. The headship of Christ over the church, which is His bride, is not a matter of dispute; it involves a relationship of order that logically requires the subjection of the church to her Head. In the apostolic teaching this logic is extended to the structure of the family: "Wives, be subject to your husbands, as to the Lord," St. Paul writes. "For the husband is the head of the wife as Christ is the head of the church, his body, and is himself its Savior. As the church is subject to Christ, so let wives also be subject in everything to their husbands" (Eph. 5:22–24). But the husband is not the supreme head, for that is an authority which belongs only to God. Accordingly, the husband too is subject: he is subject to Christ, the divine-human Savior. And even Christ, by reason of His incarnation, through which He assumed our manhood in order to redeem it (without, however, ceasing to be the truly divine Son), subjected Himself, as our fellow man, to God. Thus St. Paul admonishes the Christians in Corinth, who had been allowing the relationship between the sexes to become disorderly, "I want you to understand that the head of every man is Christ, and the head of a woman is her husband, and the head of Christ is God" (I Cor. 11:3).

This is not at all a master-servant situation. For the husband to be domineering and the wife subservient, or, contrariwise, the wife domineering and the husband subservient, is destructive of the marriage relationship, which is a relationship of unity, of oneness, not disunity. As Christ is the strength of the church ("its Savior"), so the husband is the strength of his wife, who is "the weaker sex" (I Peter 3:7). As the church desires to please her Lord (cf. I John 3:22), so the wife desires to please her husband. The marriage bond is one of mutual holiness and honor: in taking a wife to himself a man is to do so "in holiness and honor, not in the passion of lust" (I Thess. 4:4–5; I Peter 3:7). In short, marriage is a union of love, the love of the husband for his wife and the love of the wife for her husband; it is an ordered union in which both husband and wife are subject to Christ and to God, and in which the pattern of their love for each other is a reflection of the love which unites Christ and His church. Far from being self-assertive, indeed, the husband is to show love for his wife which is, like Christ's love for the church, self-denying and sacrificial. Hence the apostolic exhortation: "Husbands, love your wives, as Christ loved the church and gave himself up for her. . . . Even so husbands should love their wives as their own bodies . . . as Christ does the church," His body (Eph. 5:25–29).

The husband's headship in the family is explained by St. Paul as belonging to the order of creation itself: "For man was not made from woman, but woman from man. Neither was man created for woman, but woman for man" (I Cor. 11:8–9). But once again this is a matter of order, not lordliness. It is an order which actually establishes the oneness and interdependence of those in the marriage bond. That is why the apostle adds that "in the Lord woman is not independent of man nor man of woman; for as woman was made from man, so man is now born of woman. And all things are from God" (I Cor. 11:11–12). Under God, therefore, marriage is intended to be an institution of mutual love and interdependence, but always with respect for the order of creation with which it is stamped. In his "wedding sermon from a prison cell" Dietrich Bonhoeffer cites Colossians 3:18–19—"Wives, be subject to your husbands, as is fitting in the Lord. Husbands, love your wives"—as "a rule of life" established by God "by which you can live together in wedlock"; and he instructively applies this rule in the following incisive manner:

> You may order your home as you like, except in one thing: the wife is to be subject to her husband, and the husband is to love his wife. In this way God gives to husband and wife the honor that is due to each. The wife's honor is to serve the husband, to be a "help meet for him," as the creation story has it (Gen. 2:18), and the husband's honor is to love his wife with all his heart. . . . A wife who wants to dominate her husband dishonors herself and him, just as a husband who does not love his wife as he should dishonors himself and her; and both dishonor the glory of God that is meant to rest on the estate of matrimony. It is an unhealthy state of affairs when the wife's ambition is to be like the husband, and the husband regards his wife merely as the plaything of his own lust for power and licence; and it is a sign of social

disintegration when the wife's service is felt to be degrading or beneath her dignity, and when the husband who is faithful to his wife is looked on as a weakling or even a fool.[4]

Turning to Ephesians 5:23, Bonhoeffer says,

> Now when the husband is called "the head of the wife," and it goes on to say "as Christ is the head of the church," something of the divine splendor is reflected in our earthly relationships, and this reflection we should recognize and honor. The dignity that is here ascribed to the man lies, not in any capacities or qualities of his own, but in the office conferred on him by his marriage. The wife should see her husband clothed in this dignity. But for him it is a supreme responsibility. As the head, it is he who is responsible for his wife, for their marriage, and for their home. . . . The husband and wife who acknowledge and observe God's ordinance are "wise," but those who think to replace it by another of their own devising are "foolish."[5]

The Bible never portrays the role of the wife as one that is passive and servile. There is no suggestion that she can have no mind and will of her own, or that she cannot be a person of initiative and authority. The special sphere of the wife's authority is seen as the home, where she is in charge of all the domestic arrangements and, as the homemaker, makes provision for the care and well-being of the whole family. Hers is a sphere of concentrated activity and responsibility, as she plans and organizes the household and trains and instructs her children. The wide and varied range of her occupations is graphically depicted by the poet in Proverbs 31:10–31, where she is described as one in whom the heart of her husband trusts and as being clothed with strength and dignity. "She opens her mouth with wisdom," this encomium of the good wife continues, "and the teaching of kindness is on her tongue. She looks well to the ways of her household, and does not eat the bread of idleness. Her children rise up and call her blessed; her husband also, and he praises her." To the same effect St. Paul declares that it is the privilege and duty of wives to "rule their households" (I Tim. 5:14), and counsels that the older women "must set a high standard, and school the younger women to be loving wives and mothers, temperate, chaste, and kind, busy at home, respecting the authority of their own husbands," because in this way "the Gospel will not be brought into disrepute" (Titus 2:4–5, NEB). It is with reference to such passages that Stephen Clark observes that "the wife's role thus involves a real governmental function," for "although the husband is head of the house, the wife functions under him as someone who rules the house."[6] And he draws attention to the fact that Chrysostom calls the wife a "second authority."[7]

The order within marriage extends, further, from the husband through the wife

4. Dietrich Bonhoeffer, *Letters and Papers from Prison,* ed. Eberhard Bethge (1967), p. 50.
5. Ibid., p. 51.
6. Stephen B. Clark, *Man and Woman in Christ* (1980), p. 57.
7. Ibid. This passage from Chrysostom is quoted on p. 164.

to the children that are born to them. In a rightly ordered family the children are subject to their parents in a relationship of loving obedience. The family when duly structured is a source of strength and confidence to the children. The wisdom of the poet of old needs still to be heeded: "Hear, my son, your father's instruction, and reject not your mother's teaching; for they are a fair garland for your head, and pendants for your neck" (Prov. 1:8–9; cf. 6:20; 23:22). Timothy, for example, could count himself greatly blessed because "from childhood" he had been "acquainted with the sacred writings which are able to instruct you for salvation through faith in Christ Jesus" (II Tim. 3:15). Therefore, children are enjoined, "Obey your parents in everything, for this pleases the Lord" (Col. 3:20; cf. Eph. 6:1–3). As the head of the family the father has responsibility to ensure that his children are brought up "in the discipline and instruction of the Lord." When it is necessary to administer correction, punishment that is excessive or brutal should be avoided, as this can be harmful instead of beneficial and will lead to bitterness instead of improvement. Hence the injunction, "Fathers, do not provoke your children [to anger] lest they become discouraged" (Col. 3:21; cf. Eph. 6:4). Like the heavenly Father's chastisement of us His children, so the chastisement of children by their earthly father should be lovingly administered for their good and with the design of yielding "the peaceful fruit of righteousness" (Heb. 12:5–11).

The sphere of the Christian family and the wider sphere of the Christian church, of which it is a vital component, are concentric. Accordingly, as Christ is the head of the church, so He is also, and for that very reason, the head of the family. We will never see the ordered family in true perspective unless and until we perceive that Christ is head over all. And this brings us face to face again with the divine order of creation, because it is in the Christian church, to which the Christian family inseparably belongs, that the order of creation is being redemptively restored. Nor should we forget that the glorious consummating event will be the marriage of Him who is the great Bridegroom, when His bride the church will at last be presented to Him "without spot or wrinkle," indeed "holy and without blemish," "as a pure bride to her one husband" (Eph. 5:27; II Cor. 11:2). Nothing should be more welcome to the waiting church than the announcement of the midnight cry at the end of this age, "Behold, the Bridegroom!" as Christ appears to take His bride to Himself (Matt. 25:6), so that she may delight in the unalloyed and everlasting bliss of absolute love. This will be a time for supreme jubilation, as the seer on the isle of Patmos foresaw in the vision he received:

> Then I heard what seemed to be the voice of a great multitude, like the sound of many waters and like the sound of mighty thunderpeals, crying, "Hallelujah! For the Lord our God the Almighty reigns. Let us rejoice and exult and give him the glory, for the marriage of the Lamb has come, and his Bride has made herself ready" (Rev. 19:6–7; cf. 21:2–4; John 3:29).

Divorce

Jesus taught very plainly that a man who divorces his wife and marries someone else, or a woman who divorces her husband and marries someone else, has committed adultery—that is to say, is guilty of breaking the seventh commandment (Mark 10:11–12). This teaching comes in Christ's response to the question put to Him by the Pharisees, "Is it lawful for a man to divorce his wife?" which was designed to trap Him into saying something contradictory to the teaching of Moses, whose legislation permitted divorce under certain circumstances (see Deut. 24:1–4). Jesus did not dispute that this was part of the Mosaic law, but told His interrogators that Moses made this provision because of their hardness of heart (Mark 10:4–5). The significance of this rejoinder could not be missed by His Pharisaic critics, since throughout the Old Testament hardness of heart is a symptom of rebelliousness against God and perversion of His ordinances. But for the sinfulness of the Israelites (who in this respect were no different from the rest of humanity), there would have been no need for the Mosaic legislation. The purpose of the specific precepts and prohibitions of the law of Moses was, in large measure, to place restraints on human waywardness and provide safeguards for those who might otherwise suffer injustice.

That this was so in the case of the Mosaic enactment regarding divorce is shown not only by Christ's reference to the hardheartedness of the people but also by His direction of the Pharisees' attention to teaching of fundamental importance in the Mosaic writings. He reminded them that, as recorded in Genesis, "from the beginning of creation 'God made them male and female,'" and that the one-flesh principle of marriage means that man and wife have "become one" in a God-given union which no man is to put asunder (Mark 10:6–9). In other words, there is no place for divorce in the order of creation, which defines marriage as an indissoluble union of loving fidelity. Now it was of course precisely the order of creation that Christ came to restore; therefore the restoration of the order of creation should manifestly be taking place in His body the church, which is composed of new creatures, or renewed creations, in Christ. The Christian church, accordingly, has a special responsibility to bear witness, in its practice as well as in its doctrine, to the sanctity of the marriage bond. Of all the spheres of human society it least of all should show that ungodly hardheartedness which requires the divine standard to be accommodated to the debased level of man's fallen state.

Creation unfortunately was followed by the fall, the evil effects of which permeated and perverted the whole mass of humanity. It is a fallen world in which the church lives and works. The church itself is not yet the pure bride it will at last be. Its members, though by divine grace fully justified through faith in Him who is the propitiation for their sins (I John 2:2), are being transformed into the likeness of Christ from glory to glory (II Cor. 3:18); but none are yet fully conformed to that likeness. That is a consummation which will take place when at last Redeemer and redeemed meet face to face (I John 3:2). The church is daily engaged in a conflict not only with the fallenness of unredeemed society, with which it is constantly tempted to compromise, but also with the vestiges of fallenness within itself, which hamper its progress in holiness.

As is true of all other institutions of society, marriage has not been immune from the ill effects of the fall. Sexuality itself has been cheapened and dehumanized. Love has been lowered to lust, and self-indulgence resists commitment to another. What ws intended to be a blissful lifelong union is horribly disfigured, as all too frequently the home of harmony degenerates into an arena of warfare. And in a world where hardness of heart prevails over the graciousness of love measures become necessary to curb evil and to protect the weak. It was in this situation and for this reason that Moses sanctioned and legislated the granting of divorce; "but"—and this the church must never forget—"from the beginning it was not so" (Matt. 19:8).

The "exceptive clause" in Matthew 5:32 ("every one who divorces his wife, *except on the ground of unchastity,* makes her an adulteress; and whoever marries a divorced woman commits adultery"; cf. 19:9) has been much fussed over in modern times. Some scholars without any evidence dismiss it as a Matthean interpolation because it is not present in the parallel account in Mark's Gospel (10:11–12). Others dislike it because they are predisposed to find a multiplicity of reasons for divorce; so they likewise disallow the authenticity of this single exception. The context of the Marcan passage, to which we have already given some consideration, shows that Jesus was not in favor of indiscriminate divorce. The whole tenor of His teaching emphasizes the basic significance of the one-flesh relationship in the order of creation. Matthew, who reports His words more fully, makes it quite clear that according to the doctrine of Christ there is but one permissible ground for divorce, namely unchastity—sexual promiscuity outside the bond of marriage. This exception, of course, relates to the present fallen state of society, in which unchastity occurs, but not to the order of creation, nor, plainly, to the redemptive order of re-creation, in which there is no place for unchastity.

For the Christian believer there are certain vital considerations to take into account with regard to his (or her) sexuality. (1) Having been redeemed at the infinite cost of Christ's precious blood, he belongs totally to God, body as well as soul; therefore he is not free to do whatever he likes. (2) Being redeemed, he is set apart as holy to God, whose will is his sanctification; that necessarily involves abstention from immorality (see I Thess. 4:3, 7). (3) The Christian believer is indwelt by the Holy Spirit; his body, then, is rightly regarded as a temple of the Holy Spirit that should be kept free from defilement (I Cor. 3:16f.; 6:18f.). (4) He is also a member of the body of Christ, the church, which is to be presented as a pure bride to Him who is her pure Husband, a further compelling reason for sexual chastity. (5) Any adulterous union devastates the one-flesh principle of the marriage bond and desecrates both one's own body as a shrine of the Holy Spirit and that greater body and spiritual temple (see I Peter 2:5) which is Christ's bride.

Such considerations caused St. Paul to admonish certain members of the Corinthian church who irresponsibly asserted that all things were lawful for them, including, as the context shows, sexual intercourse with prostitutes. St. Paul counters by pointing out that "the body is not meant for immorality, but for the Lord, and the Lord for the body" (I Cor. 6:12–13). And then, to show them how monstrous is the idea that any kind of licentiousness is permissible to the Christian, he asks, "Do you not know that your bodies are members of Christ? Shall I therefore take the members of Christ and make them members of a prostitute?" To the apostle this is absolutely unthinkable. "Never!" he exclaims, and then asks further, "Do you not know that he who joins himself to a prostitute becomes one body with her?" Therefore they are urged to shun immorality, especially in view of the fact that "the immoral man sins against his own body"; this for the Christian is nothing other than to sin against the "temple of the Holy Spirit within you." And Paul reminds them forcibly and finally of this truth: "You are not your own; you were bought with a price. So glorify God in your body" (I Cor. 6:15–20).

In the light of this challenging doctrine how can we who are Christians condone the easy availability of divorce which is taken for granted in our contemporary society? How can we fail to deplore the fact that virtually one out of every two marriages in our Western civilization ends in the divorce court? How can we regard with complacency the high divorce rate within the ranks of the Christian church itself? Is it not time that we insisted on the lifelong commitment and sanctity of the matrimonial bond, and especially of *Christian* marriage, which should be a steady witness to God's order of creation and to the new order of re-creation in Christ? Distressed by the ecclesiastical timidity and disorder of his day, Dietrich Bonhoeffer called upon his German church to repent and to make this confession:

> The Church confesses that she has found no word of advice and assistance in the face of the dissolution of all order in the relation between the sexes. She has found no strong and effective answer to the contempt for chastity and to the proclamation of sexual libertinism. All she has achieved has been an occasional expression of moral indignation. She has thus rendered herself guilty of the loss of the purity and soundness of youth. She has failed to proclaim with sufficient emphasis that our bodies belong to the Body of Christ.[8]

Those who are called to positions of ministry and leadership in the church have a clear responsibility to lead exemplary lives in every respect, including sexuality. There is no question about the emphasis placed on this in the apostolic church. St. Paul insists that the bishop/elder "must be above reproach, the husband of one wife" (which does not mean solely that he should be a monogamist instead of a polygamist, but also that he should be faithful to the one-flesh marriage bond), and that "he must manage his own household well . . . ; for if a man does not know how to manage his own household, how can he care for God's church?" (I Tim. 3:4–5; cf. Titus 1:5–9). Similarly, with regard to the office of deacon he enjoins, "Let deacons be married only once, and let them manage their children and their households well" (I Tim. 3:12).

The social situation is, of course, much complicated by the selfish propensities

---

8. Bonhoeffer, *Ethics,* p. 49.

of our fallen human nature and also by the contaminating effect of compromise with worldly standards even in the church. Of the ethical problems that arise very few are so simple that a right judgment can easily be made. Parties that are genuinely innocent are seldom to be found. In the matter of divorce and remarriage, therefore, it is wise for the church to steer a firm and straight course, especially in the clear light of the emphatic biblical teaching regarding the sanctity of marriage and the family and of the solemn vows of lifelong fidelity, "for better or for worse," that belong to the institution of Christian marriage. This means that those who have been divorced and wish to be remarried should be regarded as ineligible for remarriage by the church's ministry—but not that they should be totally excluded or excommunicated from the church's fellowship, as some rigorists demand, if they enter into a new marital union by way of a civil ceremony. In many, perhaps in most, cases some measure of discipline will be desirable; but since the church is entrusted with the ministry of the gospel of grace and is the company of sinners who have been redeemed by grace, there must be room for repentance and forgiveness, and for restoration and acceptance. Thus St. Paul urged the Christians in Corinth to show love and forgiveness to the offender who after being disciplined had repented of serious sins: "So you should rather turn to forgive and comfort him," he wrote, "or he may be overwhelmed by excessive sorrow. So I beg you to reaffirm your love for him" (II Cor. 2:5–6). By taking a firm stand on Christian marriage as a permanent commitment the church will make it plain to the world that the union of man and wife is a matter of the utmost solemnity and that it accepts the teaching of Christ as binding in this as in all other respects.

The teaching we have been considering plainly implies that it is not only unwise but indeed wrong for a Christian to contract a marriage with a person who is an unbeliever. To do so would be to ignore the injunction not to "be mismated with unbelievers" (II Cor. 6:14), which, it is true, is applicable to a considerable number of relationships, but to none more appropriately than the bond of matrimony. St. Paul affirms that "a wife is bound to her husband as long as he lives," but explains that "if the husband dies, she is free to be married to whom she wishes," with the addition, however, of the important proviso, "only in the Lord" (I Cor. 7:39; cf. Rom. 7:2). For her to marry an unbeliever would be mismating. The same principle applies to a widower who remarries. There is another possibility: mismating in this sense may occur during the course of a marriage if one partner converts to the Christian faith while the other continues in unbelief. Such an eventuality does not necessarily lead to the cessation of a happy marriage, even though spiritually there is now an unequal yoke. The apostle counsels that a believing husband or wife should not divorce an unbelieving partner who wishes to maintain the marriage. The faith of the spouse who is now a Christian has a sanctifying effect on home and family: "For the unbelieving husband is consecrated through his wife, and the unbelieving wife is consecrated through her husband. Otherwise your children would be unclean, but as it is they are holy" (I Cor. 7:14). The grace of God experienced by just the one spouse brings the whole family within the sphere of God's covenant of grace. And this opens up a further possibility much to be desired, namely the conversion of the unbelieving spouse: "Think of it: as a wife you may be your husband's salvation; as a husband you may be your wife's salvation" (I Cor. 7:16, NEB). While the believing partner should thus seek to preserve the marriage, a separation should be granted if the unbelieving partner desires it. "For," St. Paul adds, "God has called us to peace" (I Cor. 7:15).

The assertion that "God has called us to peace" would seem to indicate that where there is a serious breakdown of the marriage relationship, even when both partners are believers, and peace has given way to hostility, as in the case of extreme incompatibility, it may be better for the couple to separate rather than to continue what has become an intolerable relationship. But in such a situation there should be no resort to the divorce court nor any intention of entering into a second marriage. In the case of a separation, the only courses of action countenanced by the New Testament are either thereafter to remain single or to effect a reconciliation (I Cor. 7:10–11). Where there are young children, however, it is preferable (not to use a stronger term) that the couple, despite their personal problems, seek grace from God to live peaceably together and find unity in preserving home and family for the sake of the children. This is a responsibility from which they have no right to separate themselves.

Celibacy

In the postapostolic centuries the exaltation of celibacy as a state of superior virtue and the view of the sexual intimacy of marriage as less than virtuous and even defiling led to an unnatural and unbiblical depreciation of sexuality. The procreation of children was widely held to be the sole justification for indulgence in intercourse. Clergy unmarried at the time of their ordination were forbidden to take a wife, while those who had been married before ordination, though not required to put away their wives, were thereafter to abstain from all sexual relations with them. Any man who had married a second time was regarded as ineligible for ordination—even if he had remarried only after the death of his first wife, or was living in continence, or was a widower for the second time. This ruling was based on what seems to be a misinterpretation of the apostolic stipulation that a bishop, priest, or deacon should be the husband of one wife. The uncompromising advocacy of the ascetic life by church fathers such as Tertullian, Cyprian, Ambrose, and Jerome encouraged large numbers of men and women not only to eschew marriage but also to believe that by separating themselves from the world as solitary anchorites or in monastic communities they were treading the high road to heaven. The extravagant manner in which the merit of virginity was extolled inevitably reflected adversely on those Christians who were married and had children. The result was a spirit of elitism in the church which prevailed for many centuries.

Jerome, for example, regards the celibate life as an approximation of angelic existence. In support of this opinion he cites (as others did before him) the saying of Christ that "in the resurrection they neither marry nor are given in marriage, but are like angels" (Matt. 22:30), explaining that "what others will hereafter be in heaven that virgins begin to be on earth," and that "though we rise from the dead in our own sex, we shall not perform the functions of sex."[9] Virginity Jerome likens to building with gold, silver, and precious stones on the one foundation, Christ; marriage to building with wood, hay, and stubble. He explains that the thirtyfold yield from the seed of the Word sown in good soil refers to those in wedlock, the sixtyfold yield to widows, and the hundredfold yield to those who wear the crown of virginity.[10] With respect to the counsel of St. Peter (whose "experience of the bonds of marriage" Jerome no doubt regretted) that husbands are to "give honor to the woman as to the weaker sex" (I Peter 3:7), Jerome advises us that "if we abstain from intercourse we give honor to our wives," but that "if we do not abstain it is clear that insult is the opposite of honor."[11] The virginity of Christ is adduced as the pattern of perfection for Christians, whose duty it is, as St. John writes, to purify themselves even as He is pure (I John 3:2–3; cf. 4:7); Jerome understands this to mean abstention from marriage, and interprets St. Jude's admonition that we should "hate even the garment spotted by the flesh" (Jude 23) to mean the same thing.[12]

When Jerome protests—not too convincingly—that he is not detracting from wedlock by assigning it a position inferior to celibacy, he engagingly points out that were it not for wedlock there would be no virgins, who after all are the offspring of marriage. "I praise wedlock, I praise marriage," he tells Eustochium, "but it is because they give me virgins. I gather the rose from the thorns, the gold from the earth, the pearl from the shell." He affirms that a mother whose daughter is dedicated to virginity has become "the mother-in-law of God"![13] To those who objected that in praising virginity and depreciating marriage he had taken up an extreme position Jerome retorted,

I have dealt much more gently with marriage than most Latin and Greek writers, who, by referring the hundredfold yield to martyrs, the sixtyfold to virgins, and the thirtyfold to widows, show that in their opinion married persons are excluded from the good ground and from the seed of the Father.[14]

Yet it is hard to believe that Jerome had a high view of wedlock when, in defense of his assertion that St. Paul spoke of a man and his wife "coming together" (I Cor. 7:5) because it was something "he blushed to speak of in plainer words," he

9. Jerome, *Against Jovinianus* 1.36.
10. Ibid., 1.3. See I Corinthians 3:10–15; Matthew 13:8, 23.
11. Ibid., 1.7.
12. Ibid., 1.40.
13. Jerome, Letter 22, to Eustochium, 20.
14. Jerome, Letter 48, to Pammachius, 3.

declares that this is the apostle's "modest way of indicating what he does not like to name openly, that is, sexual intercourse"; and when he observes, with reference to St. Paul's counsel that it is better for those who cannot contain themselves to marry than to burn (I Cor. 7:9), that "it is only good to marry because it is bad to burn."[15]

The intense sincerity of Jerome's convictions cannot be doubted, but it is impossible to approve the manner in which he and many others brought special pleading to their interpretation of Scripture and manipulated texts in an arbitrary and unreasonable manner to provide meanings which in most cases they could not sustain. There are certainly men and women in the Christian church for whom it is God's gift and calling to lead a celibate life for the sake of the kingdom of heaven (see Matt. 19:10–12; I Cor. 7:7–8, 25). Such persons are able, in a way that is not possible for those who are married, to fulfill special ministries, perhaps as pioneer missionaries, or as itinerant evangelists, or as servants of the displaced and destitute. Being single and free from the responsibilities of married life, they are in a special sense "anxious about the affairs of the Lord, how to please the Lord" (I Cor. 7:32, 34). For such persons there is always a need, but their calling does not reflect adversely on those who are married or on the measure of the commitment of married persons to the Lord and His service. As we have seen, the Christian home is itself an institution of God which possesses its own special blessing and sanctity.

It would be a mistake to conclude that because of their preoccupation with the worth of virginity the church fathers had no positive and scriptural teaching to give regarding the joys and responsibilities of married life to those who were in the wedded state. Even Tertullian, in the days before he embraced the ascetic extremism of the Montanist sect, spoke highly of the marriage bond:

> How can we adequately describe the happiness of a marriage which the Church binds together, the sacrament confirms, the blessing seals, the angels proclaim, and the Father ratifies? . . . How excellent is the yoke of two believers with one yoke, one discipline, one and the same service! Both are brethren, both fellow servants, there is no separation in spirit or flesh. Together they pray, they bow down, they fast, instructing, exhorting, supporting one another. . . . Together they sing psalms and hymns and challenge one another to sing better for God. When Christ sees and hears such things he rejoices and sends them his peace. Where the two of them are there he is also; and where he is the evil one is not.[16]

Yet the primary purpose of this writing was to commend to his wife (to whom he was apparently happily married) the superior virtues of widowhood and sexual abstinence in the event that he should die before her.

Chrysostom, to take another example, spoke of marriage when commenting on Ephesians 5:33: "The wife is a second authority. Let her not then demand equality, for she is under the head; nor let him despise her as being in subjection, for she is the body; and if the head should despise the body it will also perish." He therefore

15. Ibid., 16–17.
16. Tertullian, *To His Wife* 2.9.

urged the husband to "bring in love as a counterpoise to obedience," and declared that "nothing can be better than this union." Love, indeed, is "the strong tie," he explained, so that the wife, who might seem to be the loser because she is charged to show respect, is the gainer, since the principal duty, love, is charged upon the husband. And yet Chrysostom too, near the conclusion of this admirable homily on the wedded state, affirms that "those who marry thus will be but little inferior to those who live the monastic life, but little below the unmarried."[17]

In spite of their view of marriage as lower than virginity, the patristic writers are unanimous in their insistence on the sanctity of the marriage bond as a lifelong commitment, the solemn responsibilities of parenthood, and the solidarity of the family; they also with one voice condemn heterosexual relations outside of wedlock and all forms of homosexual practice, and also, of course, bestiality.[18] The unequal yoke of a Christian with an unbeliever is also categorically disapproved.

The Breakup of the Family

In Western society today the solidarity of the family as the strong nuclear unit of the community is suffering erosion of the most serious kind. The reasons for this are not difficult to discern. The assault on the concept of marriage as an outmoded and inhibiting convention incompatible with personal freedom is highly congenial to many in the current climate of social "liberation." Easy divorce is another reason for the disintegration of the family. A society in which virtually half of all the marriages now contracted are dissolved in the divorce court can hardly expect its family life to be in a healthy state. The broken home not only disrupts but actually destroys the family. Why should children who have to endure being shuttled between their estranged parents have anything but a distorted and disdainful conception of marriage and family life? Indeed, because of parental remarriages, it is becoming commonplace for children to have to adjust to growing up with two (or more) sets of "parents." In these circumstances it is unrealistic to expect our children to develop any right notion of the meaning of family solidarity and the sacredness of wedlock, or to establish stable marriages for themselves.

Another factor contributing to the disruption of the family is the now-common practice of both parents going out daily to be wage earners. There is no doubt that, with the ever-mounting cost of living and the inflated prices of even the barest necessities, it eases the economic situation considerably for a family to have two weekly paychecks instead of one. But one almost unavoidable consequence is that children return from school to empty houses which cannot fairly be called homes.

17. Chrysostom, *Homilies on the Epistle to the Ephesians* 20.

18. See, for example, the canons of the council held at Elvira in Spain early in the fourth century (C. J. Hefele, *A History of the Christian Councils, from the Original Documents, to the Close of the Council of Nicaea, A.D. 325* [1871], pp. 138ff.); see also Basil of Caesarea's letter 217, to Amphilochius (written in 375), which sets out the canonical penalties for various sexual transgressions (in *Nicene and Post-Nicene Fathers,* 2nd series, ed. H. Wace and P. Schaff, vol. 8, pp. 255ff.).

Instead of finding the loving welcome and care of a mother awaiting them, they are left to fend for themselves. It is hardly surprising that the place where they live does not prove to be for them, as it should be, a center of family unity and security. Predictably such children either drag themselves up as best they can, or they drift off into the company and indulge in the compensating habits (such as drug taking) of other untended children. Without the benefit of and consequently without concern for parental or other authority, it should not be thought strange that these children become rootless and irresponsible members of an increasingly disordered society. To imagine that in due course they will somehow make model parents and citizens and set up stable homes is altogether unreasonable.

The remedy for this aspect of social disorder is simple enough—in theory. The wife and mother should be the homemaker *who is there* as the loving focus of family life. She is, as Stephen Clark affirms, the true heart of the home:

> The wife in the household is the "heart," the "inside center" of the family. She directs a set of family activities essential to the functioning of the family. The husband is the "head." He both directs a set of family functions and is over the wife's activities, but he cannot "keep the body alive" without her.[19]

In practice, however, it is far from easy for parents who have been bringing in a double income to revert or adjust to the position of having just one breadwinner. Yet this is a price that must be paid if the family is to be rescued from the forces that now threaten its survival. And it is a price that should willingly be paid, for it is small in comparison with the cost of allowing our children to grow up in the cold climate of neglect and instability. Double money cannot compensate for the loss of family affection and cohesion. Indeed, there is ample evidence that a family which has to make some sacrifices together is enriched in more important ways and can expect to be bound into a loving and sharing unity unknown in families in which material comforts are given priority over maternal responsibilities.

Family strength benefits the whole community, not only because families, as communities in miniature, provide the cell structure of the social organism and healthy families ensure a healthy society, but also because the proliferation of families in which both parents are wage earners has contributed significantly to the critical rise in unemployment. The number of would-be wage earners now far exceeds the number of jobs available. It has been calculated that in the United States there are between forty and fifty million working women and that a far from small percentage of these women are the mothers of young children. A return to the single-wage-earner principle, at least in the case of families with growing children, would mean the release of millions of jobs and employment openings for the great numbers of young persons who are plagued with the indignity and frustration of unemployment, and thus would help to restore a more equitable

19. Clark, *Man and Woman in Christ*, p. 98.

distribution of jobs and wages. One certainly does not wish to suggest that there is anything wrong or improper about women having jobs and earning salaries. The issue is one of priorities. There are certain things of profound value that money cannot buy and for which material wealth is no substitute, and family strength is one of them.

The leaders of the so-called women's liberation movement insistently demand that women be "liberated" from what has hitherto been regarded as their distinctively womanly role in society as homemakers and bearers and raisers of children. Indeed, the home is denounced as a prison from which woman must be set free. Denying their womanhood, these women desire to be as men, and in doing so they not only despise the very essence of their own being but also overturn the only foundation on which human society can be sanely structured. They subvert the order of creation itself. They view themselves as careerists from whose course the obstacles of motherhood and childbirth must be removed. Marriage, if it is sanctioned, is treated as a two-career arrangement for the purpose of sexual self-gratification, with the result that unions that are childless by design are applauded. George Gilder has aptly commented, with reference to George and Nena O'Neill's best-selling book *Open Marriage,* that "the O'Neills *open* marriage by emptying the womb—and thus empty marriage as well."[20] It is precisely the possession of a womb that is most resented by these strident and strangely misnamed "feminists"; hence the clamor over the woman's "right" to abortion on demand. Pregnancy is disesteemed not merely as an inconvenience but as an indignity which justifies the indiscriminate termination of the new life which has been conceived. A less murderous policy, which, however, does not seem to have been considered by these feminists, would be that of hysterectomy on demand.

Wholesale hysterectomy would, in the ordinary course of events, be the road to self-imposed genocide as well as the ultimate abdication of woman from her distinctively feminine function in the human community. But it would get rid of the embarrassing uterus. A simpler but perhaps somewhat less than infallible procedure would be that of wholesale sterilization. Nor should this be dismissed as a purely fanciful notion, since scientists are busily seeking to devise laboratory techniques for the production of extrauterine test-tube babies—a dreadful misuse of time and talent, because to replace the personal and natural with the impersonal and unnatural can only prove to be disastrous folly. Thus, whether wittingly or not, these scientists are helping to substantiate the hopes of the would-be wombless feminists. But sex without reproduction is subversion of the primary purpose of sex; sex merely for the pleasure of the individual is the perversion of sex to selfish and licentious ends which will soon pall in surfeit and disgust. What is more, by depriving man of the dignity of fatherhood and woman of the joy of motherhood it will deprive both of the fullness of their humanity. Now thoroughly "equalized"—in

20. George F. Gilder, *Sexual Suicide* (1975), p. 62.

theory at least and probably by legislation—men as well as women, insofar as gender is recognized, will be demeaned to the status of "sex objects."

There is a remarkable obtuseness about the feminists of the Western world who profess admiration for the Marxist ideology which disapproves of the family as an outmoded and indeed harmful institution and postulates the complete equality of the sexes; for they seem to be unwilling to admit, let alone to learn from, the fact that the theory has not proved to be workable in practice. In the Soviet Union, for example, where women have been brought out of their homes and given full-time employment in labor and industry, it has become obvious not only that women are constitutionally unfitted for jobs involving hard physical work, but also that the emphasis on women as workers had led to a demographic crisis. Consequently, legislation has recently been enacted which debars women from several hundred occupations now seen to be unsuitable for physical and other reasons. That "the Russians have embarked on a campaign to get women off the factory floor and back into the home" is "an ironic reversal of decades of communistic ideology."[21] The feminists in our midst would be wise to pay attention to this significant development. In any case the great majority of men find that there is a humdrum routine about the jobs in which they are occupied; it must seem surprising to them, if not somewhat zany, that any woman should imagine that such routine is more fulfilling or glamorous than the work of a housewife and mother in the home. One of the main satisfactions that most men derive from their employment is that it enables them to provide for the needs and happiness of their wife and children at home; one of the main pleasures is simply having a home with wife and children to return to daily.

The researches of Margaret Mead led her to the conclusion that a woman experiences contentment and fulfillment above all when she is dedicated to "the female role of wife and mother," not when she is competing, even successfully, in the business of wage-earning.[22] Harold Voth also speaks with authority when he affirms that the mother's role is supreme:

Her contribution to mankind transcends all others in worth and yet her worth is hardly recognized by society. For her to fulfil this highest of all callings to a level of maximal effectiveness, she must be a mature, feminine woman who has a mature, masculine man by her side. Her husband provides the security for her to do her good works; he also meets her needs. Made safe, secure, and herself gratified, she can transmit her life-giving humanness—her spirit and her care, if you will—to her child. This massive infusion of life into the young child is the very basis for the perpetuation of life itself and civilization.[23]

21. Michael Binyon, *The Times* (London), 30 December 1980.
22. Margaret Mead, *Male and Female: A Study of the Sexes in a Changing World* (1949), p. 92.
23. Harold M. Voth, "Women's Liberation, Cause and Consequence of Social Sickness," in *New Oxford Review,* December 1980, p. 10. Dr. Voth is senior psychiatrist and psychoanalyst at the Menninger Foundation and clinical professor in psychiatry at the University of Kansas.

Whatever may happen in the laboratory as methods are devised for test-tube fertilization using ova and spermatozoa selected from banks kept in deep freeze and as artificial wombs are invented for the clinical gestation of resultant embryos outside of the human body, it will still be nonartificial human ova and spermatozoa from which these laboratory babies are produced. We have already warned that inhuman and unnatural manipulations of this kind can be expected to have abnormal and disastrous psychological and biological consequences for the society of mankind. We can but hope that before the current clamor for "unisex" or for the obliteration of all sexual distinction (though always, of course, with the proviso that genital eroticism be retained) hastens our race to perdition, our age may be jolted back to sanity and gain hold again of what Steven Goldberg calls "the central fact," which has persisted throughout all the generations of human history and still remains incontrovertible today—"that men and women are different from each other from the gene to the thought to the act and that emotions that underpin masculinity and femininity, that make reality as experienced by the male eternally different from that experienced by the female, flow from the biological natures of man and woman." For the women's liberationist this is the hated fact, and all the more intensely hated because it is so inexorable. Goldberg continues,

> This is the one fact that the feminist cannot admit. For to admit this would be to admit that the liberation of men and women must proceed along different and complementary lines and that the women of every society have taken the paths they have not because they were forced by men but because they have followed their own imperatives. . . . Women who deny their natures, who accept men's secondhand definitions and covet a state of second-rate manhood, are forever condemned—to paraphrase Ingrid Bengis's wonderful phrase—to argue against their own juices.[24]

Of course, as Gilder has pointed out, "the destruction of female sexuality would mean also the destruction of its male counterpart in all its significant dimensions," with the consequence that "the sexual suicide of the human race would be a *fait accompli*"; he warns, further, that "if we underestimate the danger and fail to act, merely because it is only future generations that will be directly affected, we may by an act of omission commit an act of genocide that dwarfs any in human history."[25] The evidence that abnormal and unloving relations between husband and wife and between parent and child, and homes that are empty or broken, give rise to severe psychological disturbances and to sexual disorientation, especially in children, need not be presented here. Voth affirms that "the current trend in our society away from sexual differentiation and toward unisexism and even outright identity and role reversal reflects these psychological disturbances on a grand scale"—disturbances, he explains, which "are due to the disintegration of the

---

24. Steven Goldberg, *The Inevitability of Patriarchy* (1974), pp. 228–229.
25. Gilder, *Sexual Suicide,* p. 265.

family,"[26] and which, one may add, unless corrected contribute in their turn to and accelerate the disintegrative process.

It is no coincidence that the sexual revolution of our day has been accompanied by the phenomenal growth of pornography into a multibillion-dollar business which is becoming ever more blatant in its publicity. In step with current selfist philosophy, purveyors of this merchandise proclaim the absolute freedom of the individual to achieve self-expression and self-gratification by any and every means, and advocate sexual experimentation in any imaginable way with every kind of partner. These supposedly liberating multisexual adventures, their customers are assured, may take place with members of the opposite sex, with members of the same sex, with animals, or with all together at the same time, and with the aid of specially devised instruments of stimulation. Those entrusted with the responsibilities of government have a duty to provide safeguards not only for the physical but also for the moral hygiene of the community, and they should make it their business to take effective measures to stop the open flow of sensuous sewage before all society is contaminated by its fatal filth.

The amoralism now fashionable has created a climate of complacency and permissiveness which is congenial to the growth of pornography. Even the legislative system, whose *raison d'être* is the definition and enforcement of standards of conduct, has been intimidated by the clamor of the enemies of moral standards who protest (on moral grounds of right and wrong!) that their sacred freedoms are being violated when threatened with restraints, and has shown a strange readiness to acquiesce to their claim that they have the right to print and portray whatever they like. This judicial gullibility indicates that the legal authorities themselves are not immune to the amoralistic virus. The situation is now such that massive public protest is essential if the pounding tide of indecency which is sapping the moral fiber of our civilization is to be driven back. In the United States one of the most bizarre developments is the now customary appeal to the first amendment of the Constitution as a hallowed charter which guarantees the freedom to publish without control, in print and on film, any and every kind of unseemliness. No less shocking is the measure of acceptance with which this appeal has met. How restless must the spirits of the founding fathers be as the freedom of religion they proclaimed is manipulated for the expulsion of Christianity and the enthronement of atheism in public education, and as the freedom of speech they affirmed for the purpose of protecting the expression of diverse political views within a democratic state is perverted into a blessing of the public commerce of dirty books and films!

Homosexuality

The phenomenal proliferation in the numbers of self-proclaimed homosexuals is not attributable simply to the fact that, in contrast to the concealment they had

26. Voth, "Women's Liberation," p. 11.

previously desired, homophiles have been moving out of the shadows and seeking the full light of publicity as a militant self-affirming movement. This has certainly made them visible—and audible—to an unprecedented degree. But the increase in their numbers is as real as it is apparent, and its causes are not difficult to determine. Firstly, the emphasis of popular psychotherapy on the freedom of the individual to find self-fulfillment by any and every means, the repudiation of moral standards or norms—not least in the sphere of sexual relationships—and the encouragement of erotic experimentation in the search for self-gratification as in itself healing and healthy (on the assumption that what pleases you is good for you) have predictably persuaded many to adopt or to try out the practices of "gay" eroticism or to develop sexual ambivalence, indulging themselves without regard to the gender of their partners. Secondly, the widespread display and availability of pornography and films depicting explicit sex and advocating every kind of perversion, with the abuse of young children no less than adults as the objects of sexual incontinence, have inevitably and designedly led to the multiplication of homosexual activities. Thirdly, the very considerable proportion of broken marriages and consequently of one-parent homes is conducive to sexual imbalance in the lives of growing children, for whom the loving and faithful sexual relationship of their parents exercises so important an influence on the development of their own sexual identity and stability. For example, boys who are deprived of their fathers by divorce or desertion, or whose fathers are hypercritical and unaffectionate, are more likely to be responsive to the friendly approaches of pederasts and accordingly vulnerable to corruption at their hands. Thus the breakup of the family in contemporary society contributes indirectly but nonetheless significantly to the increase of homosexuality.

Yet another factor is the general willingness of parents even in happily established households to divest themselves of their responsibility as trainers of their own children. More and more this responsibility is being shifted onto the shoulders of state and educational authorities, who cooperate by their apparent eagerness to arrogate to themselves those prerogatives that belong properly to parents. All too often parents seem to be little or not at all concerned about the things that are taught and the books that are prescribed in the schools their children attend. Regardless of whether they or their parents wish it, vast numbers of American children have become pawns in the hands of political manipulators and social experimenters, as day after day they are arbitrarily transported to be given their schooling in institutions often at a considerable distance from their home territory. This too is disruptive, not only of family authority but also of community spirit. The banishment of God from American education has opened the door for irreligion and humanistic indoctrination in the public schools. The sexual education which is now a part of the school curriculum is notoriously blatant in its anatomical explicitness and frequently illustrated with "factual" films showing, *inter alia,* methods of autoerotic stimulation. There seems to be little regard for modesty and decency, let alone chastity, and little concern to advise students that sexual activity belongs properly to the sacred and loving union of the marriage partnership as a lifelong and exclusive commitment. On the contrary, the detailed instruction on the methods and accessibility of contraception confirms that the emphasis is on how extramarital promiscuity can be made safe. In the amoral climate of contemporary education, for which the unconcern of parents is largely responsible, our children are being taught that concepts of morality and immorality are outmoded and retrogressive. Bonhoeffer's reprimand to the Germans of his day applies no less forcefully to the generation of our day:

> The Church confesses herself guilty of the collapse of parental authority. She offered no resistance to the contempt for age and idolization of youth, for she was afraid of losing youth, and with it the future. As though her future belonged to youth! She has not dared to proclaim the divine authority and dignity of parenthood in the face of the revolution of youth, and in a very earthly way she has tried "to keep up with the young." She has thus rendered herself guilty of the breaking up of countless families, the betrayal of fathers by their children, the self-deification of youth, and the abandonment of youth to the apostasy from Christ.[27]

The militant apologists of the homosexual movement claim that homosexuality belongs to the very constitution of their being, that this is the way they are made, and therefore that their homosexual disposition is perfectly natural for them, even though it may not be for others. This, however, is obviously not the case. It is special pleading of a desperate kind. Biologically, the natural use of the male genitalia in sexual relationships is for the impregnation of the female, whose genitalia are in a complementary manner designed for this use. To practice sodomy is to pervert this natural use into an unnatural misuse. Moreover, the scientific evidence indicates that no person is born a homosexual but becomes such either by choice or by being corrupted by some other person; and, as we have mentioned, psychological developments, especially in childhood, may contribute to the appearance of a homosexual inclination. As we shall see, in the Bible the practice of homosexual acts is condemned as an abomination. In any case, to saddle God or one's genes with the responsibility for one's homosexuality involves the abdication of personal responsibility, and is therefore dehumanizing. As A. W. Steinbeck has observed, "It is difficult to deny anatomy and, in a sense, anatomy is destiny. Man's very first error was to deny a destiny, and to deny the supremacy of mind-brain over body is also to deny destiny."[28]

The present situation has been well summed up by Bennett Sims, the bishop of the Episcopalian diocese of Atlanta:

> A moral offensive has been mounted against a long-cherished moral position. The consensus shaped by the Judeo-Christian tradition has always understood homosexual

27. Bonhoeffer, *Ethics,* pp. 48–49.
28. A. W. Steinbeck, "Of Homosexuality: The Current State of Knowledge," in D. J. Atkinson, *Homosexuals in the Christian Fellowship* (1979), p. 45. See also the case histories and conclusions in Leanne Payne, *The Broken Image* (1981).

orientation and homosexual genital acts as perversions of God's intention. Today this view is being aggressively challenged. A growing body of avowed and practising homosexuals, both within the church and outside it, are pressing for acceptance of homosexuality as normal and healthy. From within the church there are those who demand a radical shift from rejection to affirmation of homosexuality as a part of the creation which God deems good![29]

In October 1977, shortly after Bishop Sims issued this pastoral statement, the House of Bishops of the Episcopal Church sent out a pastoral letter plainly affirming that "it is clear from Scripture that the sexual union of man and woman is God's will and that this finds holy expression within the covenant of marriage"; consequently, "this Church confines its nuptial blessing to the union of male and female" (thus rejecting the claim that the church should be prepared to sanction and solemnize homosexual "marriages"). The letter asserted, further, that ordinands were "publicly required" by the church to fashion their personal lives "after Christ as an example to the faithful," and that "the bishops, therefore, agree to deny ordination to an advocating and/or practising homosexual person." The bishops wisely added that "in each case we must not condone what we believe God wills to redeem." On the same occasion the committee on theology of the House of Bishops drew up a "Statement on the Marriage and Ordination of Homosexuals," which confirms this decision and contains the following declaration:

> The biblical understanding rejects homosexual practice. Heterosexual sex is clearly and repeatedly affirmed as God's will for humanity. The teaching of Jesus about marriage, the teaching of Paul and other biblical writers are unanimous and undeviating in portraying heterosexual love as God's will and therefore good and normative, at the same time keeping in mind our Lord's recognition (cf. Matthew 19:12) that there is also virtue in the celibate life. It is clear from Scripture that heterosexual marriage is unanimously affirmed and that homosexual activity is condemned.

The biblical condemnation of homosexual acts is indeed quite unambiguous. In the Mosaic code, for a man to "lie with a male as with a woman" is forbidden and denounced as "an abomination" (Lev. 18:22; cf. 20:13). This is an outright condemnation of homosexual practice. For advocates of homosexuality to contend either that this condemnation is an outmoded cultic taboo or that it is not homosexuality itself which is condemned but only its practice in association with the idolatrous worship of the surrounding peoples shows an unwillingness to give heed to the biblical teaching on this matter. A moment's consideration of the context shows that it is not only homosexuality that is stringently prohibited, but also incest, adultery, child abuse, and bestiality. If the homosexuals' argument applies to one it must apply to all of these practices, a hardly conceivable possibility.

Defenders of the homosexual way of life have eagerly adopted Sherwin Bailey's reinterpretation of the account in Genesis 19 of the destruction of Sodom and

---

29. Bennett Sims, "Homosexuality: A Pastoral Statement" (1977).

Gomorrah; he postulates that it was not because of homosexual passion (something not even present in the account, it is argued) but because of the inhospitable spirit of the citizens that judgment came upon these cities.[30] But, as Richard Lovelace has remarked, "a simple reading of the Sodom story in Genesis 19 is enough to refute Bailey's thesis that inhospitality was the sole and major sin of the Sodomites"; indeed, "few exegetes who are not themselves homosexuals have adopted his view."[31] That the sin of Sodom was homosexuality has been the solid understanding of both Judaism and Christianity throughout the centuries. It is unreasonable to suppose that a failure of hospitality would suffice to provoke so devastating a divine judgment—a judgment, moreover, which thereafter was seen as an example and warning of the terror of final judgment. Christ Himself warned that "as it was on the day when Lot went out from Sodom" and "fire and brimstone rained from heaven and destroyed them all, so will it be on the day when the Son of man is revealed" (Luke 17:29–30). In the teaching of the New Testament the sin of Sodom is plainly regarded as far more serious than inhospitality. Thus we read in Jude 7 that Sodom and Gomorrah and the surrounding cities "acted immorally and indulged in unnatural lust"[32] and that "they serve as an example of those who suffer the punishment of eternal fire" (NIV; cf. II Peter 2:6). It should be noticed, further, that the wickedness of Sodom was not limited to the incident described in Genesis 19. What took place then was the culmination of their wickedness, a settled course of immoral perversion which preceded the event and brought down upon them the divine visitation. We are informed, accordingly, that the Lord had previously told Abraham that "the outcry against Sodom and Gomorrah is great and their sin is very grave" (Gen. 18:20).

In Romans 1:18–32 ungodliness and sexual viciousness are shown to be related as cause and consequence. Those who willfully and inexcusably suppress the truth of the eternal power and deity of the Creator not only darken their minds with extreme foolishness (vv. 18–23) but also degrade their bodies with sexual abuse. It is "because they exchanged the truth about God for a lie and worshiped and served the creature rather than the Creator" (v. 25), St. Paul explains, that "God gave them up in the lusts of their hearts to impurity, to the dishonoring of their bodies among themselves" (v. 24). Homosexuality is explicitly included among the "dishonorable passions" as a practice that is contrary to nature: "Their women exchanged natural relations for unnatural, and the men likewise gave up natural

---

30. D. Sherwin Bailey, *Homosexuality and the Western Christian Tradition* (1955). For a critical discussion of Bailey's thesis see Richard F. Lovelace, *Homosexuality and the Church* (1978), and Atkinson, *Homosexuals in the Christian Fellowship.*

31. Lovelace, *Homosexuality and the Church,* p. 100.

32. NIV: "gave themselves up to sexual immorality and perversion." A more literal rendering of the Greek text would be, "They practiced gross immorality and went after other [or strange] flesh." This treats the verb *ekporneuein* as an intensive compound; Michael Green suggests that the prefix *ek* may imply "against the course of nature" (*The Second Epistle General of Peter and the General Epistle of Jude* [1968], p. 166).

relations with women and were consumed with passion for one another, men committing shameless acts with men" (vv. 26–27). The fact that considerable numbers of men and women are now insisting that homosexuality is both the natural and even the godly way of life for them does not alter or annul the biblical condemnation of the practice as not only unnatural but also sinful. It is symptomatic of the disregard for holy standards in our modern society. The present easy temper of permissiveness has made possible the flood of pornography and violence which threatens to overwhelm our culture, which is so proud of its sophistication. It has also soothed the consciences of those who demand acceptance as homosexuals and who in this far from minor respect prefer to be conformed to this age rather than transformed by the evangelical renewal of the mind (Rom. 12:2).

A more appropriate description of the contemporary purveyors of pornography and perversion would be difficult to come by than that given by the apostle when he writes of persons who are "filled with all manner of wickedness, evil, covetousness, malice," who are "full of envy, murder, strife, deceit, malignity," and who are "gossips, slanderers, haters of God, insolent, haughty, boastful, inventors of evil, disobedient to parents, foolish, faithless, heartless, ruthless." He adds, in a manner that with incisive accuracy fits those engaged in this multibillion-dollar business, that "though they know God's decree that those who do such things deserve to die, they not only do them but approve those who practice them" (Rom. 1:29–32). The grave sinfulness of the practice of homosexuality explains the solemn warning that St. Paul gives elsewhere: "Do not be deceived," he says; "neither the sexually immoral nor idolaters nor adulterers nor male prostitutes nor homosexual offenders nor thieves nor the greedy nor drunkards nor slanderers nor swindlers will inherit the kingdom of God" (I Cor. 6:9–10, NIV). Similarly, it is asserted that "nothing unclean shall enter [the heavenly city], nor any one who practices abomination or falsehood" (Rev. 21:27). Thus the force of the law, with its prescriptions for right conduct, is felt by "the lawless and disobedient," or, in more specific terms, by "the ungodly and sinners, . . . the unholy and profane, . . . murderers of fathers and murderers of mothers, manslayers, immoral persons, sodomites, kidnappers, liars, perjurers, and whatever else is contrary to sound doctrine" (I Tim. 1:9–10). The plain position of the New Testament is, in short, that homosexuality is contrary to nature, contrary to law, and contrary to sound doctrine.

These passages make clear the sinfulness of homosexuality in three different respects. Firstly, homosexuality is one reprehensible sin in a whole catalogue of reprehensible sins. It cannot be detached or isolated in such a way as to make it an exception which may be condoned, excused, and accepted any more than can murder, adultery, or criminal violence. Secondly, it is as a set and willful practice or way of life that homosexuality is so unambiguously condemned, not as a propensity or inclination. To be strongly tempted or disposed to engage in homosexual activity is not in itself sinful any more than is the temptation to steal or to lie. The sin is in the doing of it, not in the being tempted to do it or anything else that is wrong. Thirdly, the grace of God freely offered through faith in Jesus Christ brings not only forgiveness of homosexual sin and of every other sin but also the power to overcome temptation and to control the urge, so that one's energies can be channeled into the pure service of others and the holy worship of God. The gospel is the dynamic life-transforming source of rebirth into the victorious life of Christ, who makes all things new (II Cor. 5:17; Rev. 21:5). Its liberating power had been gratefully experienced by the members of the church in Corinth, whose number, as we have seen, included former homosexuals as well as adulterers, thieves, and drunkards, who, thanks to divine grace, had found forgiveness for and victory over their sins. Thus St. Paul adds, "And such were some of you. But you were washed, you were sanctified, you were justified in the name of the Lord Jesus Christ and in the Spirit of our God" (I Cor. 6:9–11). The power of the gospel is no less today than it was then.

Abortion

Throughout the Bible there is no suggestion that abortion is an option for women who are pregnant; indeed, abortion is so foreign to the biblical perspective that it is not even mentioned. Quite to the contrary, the fruitful wife enjoys God's favor, and children in the home are seen as a divinely given blessing. (See, for example, Pss. 127–128.) Today the practice of abortion has become an ethical issue of the most serious magnitude. The annual figure of between fifty and sixty million abortions worldwide is staggering. In the United States one in every three pregnancies is terminated in abortion with the blessing of the federal government, which has been spending hundreds of millions of the taxpayers' dollars each year in making abortion readily available to all who demand it. Of all surgical procedures abortion is the one most frequently performed. This has necessarily involved disregard or renunciation of the Hippocratic oath, by which the medical profession has traditionally been committed to the saving, not the destruction, of life. The ethical implications of this change of attitude on the part of many members of what has hitherto been respected as an honorable profession should certainly cause concern. Even if the question whether or not an unborn fetus is a viable person should continue to be debated until doomsday, the indisputable fact remains that it is *human* life—not brutish life, but life that is being formed in the image of its Creator. The embryo that is aborted is a *human* embryo and the blood that is shed is *human* blood. The life of the fetus, moreover, is the life of an individual, and to extinguish that life is to extinguish the life of an individual.

Advocates of abortion on demand have attempted to muddy the issue by contemptuously and not too scrupulously describing the developing fetus as protoplasmic rubbish, a gobbet of meat, a nonhuman mass of tissue, or even marmalade. Feminist oracles clamor that the fetus is a part of the woman's body and that every woman has the absolute right to do whatever she likes with her own body; therefore she may abort the fetus in her womb if it pleases her to do so. The fact is, however, that the fetus within her is growing and being formed as a separate individual with an identity and an existence distinctively his or her own. Has this new human life no rights? And if it is a question of rights, what about the father whose sperm has been a vital contribution to the conception of this new life? Though the new life inherits paternal as well as maternal characteristics, abortion on demand disenfranchises the father. He becomes dispensable; he is regarded merely as the one who has caused the inconvenience of the woman's pregnancy. This is yet another pointer to the low esteem in which many now hold the historic ideals of marriage and the family. Susan Foh has ably summarized the situation:

> Regardless of whether or not the fetus is viewed as a person to be protected by the Constitution, the fetus is definitely not marmalade, rubbish, a gobbet of meat, or part of the woman's body. That the fetus is part of his mother's body has no physiological justification. He has his own unique genetic code, a combination of his mother's and father's genes. He has a separate nervous system and circulation system and his own skeleton, musculature, brain, heart, and other vital organs. The fact that the fetus is not part of the woman's body undermines the feminists' argument; the right to control one's own body does not justify abortion because the fetus is not part of the woman's body. The fetus is deliberately misrepresented in order to justify his extermination.[33]

The indiscriminate destruction of unborn children is a horrifying form of mass carnage and a further example of the inhumanity of the humanistic mind, which presumptuously grasps at being God by arrogating to man the power and the right to give and to take away life—in this case completely defenseless life. Besides, as we have previously observed, the logic which justifies the termination of life before birth can equally be used to justify the termination of life before death—that is to say, before death by natural causes. If, as proabortionists claim, it is good to abort children who are unwanted or who will be mentally or physically disadvantaged, then it is only a small step to the postulation that it is likewise good and desirable to eliminate persons who are mentally retarded or physically handicapped, or who are regarded as social or political misfits, or whose lives are judged to be no longer useful to the community. Euphemistically to call this arbitrary death sentence by the mild name of euthanasia will hardly prove comforting to those who face elimination in this way. It should be obvious that the wholesale practice of abortion, which is now a major method of limiting the number of births, must bear a heavy share of the responsibility for the increasing agedness of society. The resulting imbalance is already creating new problems as society feels the weight of the burden of having to provide support for a disproportionate number of persons who are no longer in a position to support themselves. The granting of the demand for birth control by abortion is predictably intensifying the demand for death control by euthanasia. As always, the wisdom of this age—presuming to be wiser than God—is proving to be foolishness.

33. Susan T. Foh, "Abortion and Women's Lib," in *Thou Shalt Not Kill*, ed. Richard L. Ganz (1978), p. 154.

Until recent times the church has traditionally been of one mind in the condemnation of abortion. Thus in the second century the *Epistle to Diognetus* affirmed that it was not the practice of Christians to abort unborn children;[34] and Athenagoras defined the Christian position by stating that "women who use drugs to bring on abortion commit murder and will have to give an account to God for their action."[35] In the fourth century Basil expressed a similar judgment: "The woman who purposely destroys her unborn child is guilty of murder. With us there is no nice inquiry as to its being formed or unformed."[36] Today, however, humanistic philosophers are to their surprise finding a number of professional theologians who join hands with them in their rejection of all supernaturalism and in their definition of man as a merely naturalistic phenomenon. By insisting that man is a being who has "emerged within the evolution of the forms of life on this earth" and that "the idea of supernatural divine intervention" is "simply incredible" to modern man,[37] these theologians are busily attempting to reduce Christianity to a nature religion akin to the naturalistic paganism from which the leaders of the early church were intent on dissociating Christian faith and practice. As Jeremy Jackson has said, "We may expect to find abortion practised in societies that see man in purely natural terms. The cutting short of human life is not qualitatively different from the thinning of trees or the drowning of kittens."[38]

Because it effects the termination of new human life, abortion cannot be regarded as belonging to the same classification as other operations such as tonsillectomy and appendectomy, which are designed to improve and prolong human life. It is not without good reason that many oppose abortion as an infraction of the sixth commandment. Many who belong to their number contend that there are never any circumstances which justify its practice; but in this fallen and sin-infected world of ours, in which killing is commonly justified (as self-defense or warfare against tyrants), it is difficult not to allow certain exceptions to the rule in the case of abortion, even though it is plain that the wholesale practice of abortion on demand is absolutely wrong because it is destructive of unborn life and disastrous for human society as a whole, not to mention the traumatic consequences it has for the women and girls who experience it. We should certainly be happy that what the Prayer Book described as "the great danger of childbirth"[39] is now very largely a thing of the past; yet there are still emergencies in which the decision has to be made whether to save the life of the mother or of her unborn child. Who is

34. *Epistle to Diognetus* 5.

35. Athenagoras, *Supplication for the Christians* 35.

36. Basil, Letter 188, to Amphilochius; see also Canon 21 of the Council of Ancyra (A.D. 314) and Canon 91 of the Council in Trullo (Quinisext, A.D. 692).

37. *The Myth of God Incarnate*, ed. John Hick (1977), pp. ix, 31.

38. Jeremy C. Jackson, "The Shadow of Death: Abortion in Historical and Contemporary Perspective," in *Thou Shalt Not Kill*, p. 78.

39. See "The Thanksgiving of Women after Childbirth, commonly called the Churching of Women."

prepared to dictate an immutable law by which such cases must be governed? And in cases where it is clear that both the woman and the child she is carrying will cease to live if an abortion is not performed, is it not right to save the mother and lose the child rather than to lose both lives?

There are other occasions which call for compassionate flexibility rather than intractable rigidity. Is abortion to be denied, for example, to a woman who has been brutally raped or to a little girl whose innocence has been devastated through seduction or incest? Or is the horror of their victimization to be prolonged during the months of gestation until it reaches its climax in childbirth? There may be different answers for different cases; to prescribe one answer for every case is surely at least unrealistic. The point is that while abortion is an abhorrent practice which ordinarily should be inadmissible, there will inevitably be some exceptions where, in our fallenness, it is justifiable as the lesser of two evils.

The unprecedented magnitude of the destruction of human life by means of abortion, which has been encouraged by government financing and legislation, has kept step with the development of the permissive society in which sexual promiscuity has been advocated as safe and self-fulfilling and the inconvenience of pregnancy has been readily terminable. Actually, the permissiveness of our day has had the effect of depriving sex of its joy and meaning. Excess has turned pleasure into disgust and incontinence has ended in satiety and confusion. R. F. R. Gardner has pointed out that "the most common problem now is not social taboos on sexual activity or guilt feelings about sex in itself, but the fact that sex for so many people is an empty, mechanical, and vacuous experience."[40] The true meaning and joy of sex can be recovered only by the acceptance once again of the marriage relationship as the sole proper sphere of sexual activity. Promiscuity and infidelity are no less destructive of respect for oneself and for others than of the purpose and power of the marriage bond. There are few forces more disruptive and degrading for society than the mania which treats human bodies as objects to be sexually exploited and then discarded, or the easy attitude which resorts to abortion to avoid the inconvenience of the birth and care of children.

We have seen that procreation is the primary purpose of sexual differentiation and the union of husband and wife; abortion is a rebellious reversal of that purpose and murder of divinely given life. This is a matter on which Bonhoeffer expressed himself very emphatically:

> Marriage involves acknowledgment of the right of life that is to come into being, a right which is not subject to the disposal of the married couple. Unless this right is acknowledged as a matter of principle, marriage ceases to be marriage and becomes a mere liaison. Acknowledgment of this right means making way for the free creative power of God which can cause new life to proceed from this marriage according to his will. Destruction of the embryo in the mother's womb is a violation of the right to live which God has bestowed upon this nascent life.

40. R. F. R. Gardner, *Abortion: The Personal Dilemma* (1972), p. 252.

Consequently Bonhoeffer insists that for this nascent human being to be deliberately deprived of life "is nothing but murder."[41] It is one of the grim absurdities of our time that while medical scientists are busily killing off babies *in utero,* their colleagues are no less busily working at the "creation" of babies *in vitro.*

Chastity

There is also what Gardner calls "the delight of chastity":

> the knowledge that one is keeping something very precious in trust till the great day when, unashamed and in thankfulness, one can give oneself to one's beloved, and have an intimacy which puts one's spouse in a relationship utterly different from all other people.[42]

And chastity means not only purity prior to marriage but also restraint and decency within marriage. Premarital fornication and extramarital adultery are equally excluded. In the biblical perspective chastity is essential to sanctity. "This is the will of God," St. Paul writes, "your sanctification: that each of you know how to take a wife for himself in holiness and honor, not in the passion of lust like heathen who do not know God. . . . For God has not called us for uncleanness, but in holiness" (I Thess. 4:3–7). The power of redeeming grace is such, moreover, that it is able to set free those who have been enslaved to unchastity and to give them victory where before they have suffered defeat. As we have already noticed, some members of the Corinthian church had been adulterers and homosexuals; "but," St. Paul says to them, "you were washed, you were sanctified, you were justified in the name of the Lord Jesus Christ and in the Spirit of our God" (I Cor. 6:11).

Chastity applies, accordingly, to the married as well as to the unmarried state. In marriage chastity requires maintaining the intimacies of conjugal life "in holiness and honor," neither partner denying to the other his or her conjugal rights. Though St. Paul appreciates that the unmarried state has certain advantages for those who wish to give themselves wholly to the service of the Lord, he certainly does not advocate the suppression of sexuality for those who do not have the gift of continence, but counsels that "each man should have his own wife and each woman her own husband." For those who are joined in matrimony he has this clear advice: "Do not refuse one another except perhaps by agreement for a season, that you may devote yourselves to prayer; but then come together again, lest Satan tempt you through lack of self-control" (I Cor. 7:2, 5). In the case of those who are unmarried, chastity requires sexual abstinence and the sublimation of sexuality in self-giving service and creative activity. Sexuality, marriage, and the procreation of children belong to this present life. Hereafter, Christ Himself taught, "when they rise from the dead, they neither marry nor are given in marriage, but are like the angels in heaven" (Mark 12:25), joyfully and without interruption joining in the

41. Bonhoeffer, *Ethics,* pp. 130–131.
42. Gardner, *Abortion,* p. 255.

service, praise, and adoration of the God who has created and redeemed them (Rev. 7:14–17).

A classic example of the power of the gospel to subdue the tyranny of lust and to direct the compulsions of sex into the service of God and one's fellow men is Augustine of Hippo (354–430). In his *Confessions* Augustine describes how as a young man he was deeply distressed over his inability to break free from the bonds of sexual immorality, though he longed to overcome the temptations that led him into the practice of fornication. Yet his inability was compounded by a fundamental unwillingness to give up the passions from which he, paradoxically, wished to be freed. "I beheld and loathed myself," he admitted, "but whither to flee from myself I did not discover." His cry to God for victory was not wholehearted:

> Desperately miserable, I had begged thee for chastity, saying, "Give me chastity and continence, but not yet!" For I was afraid lest hearing me thou shouldest soon deliver me from the disease of lust, which I desired to have satisfied rather than extinguished.

Still, however, "the chaste dignity of continence" beckoned him on, "extending her holy arms, full of a multitude of good examples, to receive and embrace" him, for he knew, from the witness of many, that continence was "not barren, but a fruitful mother of joys by thee, O Lord, her Husband." Finally, in his thirty-second year, the turning point came as he cried to heaven, "How long? How long must it be tomorrow, always tomorrow? Why not now? Why is there not this hour an end to my uncleanness?" And then, taking up and opening a New Testament, he read the words, "Not in reveling and drunkenness, not in debauchery and licentiousness, not in quarreling and jealousy. But put on the Lord Jesus Christ, and make no provision for the flesh, to gratify its desires" (Rom. 13:13–14). It was at this moment, Augustine gratefully acknowledged to God, that "thou didst deliver me out of the bonds of carnal desire with which I was most firmly fettered."[43] And this is still the liberating power of the evangelical message. The Christian gospel is the gateway to the Christian ethic of chastity and holy living.

43. Augustine, *Confessions* 8.6ff.

9

The Christian and the State

The Origin of Civil Government

Governmental authority, in one form or another, is and always has been a universal phenomenon. Every nation however large, or tribe however small, is governed by rulers or heads whose assigned duty is to preserve order and maintain justice in the society of which they themselves are a part. To facilitate the exercise of this authority, and to clarify and define its scope, specific laws and regulations are ordinarily approved and accepted as binding by the community as a whole. This universal "instinct" or innate recognition of the necessity of government belongs to and is a manifestation of the image of God in which man has been created. It is, in its origin, an extension or mediation of the authority of the Creator through His creature man. Thus man at his creation was entrusted with the mandate to have dominion over the earth (Gen. 1:26, 28)—to govern the earth in accordance with the will and purpose of its Creator. Subsequently the psalmist extolled the wisdom and power of God in doing so: "Thou hast given him dominion over the works of thy hands; thou hast put all things under his feet" (Ps. 8:6). Man, then, because of his constitution in the image of God is a governing being.

Even though in his fallenness man denies and perverts the divine image in which he was made, he does not—nor can he—cease to be what he constitutionally is. By the fall, however, the situation is drastically altered: man no longer governs to the glory of God and out of love for the divine will but to the glory of himself and out of love for his own creaturely will. Inevitably his rejection of the order and authority of God has plunged man and the world over which he was placed into disorder and disintegration. Man, whose blessedness consisted in being governed by God and in governing under God, has severed the line of authority leading from God through man to the rest of creation. The order of his existence has been radically disrupted and he has reaped a bitter harvest of disorder. It is tragic that man, created to govern, now has to be governed in some way by the fellows of his fallenness if all is not to degenerate into catastrophic chaos. The governing of fallen society by fallen men is a consequence of the fall itself, but at the same time it bears witness to that image in which man was created. Man has not ceased to be a governing creature. His scientific and technological achievements testify to the dominion with which he is constitutionally endowed. His abuse of these achievements for the destruction of his fellow men, his greedy exploitation of the earth's resources, and his selfish polluting of the life-sustaining environment testify to his fallenness. They attest also the need for man, who was made to govern, to be governed.

In no way, of course, does human disorder diminish or nullify the supreme rule and authority of God. As the Creator of all things, God is the sovereign Lord over the whole of His creation, and therefore over all mankind. The order which He decreed will not fail in His own good time to be established. Meanwhile His sovereignty remains unrestricted (otherwise God would not be God): its efficacy is not limited to God-fearing persons who willingly acknowledge it; it extends no less powerfully over those who rebel against it. The revolt of man totally fails to dissolve the rule of God over him. God who is the Creator and the Redeemer is also the righteous Judge of the whole world. The biblical emphasis is unmistakable: "Dominion belongs to the Lord, and he rules over the nations" (Ps. 22:28); "All the nations are as nothing before him" (Isa. 40:17); "So each of us shall give account of himself to God" (Rom. 14:12). The rhetorical address of King Jehoshaphat of Judah plainly expresses this recognition of the absolute lordship of almighty God: "O Lord, God of our fathers, art thou not God in heaven? Dost thou not rule over all the kingdoms of the nations? In thy hand are power and might, so that none is able to withstand thee" (II Chron. 20:6). Moreover, it is by the divine wisdom that "kings reign, and rulers decree what is just," and that "princes rule, and nobles govern the earth" (Prov. 8:15–16).

Human government is thus seen to be under the control of God, who is the supreme Governor. Human justice reflects the righteousness of God Himself. Indeed, government and justice are a necessity for the restraint of the injustice and disorder to which our fallenness gives rise. Human sinfulness must be contained within certain limits for the preservation of civic and communal life; therefore courts of justice and police forces are instituted as instruments for enforcing the law of the land. Even sporting contests are subject to clearly defined rules and penalties. It would hardly be a sign of divine love and care if sin were allowed to flourish unchecked, for then human society would rapidly lapse into such degradation that to be born into it would be an intolerable calamity. The authority of the state and the rule of law accordingly should be regarded as aids to our welfare, not as powers hostile to our freedom. Designed for the restraint of evil, government is not in itself evil.

The law consciousness which is implanted in the heart of every man (cf. Rom. 2:12–16), and which is essential to the realization of human dignity and responsibility, explains the existence of government as a universal phenomenon. Scripture teaches and experience confirms that there is no class or nation of mankind incapable of setting up and maintaining a state which is founded on the principles of justice and order. Everywhere, indeed, the state with its laws is a manifestation of the common or universal grace of God (as distinct from special or redeeming grace). It is universally acknowledged that the proper and necessary function of government is to promote good citizenship and to restrain those who disrupt the peace of the community. Governmental control and mutual responsibility cooperate to foster beneficial relationships at every level of human existence, not merely between statesmen and citizens, but also between employers and workers, husbands and wives, and parents and children. Thus government serves to bring dignity, decency, and equity to every normal association of persons within the state or nation. Understanding this we can all the better appreciate the frequent apostolic injunctions that citizens should honor the emperor and obey magistrates, that masters should be considerate to servants and servants diligent to please their masters, that parents should give care to the upbringing of their children, and that children should be respectful and obedient to their parents.

The responsibilities of citizenship extend, of course, to those who are in positions of governmental authority, for they too are citizens of the state and members of the nation. Their high office does not abolish their own answerability. On the contrary, their personal conduct should exemplify the standards they demand, for they too must, as fellow citizens, be bound by the laws they impose. When, moreover, it is remembered that the justice they administer is intended to reflect the justice of God Himself, it is plain that their responsibility is all the more solemn. Just as God, the supreme Judge, is no respecter of persons (Acts 10:34; Rom. 2:11; Eph. 6:9; Col. 3:25) and is Himself absolutely righteous, so too those who exercise governmental authority on earth are required to display impartiality towards all without exception—otherwise they show themselves to be betrayers of the power entrusted to them and despisers of the law they administer. Thus the judges of Moses' time were solemnly charged, "You shall not be partial in judgment; you shall hear the small and the great alike; you shall not be afraid of the face of man, *for the judgment is God's"* (Deut. 1:17). And at a later period Jehoshaphat admonished the judges he appointed: "Consider what you do, *for you judge not for man but for the Lord; he is with you in giving judgment.* Now then, let the fear of the Lord be upon you; take heed what you do, for there is no perversion of justice with the Lord our God, or partiality, or taking of bribes" (II Chron. 19:6–7). In short, the judge or ruler is dignified as the minister of God's judgment, and in the fallenness of human society universal justice continues to be the divinely ordained standard of government.

It follows that good and responsible citizenship should characterize the behavior of the Christian, who himself is the recipient of the love and justice of God's redeeming grace and whose life, consequently, should be a manifestation of love and justice to others. Living now under the supreme goodness of God's sovereignty, the Christian deplores evil, but he does not take the law into his own hands or seek to meet evil with evil. Indeed, the love by which he is now animated must embrace and care for even his enemies, for thus he manifests the power of good to triumph over evil. This is precisely the teaching of Christ as summarized by St. Paul:

Let love be genuine; hate what is evil, hold fast to what is good. . . . Never flag in zeal, be aglow with the Spirit, serve the Lord. Rejoice in your hope, be patient in tribulation, be constant in prayer. . . . Bless those who persecute you; bless and do not curse them. . . . Live in harmony with one another; do not be haughty, but associate with the lowly; never be conceited. Repay no one evil for evil, but take thought for what is noble in the sight of all. If possible, so far as it depends on you, live peaceably with all. Beloved, never avenge yourselves, but leave it to the wrath of God; for it is written, "Vengeance is mine, I will repay, says the Lord." No, "if your enemy is hungry, feed him; if he is thirsty, give him drink. . . ." Do not be overcome by evil, but overcome evil with good (Rom. 12:9–21).

This instruction provides the immediate background for St. Paul's exposition of the Christian understanding of the state and its authority.

Although it is true that Christians through the grace of the gospel have found freedom in Christ and now serve Him as Lord ("whose service is perfect freedom"), and that their citizenship is in heaven where Christ is gloriously enthroned (Phil. 3:20), yet Christ and His apostles clearly teach that Christians are to submit dutifully to those who exercise authority in this world. The reason for this is that, pending the appearance of Christ whose coming in glory they await (Phil. 3:20 again), Christians continue to be citizens of this world, or, more specifically, of particular states and nations of this world, and accordingly are still under the obligations imposed by this citizenship. Theirs is a dual citizenship: on the one hand, the temporal and passing citizenship of the present age; on the other, the abiding citizenship of the coming eternal age. The present time, in fact, is also the meantime: in this life Christians have not yet arrived at the goal on which their hope is fixed. But while concerned to be a good citizen here and now in the meantime, the Christian is also constantly aware that it is to God, the absolute authority and the source of all human authority, that he owes his primary allegiance; therefore if the authorities of the present age, whether civil or ecclesiastical, should demand of him anything that is plainly contrary to the Word and will of God he, like the apostles, must say, "We must obey God rather than men" (Acts 5:29; it is worthy of note that this response was in the first instance spoken to *religious* authorities).

Even so, these temporary authorities, fallen and fallible though they be, exist under God as instruments of common grace which operate for the general benefit of human society. They must not be dismissed by the Christian as ungodly powers which have no claim upon him. He may no longer be *of* this world, but he is still *in* it and shares in the responsibilities that belong to the community of mankind. Hence St. Paul's admonition to the members of the Roman church: "Let every person be subject to the governing authorities" (Rom. 13:1). This, presumably, was no easy lesson for them to learn, located as they were in the city which was the seat and center of the totally pagan Roman imperialism. But there were good reasons for this admonition.

1. "There is no authority except from God, and those that exist have been

instituted by God" (Rom. 13:1). Even pagan authority is authority derived ultimately from God in the very order of creation. Man could not exercise authority were the faculty to do so not God-given. Any perversion of authority is the perversion of God-given authority. Furthermore, it is due to the goodness of God's providence that, despite the fallenness of mankind, all authority is not perverted authority. As already observed, the power of civil government is one of God's means of curbing evil in our world and holding the human race back from total corruption.

2. "Therefore he who resists the authorities resists what God has appointed, and those who resist will incur judgment" (Rom. 13:2). To be irresponsible as a citizen, to rebel against government, is to rebel against authority derived from God and deservedly to have one's recalcitrance met with punishment. The Christian should always be concerned for the preservation of the due order of society.

3. The civil ruler is God's servant or minister. The purpose of government is to promote good order and contentment in the community, to maintain national harmony and productivity, and to remove, or at least restrain, whatever is harmful to social prosperity. Even a tyrant prefers his subjects to be well ordered, industrious, and governed with a show of justice, for apart from these conditions his position becomes insecure. "Rulers," St. Paul says, "are not a terror to good conduct, but to bad. Would you have no fear of him who is in authority? Then do what is good and you will receive his approval, for *he is God's servant* for your good. But if you do wrong, be afraid, for he does not bear the sword in vain; *he is the servant of God* to execute his wrath on the wrong-doer" (Rom. 13:3–4).

4. Respect for the governing authorities, moreover, is a matter of *conscience.* The Christian knows within himself that as a citizen he has obligations to the state whose authority comes from God and whose concern for order and equity in society is evidence of God's continuing care for His creation. The operation of the state in administering justice, punishing crime, and promoting the commonweal legitimates the taxation of citizens so that resources may be available for the carrying out of such purposes. Thus St. Paul instructs the Roman Christians that "one must be subject, not only to avoid God's wrath but also *for the sake of conscience";* he then adds: "For the same reason you also pay taxes, for *the authorities are ministers of God,* attending to this very thing. Pay all of them their dues, taxes to whom taxes are due, revenue to whom revenue is due, respect to whom respect is due, honor to whom honor is due" (Rom. 13:5–7). This accords fully with the famous saying of Christ that we are to "render to Caesar the things that are Caesar's, and to God the things that are God's" (Mark 12:17). The profound significance of this brief saying should not be missed, for it indicates not only that there is a sphere that rightly belongs to Caesar but also that Caesar is not God and therefore must not be respected as though he were God.

The Christian, then, should be an example of good citizenship, "submissive to rulers and authorities, . . . obedient, . . . ready for any honest work" (Titus 3:1). Likewise St. Peter's scattered readers are exhorted:

Maintain good conduct among the nations, so that in case they speak evil against you as wrongdoers, they may see your good deeds and glorify God on the day of visitation. Be subject for the Lord's sake to every human institution, whether it be to the emperor as supreme, or to governors as sent by him to punish those who do wrong and to praise those who do right. For it is God's will that by doing right you should put to silence the ignorance of foolish men. Live as free men, yet without using your freedom as a pretext for evil; but *live as servants of God.* Honor all men. Love the brotherhood. Fear God. Honor the emperor (I Peter 2:12–17).

Once again it is plain that God and the emperor are distinct and not to be confused. Our primary duty is ever to "live as servants of God." The emperor is to be honored because in his own sphere he is a minister of God. This inevitably implies that supreme authority belongs to God alone.

A further consideration is that a well-ordered state, to whose order Christians should contribute by their own good conduct, is conducive to the stability of the church and the spread of the gospel. We should therefore pray for those who are vested with authority. St. Paul accordingly urges Timothy "that supplications, prayers, intercessions, and thanksgivings be made for all men, for kings and for all who are in high positions, that we may lead a quiet and peaceable life, godly and respectful in every way"; and he explains that "this is good, and it is acceptable in the sight of God our Savior, who desires all men to be saved and to come to the knowledge of the truth" (I Tim. 2:1–4).

Perhaps, however, it may be objected that the church as the recipient of special grace is in a unique and privileged position. Has not the grace of God set her free from the demands of the law? Is it not the kingdom *of God,* rather than the kingdom of man, that is her concern? To this it should be sufficient to reply that the apostolic injunctions we have cited are addressed specifically to the church. It may indeed be said that, unlike unbelievers who rebel against the rule of God, Christians have a love of God's law, which no longer confronts them menacingly from without, but is now, in fulfillment of the promises of the new covenant, imprinted inwardly in their hearts (Jer. 31:33; Ezek. 11:19). Thus they should not only be eager to promote justice and honor in the state but also should show themselves to be the most law-abiding of all citizens.

The Christian in a Pagan State

But, it will be asked, what should be the attitude of the Christian church when it is placed under the rule of an oppressive tyrant or a pagan government which has no liking for the work and witness of the church? It should be clearly understood, to begin with, that godless governments in no way nullify or diminish the supreme sovereignty of almighty God; nor by opposing God's will are they able to hinder the achievement of what He purposes. Scripture, indeed, sees pagan and heathen states as actually advancing God's purposes, albeit unconsciously and unwillingly. They may be instruments of divine judgment, as when the unfaithful Israelites are told, "Because you did not serve the Lord your God with joyfulness and gladness of heart . . . therefore . . . the Lord will bring a nation against you from afar" (Deut. 28:47–49), and when for the same reason Assyria is called "the rod of [God's] anger" and "the staff of [his] fury" (Isa. 10:5). Cyrus, the Persian monarch, is even described as God's "shepherd" and "anointed," because he is an instrument, though unwittingly, under the divine control (Isa. 44:28; 45:1; cf. Prov. 21:1; Hos. 13:11). Nebuchadnezzar, the Babylonian king, is designated "God's servant" on the occasion when God declares through His prophet, "It is I who by my great power and my outstretched arm have made the earth, with the men and animals that are on the earth, and I give it to whomever it seems right to me" (Jer. 27:5; cf. Ezek 29:19–20). In the Book of Daniel God is praised as the One who "removes kings and sets up kings," and Nebuchadnezzar, whose dream of the great image is interpreted as a prediction of a sequence of powerful kingdoms, is brought to the realization that "the Most High rules the kingdom of men, and gives it to whom he will" (Dan. 2:21, 36–45; 4:17; 5:21).

This teaching is emphatically confirmed by Jesus who, when Pontius Pilate asked Him, "Do you not know that I have power to release you, and power to crucify you?" replied, "You would have no power over me unless it had been given you from above" (John 19:10–11). Even the most wicked deeds of men do not in any way incapacitate God in the exercise of His supreme authority; on the contrary, though they do not know it and certainly do not intend it, their wickedness is actually overruled for the advancement of the divine purposes. The most notable example of this is the condemnation and crucifixion of Jesus, which, while the most sinful of deeds, was used by God to fulfill His plan for our redemption. This consideration does not make the deed any less sinful and reprehensible, but it shows the futility of rebellion against God and demonstrates how even the wrath of man is turned to the praise of God (Ps. 76:10). It also explains the apostolic perception that the evil done to Jesus was "in accordance with the definite plan and foreknowledge of God," and that Psalm 2 (the raging of nations, peoples, kings, and rulers "against the Lord and his anointed") was remarkably fulfilled when, in an unrighteous alliance, Herod, Pontius Pilate, the Gentiles, and the peoples of Israel "gathered together" to do, not by their will but by God's, "whatever [God's] hand and [his] plan had predestined to take place" (Acts 2:23; 4:24–28). And so it was their will that was nullified and the divine will that prevailed, for the purpose of the coming of the Good Shepherd was precisely to lay down His life for the sheep: His coming was a manifestation of His power, and not only His rising from the dead but also His dying itself was the exercise of that power. Hence His declaration: "I lay down my life, that I may take it again. No one takes it from me, but I lay it down of my own accord. I have power to lay it down, and I have power to take it again" (John 10:17–18; cf. 10:11).

We see, then, that Scripture has a high view of the authority of the state, while at the same time it presents that authority as itself coming under the supremely sovereign authority of God, the Creator and Ruler of all. The Christian who is placed under a government which is antipathetic to the gospel should remember that the civic environment in which Christ Himself and His disciples lived and witnessed was essentially hostile to them and that the New Testament doctrine of the state and its authority was propounded under the pagan rule of imperial Rome. As the early history of the church shows, this government readily oscillated between toleration and persecution of the Christian faith. Yet, despite the state's non-Christian character, members of the church accepted the responsibilities of citizenship with all seriousness. They obeyed the duly appointed magistrates, they paid taxes, they honored and prayed for the emperor. It would, however, be wrong to conclude that they always concurred with the attitude or the decrees of the government. As a Roman citizen, St. Paul on occasion complained when his rights were being violated, and exercised his privilege of appealing his case to the emperor (see Acts 16:35–40; 22:22–29; 25:8–12). And in the event that the state ordered the public denial of the lordship of Christ, the Christian's citizenship in heaven took precedence over his citizenship in this world and he followed the way of civil disobedience—but always with the understanding that, since he was still under the authority of the secular power, he had to be prepared to submit to the punishment imposed by the state for his disobedience, knowing that this frequently meant flogging, imprisonment, and even death. Hence the history of the Christian martyrs, who chose to deny the lordship of Caesar and die rather than deny the lordship of Christ.

The ethical responsibilities of the Christian in a hostile state are not fulfilled by passive citizenship. Even though he may to a greater or lesser degree be a suffering citizen, he still should regard himself as having a positive contribution to make. His is a voice to be raised for the promotion of truth and the denunciation of error and injustice. In this manner he learns the costliness of discipleship, but he also enters into the blessing that Christ promised when He said, "Blessed are you when men revile you and persecute you and utter all kinds of evil against you falsely on my account" (Matt. 5:11). The qualification is important: suffering for its own sake is of no account; the only suffering that can rightly be described as Christian suffering is suffering on Christ's account, not for one's own sake but for His sake. Punishment, moreover, must be undeserved in that the Christian citizen should be a good citizen who is innocent of criminal offense. In other words, the Christian citizen when he is persecuted because of the faith he professes should follow the example of Christ who, falsely accused and unjustly condemned, "when he was reviled . . . did not revile in return; when he suffered . . . did not threaten; but trusted to him who judges justly" (I Peter 2:23). The One of whom this is written spent His life blamelessly before God and man, doing good, speaking the truth, and proclaiming the kingdom of heaven.

Nor did Jesus forbear to speak out against error and falsehood. His most vehement censures were pronounced against the hypocrisy, the casuistry, and the superstition of the scribes and Pharisees, whom He called "blind fools," "blind guides," "whitewashed tombs," "serpents," and a "brood of vipers" (Matt. 23:17

24, 27, 33), simply because He could not overlook the way in which they were smothering God's Word with their traditions and leading the populace to perdition. Herod, who was planning His death, He described as "that fox" (Luke 13:32). But His righteous anger arose from a heart of compassion, as His lament over Jerusalem and its inhabitants, recorded in these same passages, so dramatically reveals (Matt. 23:37–38; Luke 13:34). It was concern for the holiness of God and for true spiritual worship that stirred Him to take a whip to those whose greed caused them to desecrate the house of God (John 2:13–16). So also the Christian citizen has a duty to denounce what is wrong, not for his own sake, but for the benefit of others, compassionately and in the name of Christ who gave Himself to redeem the world.

A notable example of the dual citizenship of which we have spoken is provided in the case of Daniel, whose enemies, unable to find any fault or ground for complaint in him with respect to the laws of the state, plotted his destruction by devising a decree requiring every citizen to worship no god except Darius the Persian king. Daniel, though a faithful minister of this heathen king, and knowing that the penalty for disobedience to this decree was to be cast to the lions, opened wide the windows of his house and in the sight of all "got down upon his knees three times a day and prayed and gave thanks before his God, as he had done previously" (Dan. 6:10). As Jesus would later say to Satan, citing the words of Holy Scripture, Daniel said in effect to the world in his day, "You shall worship the Lord your God and him only shall you serve" (Matt. 4:10; Deut. 6:13). So also the apostles Peter and John said to those who threatened them with dire consequences if they did not cease to speak and teach in the name of Jesus: "Whether it is right in the sight of God to listen to you rather than to God, you must judge; for we cannot but speak of what we have seen and heard" (Acts 4:19–20).

In point of fact, the concept of a Christian state is not found in the pages of the New Testament. No doubt rulers and magistrates who themselves are governed by Christian principles are much to be desired and should be accounted a blessing in the life of a nation, but the official Christianization of a country or an empire creates problems of its own in this fallen world of ours. It is sufficient to recall that when, following the conversion of Constantine in the fourth century, Christianity became the imperially approved religion, great numbers of people who were seeking their own advantage hurried to join the Christian ranks without knowing or caring what the distinctive demands of the gospel were. A numerical increase of this kind could hardly lead to anything other than an increase in shallowness and hypocrisy within the church. A genuinely Christian state can be a reality only if all its citizens are genuinely Christian believers. This reality will come to pass, but only hereafter with the setting up of God's eternal kingdom of love and righteousness whose populace will be composed entirely of those who have been redeemed and brought to glory by the grace of almighty God. Meanwhile even the best kingdoms of this age will have a large admixture of spiritual superficiality and ungodliness, and the best the church can hope for is a government that is impartially administered and that grants to Christians the freedom to worship and to evangelize. There is, however, no reason to think that Christ's true followers will at any time be free from hostility and misunderstanding on the part of those who have no sympathy for the faith they profess. Christians, therefore, should heed the wise counsel of St. Peter concerning the manner in which they should conduct themselves as citizens in the present age:

> Beloved, do not be surprised at the fiery ordeal which comes upon you to prove you, as though something strange were happening to you. But rejoice in so far as you share Christ's sufferings, that you may also rejoice and be glad when his glory is revealed. If you are reproached for the name of Christ, you are blessed, because the spirit of glory and of God rests upon you. But let none of you suffer as a murderer, or a thief, or a wrongdoer, or a mischief-maker; yet if one suffers as a Christian, let him not be ashamed, but under that name let him glorify God. . . . Therefore let those who suffer according to God's will do right and entrust their souls to a faithful Creator (I Peter 4:12–16, 19).

Christian believers in every age, including our own, have unhesitatingly chosen "the fiery ordeal" of persecution at those times when the will of the state has been in conflict with the will of God. For instance, Polycarp, the aged bishop of Smyrna, when urged by the Roman proconsul to gain his freedom by reviling Christ, replied, "I have been his servant for eighty-six years and he has done me no wrong. How then can I blaspheme my King who saved me?" On being threatened with burning he told the proconsul, "You threaten that fire which burns for a season and after a little while is quenched; for you are ignorant of the fire of the future judgment and eternal punishment, which is reserved for the ungodly." It is recorded, further, that after being bound to the stake Polycarp raised his eyes heavenward and said,

> O Lord God Almighty, the Father of thy beloved and blessed Son Jesus Christ, through whom we have received the knowledge of thee, the God of angels and powers and of all creation and of the whole race of the righteous, who live in thy presence; I bless thee for that thou hast granted me this day and hour, that I might receive a portion amongst the number of martyrs in the cup of thy Christ unto resurrection of eternal life, both of soul and of body, in the incorruptibility of the Holy Spirit. May I be received among these in thy presence this day, as a rich and acceptable sacrifice. . . . For this cause, yea and for all things, I praise thee, I bless thee, I glorify thee, through the eternal and heavenly High Priest Jesus Christ, thy beloved Son, through whom with him and the Holy Spirit be glory to thee both now and evermore. Amen.[1]

The Christian, of course, does not have to wait for the day of persecution to remind the state authorities that they derive their power from God and are themselves ultimately answerable to God. The church, which is the community of believers, has a civic obligation to encourage governments in the way of justice and

---

1. *Letter of the Smyrnaeans on the Martyrdom of Polycarp* 9, 11, 14. The translation is mainly J. B. Lightfoot's. Polycarp was martyred c. A.D. 155.

ethical responsibility, and thus to stimulate and render sensitive the conscience of the state. As citizens, moreover, Christians should be attentive to the calling, where circumstances make this possible, to influence the course of events, not merely as good citizens, but also as parliamentarians and as members of local government. William Wilberforce's decision to enter Parliament rather than seek holy orders was largely due to the persuasion of John Newton, who discerned his outstanding gifts and qualifications for leadership in government. The effectiveness of Wilberforce's impassioned campaigning for the abolition of slavery needs no elaboration here. There is always necessity for the Christian to exercise his citizenship seriously, in action as well as in word, for the benefit of society and the affirmation of justice and dignity for all.

The Atheistic State

Quite distinct from the religiously neutral state of paganism and the well-disposed (perhaps even nominally Christian) state is the atheistic or antitheistic state as depicted in Revelation 13, where St. John describes his vision of the tyrant or beast arising from the sea, bearing a blasphemous name, and wielding quasi-omnipotent authority that is derived from the dragon which represents Satan. The apostle sees the worship of men being offered to the dragon and the beast, and he hears blasphemies being uttered against God by the beast as he makes war on the saints and as his power, quasi-omnipresent as well as quasi-omnipotent, extends over all the peoples of the earth. Another beast is then observed, arising out of the earth and with two horns like a lamb, that is, like a quasi-redeemer: however, he speaks like the dragon and exerts all the authority of the first beast as he makes the earth's inhabitants worship the first beast and deceives them by the marvelous signs he performs. Moreover, all are forced to bear the mark of the beast on their hands and foreheads or else to be outcasts from society. The number of the beast is a trinitarian number, 666—in other words, a mocking parody of the Holy Trinity, for this anti-God figure is at the same time a would-be god, though in fact, of course, a "no-god." (Six, the number of man, falls short of seven, the number of divine perfection; 666 thus represents a humanistic trinity.)

This vision, then, portrays a state of anti-God totalitarianism which is essentially a fusion of politics and religion, for antitheism is no less radically religious than theism: man, the worshiping creature, worships either the true God or the humanistic substitute for the true God. The mark of the beast is the attempt of Satan to obliterate the image of God which is constitutive of man's being. In such a state the Christian, no matter how well behaved, cannot be a good citizen, since the profession of faith in Christ and the worship of God as his Creator and Redeemer have been made a capital offense and the unpardonable crime. Atheistic totalitarianism deprives Christians not only of freedom of worship and the right to bring up their children in the Christian faith but also of political power. The very fact that they are followers of Christ brands them as criminals who are fittingly confined in prisons and concentration camps or as unbalanced nonconformists who should be immured in madhouses or subjected to "remedial" treatment in psychiatric hospitals. To the authorities of such a state those who profess the Christian faith can but say, "God whom we serve is able to deliver us . . . out of your hand. . . . But if not, be it known to you . . . that we will not serve your gods or worship the golden image which you have set up" (cf. Dan. 3:17–18).

The vicious brutality of the totalitarian state is vented on all who are categorized as religiously, ethnically, or academically incompatible with the system, and also on any who are imagined to pose a threat as potential rivals to those who have seized power. The present-day tyranny of atheistic communism in Russia and China and other countries has been responsible for the "elimination" of scores of millions of inoffensive citizens. The horrifying facts of such ruthless extermination are well documented and attested. Yet the ideology these governments profess claims to be designed for the removal of inequity and injustice from society! The state that has become the destroyer of its citizens rather than their protector is manifestly branded with the diabolical stamp. The question then arises whether the Christian has not a duty *as a citizen* to do as far as he may be able what the state is failing to do.

Must not the Christian citizen, and for that matter any citizen who is conscientiously concerned about the dignity and the sanctity of human life and the rights of inoffensive persons, be prepared to take action for the purpose of protecting those whom a tyrannical government is intend on destroying? Who will argue that those who courageously provided sustenance and a secret hiding place in their homes for Jewish citizens in defiance of Hitler's decree for their "liquidation" were not acting laudably and responsibly? But then does not this same line of logic lead even further to the justification of taking action to rescue the state and its citizenry as a whole from the annihilating power of totalitarian tyranny? Just as in self-defense or in defense of another person it is permissible to strike down an attacker, is it not possible that a crisis may arise when it becomes permissible to strike down a tyrant for the saving of a nation? Was the megalomaniacal despotism of Hitler more sacrosanct than the German people he was leading to destruction (even though it is true that the German people were not as a whole free of responsibility for allowing Hitler to gain the absolute power that he seized)?

It was questions such as these that exercised the minds and consciences of a number of German officers and pastors as they saw their great nation being led to moral and spiritual as well as physical destruction by Hitler and his henchmen. Only after much anguished soul-searching did these men, one of whom was Dietrich Bonhoeffer, reach the decision that it was their duty to take action to rid their country of this tyranny, fully aware of the dire consequences which would overtake them should they fail. The attempt on Hitler's life was made on 20 July 1944; it was unsuccessful. It was made conscientiously before God and responsibly as citizens who felt compelled to do what those who wielded power in the state were failing to do: to restrain violence, injustice, and genocidal inhumanity. In planning tyrannicide these men were not impelled by selfish egotism or the lust for power, but by concern for the common good. It is instructive that one of the conspirators who was a theologian clearly saw himself involved in the plot as a citizen—as a Christian citizen, certainly—rather than as an ecclesiastic, and openly declared when he was brought to the gallows, "I die as a traitor, not as a pastor."[2] Although a people may appear to be somewhat helpless and easily deceived by the political manipulations of evil men who lie their way into power, it is impossible for them to escape a measure of culpability for their irresponsible apathy as citizens of the state, for this political indifference contributes materially to the creation of a social climate that is congenial to the establishment of tyranny. The question which then arises, and which must be decided in the crucible of the intolerable situation that prevails, is whether drastic action is justifiable for the purpose of counteracting the evil resulting from the failure of the citizenry to act sensibly, by political means, at an earlier stage.

A nation finds itself in an acutely critical situation, ethically as well as politically, when a tyrant who has obtained power places himself above the law of the land and acts as though he were answerable to none for his misdeeds. It was the development of such a situation in Germany that appalled Dietrich Bonhoeffer as he earnestly searched his own as well as the national soul. He wrestled with the question how to challenge what he described as "the great masquerade of evil" which "has wrought havoc with all our ethical preconceptions" and which "for the Christian man who frames his life on the Bible simply confirms the radical evilness of evil."[3] It was plain to him that Nazi despotism had produced "a rich harvest of bravery and self-sacrifice, but hardly any civil courage."[4] As he pondered the agonies of his people from a prison cell he perceived not only that "the deliberate transgression of the divine law on the plea of self-preservation has the opposite effect of self-destruction," but also that "nobility springs from and thrives on self-sacrifice and courage and an unfailing sense of duty to oneself and society."[5] The fierce irresponsibility of tyranny gains its strength from the failure, the abdication, of responsibility on the part of the citizenry. Bonhoeffer well knew that there is a world of difference between suffering passively under a totalitarian regime and suffering responsibly in opposition to it:

> It is infinitely easier to suffer in obedience to a human command than to accept suffering as free, responsible men. It is infinitely easier to suffer with others than to suffer alone. It is infinitely easier to suffer as public heroes than to suffer apart and in ignominy. It is infinitely easier to suffer physical death than to endure spiritual suffering. Christ suffered as a free man alone, apart, and in ignominy, in body and in spirit, and since that day many Christians have suffered with him.[6]

2. Helmut Thielicke, *Theological Ethics* (1969), vol. 2, p. 345.
3. Dietrich Bonhoeffer, "After Ten Years," in *Letters and Papers from Prison* (1953), p. 135.
4. Ibid., p. 137.
5. Ibid., p. 141.
6. Ibid., p. 144.

In saying this he made it emphatically plain that "we are not Christs, we do not have to redeem the world by any action or suffering of our own," but rather that "we are instruments in the hand of the Lord of history."[7] Bonhoeffer is now commonly venerated as a Christian martyr; but his death would be more justly regarded as that of a Christian citizen who displayed remarkable civil courage, responsibility, and equanimity—even at the expense of losing his life—as he sought to honor God and serve his suffering fellow citizens in a scene of intolerable disintegration.

The possibility of a situation arising in which an act of tyrannicide is defensible is acknowledged by Karl Barth, who points out that "Calvin did not absolutely rule out the possibility of tyrannicide";[8] Barth warns, however, that "anyone who thinks that he is called to do this, along with all the other things that he has to consider, must be very sure (1) that he can justify himself factually, and (2) that he can really appeal to a call."[9] The nature of the call Barth does not specify, but presumably he means a call of duty to defend society by ridding the nation and the world of an intolerable monster.

There is, however, another ethical question which presents itself, at least in the case of the officers who planned to kill Hitler: had they not sworn an oath of loyalty and obedience to him as their Führer? Is it justifiable for Christians (as they professed to be) to disregard such an oath? In response to this problem it may be observed, firstly, that the taking of an oath implies that one binds oneself before almighty God, who is absolute truth and absolute power, to a particular promise or course of action, with the further implication that, should one fail to honor one's word, the judgment of God is invoked upon oneself. An oath therefore is an undertaking of the utmost solemnity, sworn, whether explicitly or implicitly, in the presence of and subject to the judgment of almighty God. Secondly, it follows from this that an oath would be meaningless were it not commonly acknowledged that there is a power and an authority supreme over all earthly power and authority, greater than both the one who swears the oath and the one to whom it is sworn, and that obedience is owed to this Supreme Being before all others. Thus an oath of loyalty sworn to Hitler or any other earthly authority loses its validity if the one who has thus bound himself is ordered to do something contrary to the will of God (such as to put Jews in gas chambers or to betray one's parents). Indeed, it may be said that the leader who develops into a tyrant is the one who is guilty of bad faith. Thirdly, if it is an irreligious oath, as for example in the case of a regime which officially denies the existence of God, the situation is in the ultimate sense ridiculous, because (as the Christian knows) the sinful and fallen state of humanity is such that no man's word can be fully trusted (hence the occasion for oaths). Consequently the godless tyrant must realize—if he has any common sense—that he can trust

7. Ibid., p. 145.
8. See John Calvin, *Institutes of the Christian Religion* 4.20.30–31.
9. Karl Barth, *Ethics,* ed. Dietrich Braun, trans. Geoffrey W. Bromiley (1981), pp. 149–150.

nobody, no matter how solemnly oaths may be given. It is equally well for others to recognize that the word of the godless tyrant cannot be trusted either in the domestic or in the international sphere.

When Herod Antipas, pleased with the dancing of the daughter of Herodias, "promised with an oath to give her whatever she might ask," and she, prompted by her mother, asked for the head of John the Baptist, we are told that he was sorry, but that "because of his oaths and his guests he commanded it to be given" (Matt. 14:1–12). However, the honorable course of conduct for him would have been to disregard the rashly given oath and the comments of his guests and to refuse to do what his conscience told him was wrong in the sight of God.[10] As for the Christian, his absolute loyalty is owed to God alone, and he should be careful not to bind himself by oaths without including the qualification that he can do nothing contrary to God's will—even though, as we have said, this proviso is really implicit in the taking of any oath.

This discussion may lead one to inquire whether it is ever permissible or pardonable for a Christian to tell a lie. Lying is rightly considered as forbidden by the ninth commandment, but the question is essentially this: is lying, when judged to be the lesser evil, justified in order to prevent the perpetration of the greater evil? Is it not preferable to lie, for example, in order to save the life of an innocent victim rather than to tell the truth and see that person destroyed? To take a biblical illustration, Rahab, who saved the lives of the two Israelite spies by hiding them in her house and then by lying to the men who had been sent to arrest them, was thereafter held in honor for what she had done, though the record does not say specifically whether her lying was commended or condemned (Josh. 2; cf. Heb. 11:31). The impression is, however, that her action as a whole was accepted as praiseworthy. If her lie was condoned, it must be taken as a case of accommodation to the prevailing fallenness and degeneracy of human society. Another example of this is the condoning of divorce where adultery has taken place, though the divinely appointed standard for marriage is that of lifelong union (see Matt. 19:3–9).

Who will say that it is not reasonable for a starving man to break the eighth commandment by helping himself to food that does not belong to him and thus to preserve his life, or for someone else to do this for him? David and his band staved off their hunger by taking bread that not only was not theirs but also was holy. Jesus Himself did not condemn this action when He challenged His critics: "Have you not read what David did, when he was hungry, and those who were with him: how he entered the house of God and ate the bread of the Presence, which it was not lawful for him to eat nor for those who were with him?" (Matt. 12:3–4). Similarly, Scripture envisages and recounts occasions when killing, which is for-

10. As Alfred Plummer observes, for Herod "to have broken the rash oath, into which he had been entrapped, would not have been sin, but repentance" (*An Exegetical Commentary on the Gospel according to S. Matthew* [1909], p. 202).

bidden by the sixth commandment, is allowable, as in the cause of justice or in self-defense. (The problems associated with killing are discussed in the next section.) The distinction between the lesser and the greater of two evils should, however, ordinarily be made only in emergencies. It should not be applied as a standard for everyday conduct. Lying, thieving, and killing are still evils. The distinction, where it is justified, is further evidence of the corruption and confusion of society and its relationships by the sinfulness of man. The ethical dilemmas we face are the consequence of our fallenness.

The intractability of the problem is apparent in the thought of Augustine, who, while holding that lying is always a sin, at first countenanced the permissibility of lying when it is the lesser of two evils, provided that eternal good results from it.[11] Yet he later adopted a more rigid position, arguing that if some sins such as lying are occasionally allowable the way will be opened to the commission of every kind of wickedness, with the result that no deed, no matter how outrageous, will be outlawed. He asked, further, what could be more absurd than to say that some lies are just, since this amounts to saying that some things are just which are unjust.[12] But this is precisely our dilemma. Our fallen world is no longer the ideal world it once was nor the perfect world that it is destined to be in Christ. The ethical problems we face are created by our fallen state. It is true that the power of God is supreme, but we are still not separated from our own frailty or from the perplexities of our relationships with others.

Let us illustrate this by an event that took place in the sixteenth century. In June of 1555 five Protestant pastors who were on their way to the Piedmontese valleys were seized and imprisoned at Chambéry in France, where they were sentenced to death by burning. On July 25 they wrote a letter to the pastors in Geneva describing how during their interrogation they had denied any knowledge of Reformed services in the valley of Pragela, and explaining that they had resorted to this falsehood not for their own sakes but because they believed that the alternative to lying, telling the truth, would expose a large number of persons, including women and children, to persecution and death. They spoke further of the anguish with which this decision had been made.[13] Calvin responded compassionately and assured them that the prudence with which they had answered their interrogators was "truly according to the Spirit of God and not according to worldly guile."[14] But at the beginning of August the captive pastors wrote again to Geneva, now altogether deploring the falsehood they had told because, as things had turned out, it had not effected the good result intended by them.

> Gentlemen and most dear brethren, we have been greatly comforted by the letters which you have kindly written us, especially in seeing by them that your customary

11. Augustine, *De mendacio* (written c. A.D. 395).
12. Augustine, *Contra mendaciam* (written c. A.D. 420).
13. *Ioannis Calvini opera quae supersunt omnia* (1875), vol. 15, cols. 694ff.
14. Ibid., col. 708.

magnanimity has supported us despite our fault, which cannot be described as small, as its effects show us all too clearly. Have we achieved anything by what we have done? Have we, by our misguided prudence, prevented what we feared from happening? Alas, no. For three or four days later, when we were still sorrowing over our fault, the news came that Satan was inflicting his fury on those whom we wished to preserve. Our grief was then redoubled, and we knew very well that this was for our humiliation, having learnt that the prudence of men cannot prevent the providence of God. We have in ourselves more than enough imperfections to keep us lowly before God; but this one is so obvious that it exceeds all others. The Lord has caused us to feel this most vividly so that for the rest of our lives we may be humbled by it; yet he is willing to pardon us, as we believe he has already done.[15]

How are we to judge between the benevolent intention which motivated the false information given by these prisoners and their own subsequent self-condemnation? Would they have taken a different view of things if their dissembling had produced the desired effect? We may at least learn from Calvin, who showed no condemnation but only compassionate understanding of the way they had acted.

The Christian and Warfare

The debate regarding the involvement of Christians in military service and the waging of warfare is nothing new in the history of the church. In the New Testament, certainly, it is nowhere explicitly asserted that for a Christian to serve in the armed forces is inappropriate or inadmissible. Had this been the New Testament position, we would expect that Peter would have required Cornelius to surrender his commission on becoming a Christian, that Jesus would have qualified His praise of the faith of the centurion whose servant He healed, and that John the Baptist would have told the soldiers who asked him what they should do that they should give up their soldiering, instead of merely admonishing them to stop using violent and dishonest means to enrich themselves and to be content with their wages (see Acts 10:24–48; Matt. 8:5–13; Luke 3:14). Moreover, the Christian is repeatedly described as a soldier who is engaged in spiritual warfare: he is to "wage the good warfare" and to "fight the good fight" as "a good soldier of Christ Jesus"; in the unrelenting conflict with the forces of evil he is to put on "the whole armor of God"; and he remembers not only his Master's assertion that by His coming to us He has brought not peace but a sword, but also the wonderful promises that have been given to those who overcome in this warfare (I Tim. 1:18; 6:12; II Tim. 2:3; 4:7; Eph. 6:11; Matt. 10:34; Rev. 2:7, 11, 17, 26–29; 3:5, 12, 21). If, as some wish to persuade us, the very concept of warfare is incompatible with the will of God and the way of the Christian, it is impossible to explain the free use of this military terminology.

To dismiss it as mere terminology, as no more than literary metaphor and

---

15. *The Register of the Company of Pastors of Geneva in the Time of Calvin,* ed. and trans. P. E. Hughes (1966), pp. 311–312.

imagery, will not do, for Christ and His apostles are clearly speaking of real warfare—warfare, it is true, that is spiritual, but which for that very reason is more intense and perilous than physical warfare. Precisely because "we are not contending against flesh and blood, but against the principalities, against the powers, against the world rulers of this present darkness, against the spiritual hosts of wickedness in the heavenly places"—in short, against our implacable foe Satan and his armies—we, who are weak in ourselves, need the armor and the equipment which God supplies (Eph. 6:10–13). Indeed, this warfare starts in heaven (Rev. 12:7). God's army, "arrayed in fine linen, white and pure," cleansed from all defilement by the blood of the Lamb (Rev. 19:14), is led into battle by its Redeemer, the "King of kings and Lord of lords" (Rev. 19:16), who "is called Faithful and True and in righteousness judges and makes war" (Rev. 19:11). It is essential to see that the coming of Christ to our world belongs inseparably to this warfare. In the incarnation, life, death, resurrection, and glorification of the eternal Son, God is actively waging war. Christ's coming was at the same time Christ's conquest. The purpose He achieved was to defeat, disarm, and destroy His and our strong enemy (Luke 11:21–22). He took our human nature and made it His own at Bethlehem for this reason: "that through death he might destroy him who has the power of death, that is, the devil, and deliver all those who through fear of death were subject to lifelong bondage" (Heb. 2:14–15).

Despite appearances, Jesus' death was not His helpless subjugation but His active conquest. Even His passive submission was determined by the power of His divine will. The cross is the critical heart of His cosmic warfare. The worldly judges who condemned and killed Him had no power of their own but only such power as was given from above (John 19:10–11; Matt. 26:63–66). What looked like His defeat was in fact His triumph. It is no less than His victorious achievement of the purpose which brought Him to our world. That is why He was able to affirm with complete confidence, "No one takes [my life] from me, but I lay it down of my own accord. I have power to lay it down, and I have power to take it again" (John 10:18).

The cross is God's battlefield. It is the scene of Satan's defeat because it is the place of the triumph of God's love in union with His holiness. There the outpouting of divine grace and the demands of divine justice are victoriously brought together. Divine love cannot be isolated from divine judgment. The cross is God in action for us. There God Himself, in the person of the incarnate Son bearing our sins and enduring their penalty, meets the demands of His justice, and this is simultaneously the manifestation of His pure love for us. God propitiates Himself in order to procure our redemption. "In this is love," St. John writes, "not that we loved God but that he loved us and sent his Son to be the propitiation for our sins" (I John 4:10). We are invited to receive the perfect righteousness of Christ in exchange for our sins which God has dealt with at Calvary. St. Paul explains this holy and gracious exchange in the following way: "God was in Christ reconciling the world to himself. . . . For our sake he made him to be sin who knew no sin, so that in him we might become the righteousness of God" (II Cor. 5:19, 21). Though nailed to the cross by wicked hands, the incarnate Son was not offered up by alien powers: His offering was His own self-offering. He both presents the offering and is the offering. He Himself is both priest and victim (Heb. 7:27; 9:14; 10:11–14).

The meeting of justice and mercy at Calvary is the true ground of the believer's justification before God. It is only because God acts in justice as well as in love at the cross that the sinner is justified there (Rom. 3:26). P. T. Forsyth, who had a profound perception of the holy love of God, has well said,

> For the average Christian mind love and judgment are contraries; and the action of love is to provide an escape from judgment. But that is not the Christian revelation at all. It is fatal to it. It is immoral. It is not God's account of his love in the only place where he reveals it—in the Bible, in Christ, in the Cross.[16]

As God's battlefield the cross is also the place of bloodshed, where the blood of God incarnate is poured out in reconciling death. To quote Forsyth again:

> The Cross, by a holy war, sought first the righteousness of God, and only then and thereby, the wellbeing of man. . . . Our relation to the God of the universal and holy Cross is the foundation of all morality. . . . Death, viewed from the Cross, is not resigned suffering, and not impressive suffering. Christ did not die just to show how god-like a meek death could be made, nor even to show with the last emphasis how loving God is; but to hallow the Holy Name, to secure the real and universal righteousness, to destroy the work of the prince of this world, to judge him to death, and to set up the Kingdom of God on earth.[17]

Within the pages of the New Testament, then, the Christian life is portrayed as one of unremitting spiritual warfare against the forces of evil, and Satan and his followers are shown to be destined for defeat and judgment. It follows that the concept of warfare is, pending the final judgment, fully compatible with the Christian perspective. This should not be taken to mean, however, that the notion of warfare and participation in this power struggle are congenial to the Christian mind. Warfare by its very nature is hard and unpleasant, and it is justified only for the purpose of overcoming evil and establishing peace. Accordingly, warfare is only for the present age; it does not belong to the ultimate and permanent state of things: it is waged with a view to the setting up of Christ's eternal kingdom of righteousness (see Isa. 9:6–7; II Peter 3:13; Rev. 21:1–4).

But this is far from being a merely spiritual expectation which promises the cessation of spiritual conflict, for the physical realm is inevitably involved in it. We look for the renewal of all creation, the appearance of the new heavens and the new earth, in which physical warfare and suffering and death will belong to the past and the future will be marked by everlasting peace, physical as well as spiritual.

16. P. T. Forsyth, *The Christian Ethic of War* (1916), pp. 184–185.
17. Ibid., pp. 140–141.

At the physical level warfare against disorder and injustice is waged not only by armies of soldiers but also by police forces and magistrates; the latter two, as we have seen, being designed for the preservation of social justice and security, wield their authority under God as His ministers. International warfare for the purpose of opposing what is evil and restoring justice and security is an extension of the domestic struggle. Karl Barth, indeed, postulates a logical connection between the act of an individual who kills in self-defense and both capital punishment and national warfare. Capital punishment is society's defense of itself against the aggression of the violent criminal, and warfare is the nation's defense of itself against the aggression of a violent enemy. "War," he writes, "is the execution which a people organized as a state, on account of its will to live, performs on another people which threatens its will to live."[18] The question now to be discussed concerns the responsibility of the Christian regarding the taking up of arms and participation in military conflict.

The Just War

The sixth commandment, "You shall not kill" (Exod. 20:13), plainly raises the question of the legitimacy of engaging in warfare. There are many factors other than killing that enter into military strategy, but it cannot be denied that killing is inseparable from the concept and the history of warfare. Is the waging of war therefore an infraction of the sixth commandment? That it is not necessarily so regarded is obvious from the Old Testament itself, which records many instances of warfare waged by the Israelites, themselves subject to the law of Moses, with the approval and at the command of God. This does not mean, of course, that all warfare is justifiable. The savage subjugation of peoples by greedy aggressors is in no way sanctioned. Throughout the centuries it has been acknowledged that there is such a thing as a just war and that this is the only kind of war that can be approved. Cicero (to take an example from among the pagan authors) insisted that the rules of war must be strictly observed by the state and that in international disputes discussion should take precedence over resort to physical force. "The only excuse for going to war," he asserted, "is that we may live in peace unharmed; and when the victory is won, we should spare those who have not been blood-thirsty and barbarous in their warfare." He maintained, further, that "no war is just unless it is entered upon after an official demand for satisfaction has been submitted or warning has been given and formal declaration made." Even so, the imperialist mind of his time reveals itself when he speaks, without censure, of "wars which have glory for their end," though he adds that these should "be carried on with less bitterness."[19] On another occasion Cicero writes that "a war is never undertaken by the ideal state, except in defence of its honor or its safety"; that "those wars are

18. Barth, *Ethics,* p. 154; see also pp. 149ff.
19. Cicero, *De officiis,* trans. W. Miller (Loeb edition), 1.11–12.

unjust which are undertaken without provocation," since "only a war waged for revenge or defence can actually be just"; and that "no war is considered just unless it has been proclaimed and declared, or unless reparation has first been demanded."[20]

Among the Christian authors Tertullian was one who held that it is improper for a Christian to involve himself in military service, or, for that matter, to accept appointment to any civil office. The military oath, he contended, places the Christian impossibly under two lords, Caesar as well as God. Although he granted that the people of Israel had had famous military leaders and had engaged in warfare, and that soldiers had not been dissuaded from their profession by John the Baptist or by Jesus, he maintained that in disarming Peter, the Lord subsequently unbuckled the sword of every soldier.[21] The reference is to the occasion of the arrest of Jesus, when Peter drew his sword and struck the slave of the high priest, evoking from Jesus this rebuke: "Put your sword back into its place; for all who take the sword will perish by the sword" (Matt. 26:52). In the century after Tertullian, following the "Christianization" of the Roman Empire under Constantine, Basil of Caesarea was pleased to find he could write as follows to a military officer: "I have learnt to know one who proves that even in a soldier's life it is possible to preserve the perfection of love to God, and that we must mark a Christian not by the style of his dress, but by the disposition of his soul."[22]

Augustine deplored all warfare, including the waging of just wars which are made necessary by human wrongdoing—wrongdoing that in itself is deplorable even if it does not give rise to warfare.[23] That there are *just* wars which are *necessary* is a consequence of the fallenness of human society. It is not wrong or forbidden, he held, for a Christian to take up arms in the cause of justice. "Do not think it is impossible for any one to please God while engaged in active military service," Augustine wrote to Boniface in 418. As biblical instances of the sanction of military action he cited David, the centurion whose faith Jesus praised, Cornelius, and the soldiers whom John the Baptist told to be content with their wages. A Christian, however, cannot lend himself to warfare in an ungodly cause: "Think of this first of all when you are arming for the battle, that even your bodily strength is a gift of God; for, considering this, you will not employ the gift of God against God." It is a paradox of our fallen situation that the proper purpose of warfare is the establishment of peace; victory, moreover, should be tempered with mercy:

Peace should be the object of your desire; war should be waged only as a necessity, and waged only that God may by it deliver men from the necessity and preserve them in peace. For peace is not sought in order to kindle war, but war is waged in order that peace may be obtained. Therefore, even in waging war, cherish the spirit of

20. Cicero, *De re publica*, trans. C. W. Keyes (Loeb edition), 3.23–24.
21. Tertullian, *De idololatria* 19.
22. Basil of Caesarea, Letter 106.
23. Augustine, *De civitate Dei* 19.7.

204 Christian Ethics in Secular Society

a peace-maker, that, by conquering those whom you attack, you may lead them back to the advantages of peace. . . . Let necessity, therefore, and not your will, slay the enemy who fights against you. As violence is used towards him who rebels and resists, so mercy is due to the vanquished or the captive, especially in the case in which future troubling of the peace is not to be feared.[24]

There is, indeed, a merciful aspect to the waging of a just war. As Augustine points out in another of his letters, for God to allow crimes and vices to go unpunished is a more terrible judgment than for Him to curb them by affliction. Thus it can be said that "He afflicts in mercy."

> And in mercy also, if such a thing were possible, even wars might be waged by the good, in order that, by bringing under the yoke the unbridled lusts of men, those vices might be abolished which ought, under a just government, to be either extirpated or suppressed.[25]

The evils which make just wars necessary he describes elsewhere as follows:

> The real evils in war are love of violence, revengeful cruelty, fierce and implacable enmity, wild resistance, and the lust of power, and such like; and it is generally to punish these things, when force is required to inflict the punishment, that, in obedience to God or some lawful authority, good men undertake wars, when they find themselves in such a position as regards the conduct of human affairs, that right conduct requires them to act, or to make others act, in this way.[26]

Such passages classically present the case for the just war.

The principle of the just war was reaffirmed in later centuries by Thomas Aquinas and John Calvin (to select but two out of many scholars that could be cited). The former postulated three requirements for what might be designated a just war. The first of these states that it is the right not of any private citizen but of the ruling authority of a nation to declare and wage war, since it is the function of government to protect the nation as a whole as well as the individuals who constitute the national entity.

> It is not the business of a private individual to declare war, because he can seek for redress of his rights from the tribunal of his superior. Moreover, it is not the business of a private individual to summon together the people, which has to be done in wartime. And as the care of the common weal is committed to those who are in authority, it is their business to watch over the common weal of the city, kingdom, or province subject to them. And just as it is lawful for them to have recourse to the sword in defending that common weal against internal disturbances, when they punish evil-doers, according to the words of the Apostle (Rom. xiii.4): "He beareth not the sword in vain: for he is God's minister, and avenger to execute wrath upon him that doeth evil"; so too it is their business to have recourse to the sword of war in

24. Augustine, Letter 189, to Boniface.
25. Augustine, Letter 138, to Marcellinus.
26. Augustine, *Contra Faustum Manichaeum* 22.74.

defending the common weal against external enemies. Hence it is said to those who are in authority (Ps. lxxxi.4): "Rescue the poor and deliver the needy out of the hand of the sinner."

Secondly, Aquinas asserts that "those who are attacked should be attacked because they deserve it on account of some fault." And he declares, thirdly, that "it is necessary that the belligerents should have a rightful intention, so that they intend the advancement of good or the avoidance of evil." He follows Augustine in affirming that "those who wage war justly aim at peace, and so they are not opposed to peace."[27]

Calvin argues that "man is under a twofold government" and that "Christ's spiritual kingdom and the civil jurisdiction are things completely distinct." Nonetheless he insists that "this distinction does not lead us to consider the whole nature of government a thing polluted, which has nothing to do with Christian men," since it has "its appointed end, so long as we live among men, to cherish and protect the outward worship of God, to defend sound doctrine of piety and the position of the church, to adjust our life to the society of men, to form our social behavior to civil righteousness, to reconcile us with one another, and to promote general peace and tranquillity." He judges that wars which are undertaken to execute public vengeance are lawful. "Both natural equity and the nature of the office dictate that princes must be armed," he writes, "not only to restrain the misdeeds of private individuals by judicial punishment, but also to defend by war the dominions entrusted to their safekeeping, if at any time they are under enemy attack"—but with the proviso that "everything else ought to be tried before recourse is had to arms."[28] Thus it is reasonable to conclude, as does Article 37 of the Church of England, that "it is lawful for Christian men, at the commandment of the magistrate, to wear weapons, and to serve in the wars."[29]

Conscientious Objection

There are Christians, however, who have felt unable in conscience to accept this conclusion and who as conscientious objectors have refused to involve themselves in warfare. Conscientious objection is itself divisible into two categories which may conveniently be designated passivism and pacifism.

27. Thomas Aquinas, *Summa Theologica* 2.2.40.

28. Calvin, *Institutes* 4.20.1, 2, 11, 12.

29. This clause together with the rest of the Article was omitted in the revision adopted by the American Episcopal Church in 1801, when the original Article 37 was replaced by the following: "The power of the civil magistrate extendeth to all men, as well clergy as laity, in all things temporal; but hath no authority in things purely spiritual. And we hold it to be the duty of all men who are professors of the Gospel, to pay respectful obedience to the civil authority, regularly and legitimately constituted." Though no longer explicitly stated, approval of participation by Christians in military service is implicit in this reformulation.

Passivism demands the renunciation of the use of violence under any circumstances. Violence, viewed as intrinsically evil, must never be met by violence; indeed, passivists believe that violence can ultimately be overcome by nonviolence. Their charter for the ethic of nonviolence is the Sermon on the Mount, and in particular the dominical injunction, "Do not resist one who is evil. But if any one strikes you on the right cheek, turn to him the other also" (Matt. 5:39). They take Christ's passive endurance of the violence He received at the hands of those who assaulted Him and put Him to death as the model for their own nonresistance (cf. I Peter 2:23), and they seek to follow the apostolic precepts to repay no one evil for evil and, instead of being overcome by evil, to overcome evil with good (Rom. 12:17, 21). The use of violence, accordingly, for any purpose whatsoever is abjured, including of course the violence of military action.

Such idealism, however, though prompted by the best of intentions, is hopelessly inappropriate in view of the realities of the human situation. It totally lacks the dimension of justice and judgment, and therefore of moral responsibility. Strictly applied, it requires that a disobedient child not be punished, that assault against one's own person not be resisted, and that no force be used to restrain the thug who is attacking one's wife or kidnapping one's daughter, for the difference between all such countermeasures and the violence of warfare is only one of degree. If consistent with itself, it must demand, in Tolstoyan fashion, the abolition not only of national armies but also of police forces, courts of law, and places of detention for criminals. Concerned with love and not at all with justice (though, as we have seen, the two are allied with, not antithetical to, each other), it actually becomes a moral abdication and a renunciation of ethical duty. It fails to understand that in going to the cross the "passive Jesus" was in reality waging active warfare against the kingdom of evil. It leaves out of account His display of righteous indignation and His wielding of a whip. And it is blind to the fact that the Sermon on the Mount was addressed by Jesus not to society or the world at large, but to His own disciples who, when facing opposition and violence for His sake—a result of confessing Him before men—were to endure such hostility joyfully and without retaliation. Nor does it notice that Christ's coming to save the world was inseparably linked to His fulfillment of the law and the righteousness it enjoins (a point made clear in the same sermon—see Matt. 5:17–20).

As Augustine pointed out, the nonresistance and the turning of the other cheek found in the Sermon on the Mount require "not a bodily action but an inward disposition"; to suggest that Christ was setting aside the moral law is an inexcusable misrepresentation of His teaching:

> It is mere groundless calumny to charge Moses with making war, for there would have been less harm in making war of his own accord than in not doing it when God commanded him. And to dare to find fault with God himself for giving such a command, or not to believe it possible that a just and good God did so, shows, to say the least, an inability to consider that in the view of divine providence, which pervades all things from the highest to the lowest, time can neither add anything nor

take away, . . . while in men a right will is in union with the divine law, and ungoverned passion is restrained by the order of divine law.[30]

To the same effect, D. Martyn Lloyd-Jones has in our own day warned that we must not think of the Sermon on the Mount "as being a new kind of law to replace the old Mosaic law," especially because "it is rather a matter of emphasizing the spirit of the law." He insists, moreover, that its teaching "has nothing whatever to do with a man who is not a Christian," and that consequently "to advocate this teaching as a policy for a country or a nation is no less than heresy." Nor does it provide ethical instruction for the Christian with regard to his relationship as a citizen to his country's government, for the essence of the teaching of Jesus in the sermon is that "if we are to be truly Christian we must become dead to self."[31]

The moral irresponsibility of passivism has been depicted with characteristic penetration by P. T. Forsyth, who perceived it to be the opposite of conscientious because it "deposes conscience as the agent of God." "That," he wrote, "is what I do if I do not resist evil but leave God to intervene if he wants it resisted. I leave him to take moral responsibility, I take none." Passivism, in fact, "crushes moral action."[32] God, after all, has entrusted a sword to the state: to follow a line of passive detachment is to shirk one's duties and obligations as a citizen. Thus in effect the passivist either denies that apart from the private conscience there is such a thing as a national conscience, or acts as though the Christian has no part in the national conscience when his country has to defend itself against aggression from without or calls its citizenry to arms in the cause of international justice and peace. To quote Forsyth again:

> Not to resist is to be accessory. It is to leave the door open for the robber. Passivity is complicity. And it is profaning Christ to use his precepts of love to erase the distinction between good and evil, freedom and crime. . . . It is the ethic of a religion which practically ignores the wrath of God, and finds either no real place in the Saviour for the Cross, or no place in the Cross for more than sacrifice—none for divine judgment. . . . This is a religion in which the sympathetic and mystical has dislodged the ethical, and it tends to destroy Christianity as the religion of moral redemption.[33]

Pacifism, on the other hand, displays an attitude that is more positive, in that it acknowledges the claims of the state upon its citizens. The Christian pacifist does not disavow his civil responsibilities. He believes, however, that it is wrong for him to bear arms and to kill others, even though they are enemies who threaten the security of his nation; and he asks the state to respect these scruples. At the same time, however, he affirms his willingness to serve his country as a noncombatant, for instance, by ministering to the wounded on the battlefield as a medical orderly

30. Augustine, *Contra Faustum Manichaeum* 22.76, 78.
31. D. Martyn Lloyd-Jones, *Studies in the Sermon on the Mount* (1959), vol. 1, pp. 273ff.
32. Forsyth, *The Christian Ethic of War,* pp. 74–75.
33. Ibid., pp. 82–83.

or an ambulance driver, or by making himself available for some occupation at home which is regarded as essential to the war effort or the survival of his country. Thus the pacifist takes into account that he is here and now a citizen of an earthly kingdom as well as a citizen of the kingdom of heaven. His understanding of the total situation is deficient, however, because he fails to grasp that the spiritual warfare against the satanic forces of evil is still being waged, even though the decisive victory has been won at Calvary, and that the everlasting reign of peace and righteousness, when there will be no more war and no more death, is still future.

Meanwhile, pending the final destruction of these satanic forces and the complete elimination of evil from God's creation, it is sheer folly to imagine that disarmament, the signing of pacts, and the establishment of international leagues will effect the removal of strife and bloodshed from the human scene. But this does not imply that the Christian, whether a pacifist or a combatant, should not do all in his power to preserve peace at home and throughout the world. The irony, as we have said previously, is that there are times when the cause of peace is served by going to war, whether it be in self-defense or to prevent a ruthless bully from overrunning a free people and obliterating their national identity. Thielicke has realistically observed that "the fallen world knows peace only under the threat of violence" and that the peace of this interim age between the two comings of Christ is "an armed peace."[34] This realization serves to underline the absurdity and irrationality of fallen man.

There are some, indeed, who judge that the development of nuclear armaments has changed the character of warfare in so fundamental a manner that any concept of a just war is now completely outmoded: nuclear warheads are so devastating and indiscriminate in their destructiveness that the only realistic view of any future war is not of the victory of one side and the defeat of the other, but of the annihilation of the human race—or of a large part of it—and the demolition of civilization. To believe that there no longer is such a thing as a just war is, however, an unacceptable point of view, even though it is indisputable that the prospect of nuclear warfare is horrifying in the extreme. For one thing, the propensities of human nature in its fallenness remain the same, and greed and injustice, whether at the interpersonal or the international level, continue among us and need to be opposed in the name of freedom and righteousness. The principle of the just war, then, must not be treated as an obsolete relic of past history. The smothering of the national conscience can bring about the smothering of the nation. The global power struggle, which is now more than ever a fact of everyday life, makes it altogether unrealistic to imagine that the manufacture of nuclear weaponry can be outlawed by mutual agreement, or that unilateral disarmament by one power will induce the other to repent and follow suit.

For another thing, it must be questioned whether, as Thielicke maintains, "the nuclear age confronts us with a change, not merely in the form, but in the very

34. Thielicke, *Theological Ethics,* vol. 2, p. 465.

nature of war," in a word, a change that is "radical."[35] War is, and always has been, the most ghastly consequence of the fallenness of the human race. From the murder of Abel by his brother Cain, it is, and always has been, fratricide—the killing of man by his fellow man, both of whom are made in the image of God. It springs from the greed, envy, and hatred in the human heart. Thus St. James writes, "What causes wars, and what causes fightings among you? Is it not your passions that are at war in your members? You desire and do not have; so you kill. And you covet and cannot obtain; so you fight and wage war" (James 4:1–2). The war within oneself leads to war with others, and the necessity for unjust violence to be checked by just violence follows. In this way the true nature of warfare is defined, whether it be against crime or against international aggression. To picture the wars of earlier ages as conflicts in which the combatants injured only themselves is sheer romanticism. Warfare has always been brutal and has always savagely brought suffering to the innocent. It has always been commonplace in warfare for women and children to be raped, enslaved, and slaughtered, for homes to be destroyed and lands devastated, and for tyrants to be inflamed with genocidal fury.

The invention of nuclear weapons has introduced a new dimension but not a radical change in the nature of war. It portends a colossal intensification in the destructive horror of war and it extends the range and distance over which hostilities may be conducted. But this is only the latest development in a long sequence of developments throughout the history of warfare which have successively increased the scope of conflict. The use of bows and arrows must have seemed a great advance over hand-to-hand combat, and much more so the making of firearms, until now in our day the nations are armed with intercontinental missiles of amazing power and accuracy. The next stage to be anticipated is the waging of war in and from outer space. These are terrifying prospects for all, and especially for those who have cut themselves off from the grace and power of God. As in the days of Noah, when the earth was filled with violence (Gen. 6:11), God's people should be heralds of righteousness (II Peter 2:5), calling others to repentance and faith and warning them of coming judgment. This is the only radical way of averting the next world war, though Christians should also do everything possible within the civil realm to preserve peace and security. In doing so, however, they must never forget that the divine love is ever a holy love, that mercy and justice belong together, and that the cross of Christ is the seat of judgment as well as the throne of grace.

Dietrich Bonhoeffer postulates a distinction between killing that is arbitrary and killing that is justifiable. The former is defined by him as the deliberate destruction of innocent life. Killing of the enemy in war is not arbitrary, for, Bonhoeffer explains, "even if he is not personally guilty, he is nevertheless consciously partici-pating in the attack of his people against the life of my people and he must share in bearing the consequences of the collective guilt." Nor does Bonhoeffer regard the

35. Ibid., pp. 420, 473.

killing of civilians in war as arbitrary, "so long as it is not directly intended but is only an unfortunate consequence of a measure which is necessary on military grounds."[36] The greatly increased destructiveness of modern weapons and warheads is undoubtedly making the distinction between military and civilian personnel much more difficult to sustain in this respect. The resulting dilemma is illustrated by the decision of President Truman to drop atomic bombs on Japanese cities, where there was no possibility of discriminating between military and civilian victims. Indeed, it was recognized that these were primarily civilian targets, but the decision was held to be justified on the grounds of military necessity, as a means of bringing the war to an end and saving many lives that would otherwise have been destroyed. Yet it must be admitted that this action was simply an intensification of the bombing of cities (with their largely civilian populations) which had started in the First World War, and which in turn had been preceded in past centuries by the destruction of cities and their populations by cannonades or assaults of various kinds. The world powers appear to be nearing the brink of Armageddon, which will be the war to end all war—not, however, because of the self-destruction of mankind, but because God finally will intervene to defeat the demonic forces of evil and to shake the world for the last time, "in order that what cannot be shaken may remain" (Heb. 12:25–27).

The International Christian

While Christians as individuals are citizens of particular states and owe responsible allegiance to those states, yet corporately they constitute the church, which, as the body of Christ, is one and worldwide. The Christian perspective, therefore, cannot be merely insular. Since they are charged to be Christ's witnesses to the ends of the earth, Christians should feel and show compassion for others that is truly international in scope. The hallmark of their lives should be "righteousness and peace and joy in the Holy Spirit" (Rom. 14:17), as they "strive for peace with all men" (Heb. 12:14). Christians, having themselves found inward peace by the blood of Christ's cross and knowing that divine blessing is promised to peacemakers (Col. 1:20; Matt. 5:9), have a duty to seek and pray for peace among the nations, for this, while desirable in itself, is also conducive to the progress of the gospel. How can the Christian's concern for others be limited to his own country or to fellow believers when he knows that the great company of the redeemed comes "from every nation, from all tribes and peoples and tongues," and that the whole world has been set before him as his field for mission and well-doing? (Rev. 7:9; Matt. 28:19).

The need for military preparedness in the interests of national defense and as a deterrent to international aggression can hardly be doubted, given the paradoxes and contradictions of our fallen world; nonetheless Christians should be deeply

36. Bonhoeffer, *Letters and Papers*, pp. 115–116.

disturbed over the astronomical sums that are being spent on the manufacture and stockpiling of death-dealing armaments, not only because this economic profligacy is symptomatic of the frenetic insanity of the never-ending arms race, but also because even a fraction of this vast expenditure would suffice to feed the starving, clothe the naked, shelter the homeless, and minister to the destitute who in their millions are mutely and despairingly looking for help. Care for them should be the highest priority of those peoples who have more than enough. It is right and proper for the Christian citizens of such countries to remind those in authority of their human responsibility to take effective action to alleviate the suffering of so many millions. At the same time it is incumbent on both Christian individuals and the Christian church to take every possible action to bring food, clothing, and shelter to these multitudes. Least of all is it open to those who profess to follow Jesus Christ to "pass by on the other side" as though this were no concern of theirs (see Luke 10:31).

The principle of godly compassion was laid down long ago by Moses:

If there is among you a poor man, one of your brethren, . . . you shall not harden your heart or shut your hand against your poor brother, but you shall open your hand to him, and lend him sufficient for his need, whatever it may be. Take heed lest there be a base thought in your heart, . . . and your eye be hostile to your poor brother, and you give him nothing, and he cry to the Lord against you, and it be sin in you. You shall give to him freely, and your heart shall not be grudging when you give to him; because for this the Lord your God will bless you in all your work and in all that you undertake (Deut. 15:7–10).

This principle, which was at first given only to the Israelites, is now universal in Christ. So also the psalmist declares the blessedness of those who consider the poor and incites us to "give justice to the weak and the fatherless," to "maintain the right of the afflicted and the destitute," and to "rescue the weak and the needy" (Ps. 41:1; 82:3–4). St. James advises us that "religion that is pure and undefiled before God" involves not only "keeping oneself unstained from the world" but also "visiting orphans and widows in their affliction" (James 1:27).

Can we who are Christians ever forget that it was precisely when we were "wretched, pitiable, poor, blind, and naked" (Rev. 3:17) that the Lord mercifully came to our aid, deliberately by His incarnation impoverishing Himself, even to the death of the cross, in order that through His grace we might be enriched? "For you know the grace of our Lord Jesus Christ," the apostle Paul writes, "that though he was rich, yet for your sake he became poor, so that by his poverty you might become rich" (II Cor. 8:9; cf. Phil. 2:6–8). So we should follow the example of Him who is the Good Samaritan par excellence and, in obedience to His command to "go and do likewise" (Luke 10:37), identify ourselves compassionately with those who are in the depths not merely of spiritual but also of material destitution. Saved to serve, how blessed will those be who hear the commendation of their Lord:

I was hungry and you gave me food, I was thirsty and you gave me drink, I was a stranger and you welcomed me, I was naked and you clothed me, I was sick and you visited me, I was in prison and you came to me. . . . Truly, I say to you, as you did it to one of the least of these my brethren, you did it to me (Matt. 25:35–40).

Thus to minister to others in Christ's name and for His sake is our privilege as well as our responsibility. It is the continuation of His healing and reconciling work here on earth. And this is the true heart and mainspring of the Christian ethic.

O Lord, we beseech thee mercifully to receive the prayers of thy people who call upon thee; and grant that they may both perceive and know what things they ought to do, and also may have grace and power faithfully to fulfil the same; through Jesus Christ our Lord. Amen.

Collect of the First Sunday after the Epiphany, Book of Common Prayer.

Select Bibliography
of more recent works

Barclay, William, *Ethics in a Permissive Society* (New York, 1971).

Barry, F. R., *Christian Ethics and Secular Society* (London, 1966).

Barth, Karl, *Ethics,* ed. Dietrich Braun, trans. Geoffrey W. Bromiley (New York, 1981).

Bonhoeffer, Dietrich, *Ethics,* ed. Eberhard Bethge (New York, 1964).

Brinkley, Luther John, *Contemporary Ethical Theories* (New York, 1961).

Brunner, Emil, *Man in Revolt,* trans. Olive Wyon (London, 1939).

————. *Justice and the Social Order,* trans. Mary Hottinger (London, 1945).

————. *The Divine Imperative,* trans. Olive Wyon (Philadelphia, 1947).

Clark, Gordon Haddon, and Smith, T. V., eds., *Readings in Ethics* (New York, 1931).

Clark, Stephen B., *Man and Woman in Christ* (Ann Arbor, 1980).

Ellul, Jacques, *To Will and to Do,* trans. Edward Hopkin (Philadelphia, 1969).

————. *The Ethics of Freedom,* trans. Geoffrey W. Bromiley (Grand Rapids, 1976).

Ferm, Vergilius, ed., *Encyclopedia of Morals* (New York, 1956).

Forell, George Wolfgang, ed., *Christian Social Teachings: A Reader in Christian Social Ethics from the Bible to the Present* (New York, 1966).

————. *History of Christian Ethics,* Vol. 1, *From the New Testament to Augustine* (New York, 1966).

Forsyth, P. T., *The Christian Ethic of War* (London, 1916).

Geisler, Norman, *Ethics: Alternatives and Issues* (Grand Rapids, 1971).

Hammond, Thomas C., *Perfect Freedom: An Introduction to Christian Ethics* (London, n.d.).

Hastings, James, ed., *Encyclopedia of Religion and Ethics,* 13 vols. (New York, 1908–28).

Henry, Carl F. H., *Christian Personal Ethics* (Grand Rapids, 1957).

————. *Aspects of Christian Social Ethics* (Grand Rapids, 1964).

————. ed., *Baker's Dictionary of Christian Ethics* (Grand Rapids, 1973).

Inge, W. R., *Christian Ethics and Modern Problems* (London, 1930).

Kirk, Kenneth E., *Conscience and its Problems: An Introduction to Casuistry* (London, 1927).

Lehmann, Paul Louis, *Ethics in a Christian Context* (New York, 1963).

Long, Edward LeRoy, *A Survey of Christian Ethics* (New York, 1967).

Macquarrie, John, ed., *Dictionary of Christian Ethics* (Philadelphia, 1967).

Maritain, Jacques, *Moral Philosophy* (New York, 1964).

Melden, Abraham Irving, *Ethical Theories: A Book of Readings* (New York, 1951).

Mott, Stephen Charles, *Biblical Ethics and Social Change* (New York, 1982).

Mowrer, O. Hobart, ed., *Morality and Mental Health* (Chicago, 1967).

Murray, John, *Principles of Conduct: Aspects of Biblical Ethics* (London, 1957).

Niebuhr, H. Richard, *Christ and Culture* (New York, 1951).

Niebuhr, Reinhold, *Moral Man and Immoral Society* (New York, 1932).

————. *An Interpretation of Christian Ethics* (New York, 1935).

————. *The Nature and Destiny of Man,* 2 vols. (New York, 1941, 1943).

Osborn, Eric Francis, *Ethical Patterns in Early Christian Thought* (New York, 1976).

Outka, Gene H., and Ramsey, Paul, eds., *Norm and Context in Christian Ethics* (New York, 1968).

Pannenberg, Wolfhart, *Ethics,* trans. Keith Crim (Philadelphia, 1981).

Ramsey, Paul, *Basic Christian Ethics* (New York, 1950).

————. *War and the Christian Conscience* (New York, 1961).

————. *Deeds and Rules in Christian Ethics* (New York, 1967).

————. *The Just War* (New York, 1969).

Stob, Henry, *Ethical Reflections: Essays on Moral Themes* (Grand Rapids, 1978).

Thielicke, Helmut, *Theological Ethics,* 3 vols. (Grand Rapids, 1979).

Troeltsch, Ernst, *The Social Teaching of the Christian Churches,* trans. Olive Wyon (New York, 1931).

Waddams, Herbert, *A New Introduction to Moral Theology* (New York, 1965).

White, R. E. O., *Christian Ethics: The Historical Development* (Atlanta, 1981).

Index of Authors
and Subjects

Index of Scriptural References

Genesis

1:21–22—150
1:26—183
1:26–31—19
1:27—149
1:28—149, 183
1:28–31—23
1:31—19
2:17—22, 47
2:18—152
2:23—152
2:24—152
3—21
3:4—21
3:12—62
3:17–19—23
6:11—209
9:5–6—119
18:20—174
19—173, 174

Exodus

20—48
20:2—48
20:13—202

Leviticus

4—61
11:44–45—20
18:5—51
18:15—47
18:22—173
19:2—20, 59
19:18—48
20:13—173

Numbers

15:22–31—61
35:16–21—118

Deuteronomy

6:4—15
6:4–5—48
6:13—191
8:3—97
15:7–10—211
24:1–4—158
28:47–49—189

Joshua

2—197

II Chronicles

19:6–7—185
20:16—184

Nehemiah

9:29—47

Job

34:22—24

Psalms

2—189
19:7–11—52
22:28—184
41:1—211

51:4—16
51:10—16
51:13—16
68:6—152
76:10—189
82:3–4—211
119:97—52
127–128—176

Proverbs

1:8–9—157
6:20—157
8:15–16—184
21:1—189
23:22—157
31:10–31—156

Isaiah

9:6–7—201
10:5—189
40:6–8—22
40:17—184
53:6—117

Jeremiah

2:17—23
2:19—23
4:18—23
6:19—23
27:5—189
31:33—52, 188

Ezekiel

11:19—52, 188
18:4—47